**Bahrain, Qatar, and the United
Arab Emirates**

Bahrain, Qatar, and the United Arab Emirates

Colonial Past, Present Problems,
and Future Prospects

Muhammad T. Sadik
American University of Beirut

William P. Snavely
University of Connecticut

309.1536
5.1256

Lexington Books
D.C. Heath and Company
Lexington, Massachusetts
Toronto   London

Research grants from the Graduate Program in Development Administration at the American University of Beirut, from the Ford Foundation, and from the Research Foundation of the University of Connecticut made possible the collection of data for this study. The views expressed are solely those of the authors, however, and the institutions providing funds for the research support bear no responsibility for them.

Published simultaneously in Canada.

Printed in the United States of America.

International Standard Book Number: 0-669-84517-5

Library of Congress Catalog Card Number: 72-5306

To Ifraj A. Sadik
    Alice P. Snavely

Contents

List of Charts and Figures

List of Tables

Preface

The nine small city states which are the subject of this study are of far greater interest and importance than their mere size alone would suggest. They are strategically located on the shipping routes to the rich oil producing countries of Saudi Arabia, Kuwait, Iraq and Iran. In addition, four of these tiny states have oil resources which are currently being tapped, and there are possibilities that oil may be found in some of the others as well.

Except for oil, the known resource endowments of this area are extremely meager. All of these countries have suffered from serious poverty, and only those which have been fortunate to discover oil have been able to make significant developmental progress.

Until the past few years, these nine countries remained in relative oblivion. They all had formal agreements with Great Britain which assigned responsibility for their physical protection and for the administration of their foreign relationships to her. It was Britain's announcement at the end of the 1960s that it intended to withdraw its protective shield from the Arabian Gulf area at the end of 1971 which suddenly thrust these small countries upon the world stage. Their strategic importance in relation to the power vacuum to result from Britain's withdrawal made them attractive pawns, indeed, in the game of international politics. Without Britain's protection, only two alternatives seemed to face these countries. One was to fall, individually, under the domination of other, more powerful countries. The other was to form some kind of union or federation among themselves. Seven of these states wisely followed the latter course in late 1971 and early 1972 in forming the United Arab Emirates.

Given the discovery of oil in four of these states and the recent major political changes, these Gulf city states have become a dynamically developing area which is a fascinating subject of study for social scientists. They represent an exceptionally good laboratory for studying the interrelated processes of political, social, economic and administrative growth and development.

Very little has been written so far about the development of the area, either in Arabic or English; and interested scholars and students have been seriously handicapped by the lack of published statistical data. It is the objective of this study to present a wide range of data about these nine countries and to offer some tentative propositions about the significance of some of the variables involved in the complex process of development in this region. Since development is a multidimensional process, an interdisciplinary approach has been followed.

The authors are grateful for the generous cooperation of the many government officials in these countries who helped them in the compilation of data and in supplying information about developmental problems and plans. In a sense, this is their book also, for without this assistance it could not have been written.

It is the authors' intention to continue with research in this area and to analyze various problems in greater depth in future studies. Constraints of length and time made it impossible to probe more deeply in the present volume.

Many others have played a part in the preparation of this study. It is not possible to acknowledge them all by name, but among those deserving of special mention are Mr. Adnan Darmish who served so effectively as a research assistant, Miss Salwa Younis, who typed the first draft, Mrs. Rosalind Fuchs who typed the many difficult tables, Mrs. Charlotte Ritchie who typed the final draft of the manuscript and made it possible for the authors to meet the publisher's deadline, and Mrs. Muriel Scotta who helped to coordinate the secretarial work on the study. Mrs. Bernice Colt provided invaluable editorial assistance in the compilation of her excellent index.

The authors also wish to express their appreciation for the financial support of the study contributed by the Graduate Program in Development Administration of the American University of Beirut, the Ford Foundation, and the Research Foundation of the University of Connecticut. We hasten to add that the authors, alone, bear the responsibility for the views expressed and conclusions reached.

Finally, we wish to express our gratitude to our families for their patience and forbearance in the face of time diverted from them to the writing of this book.

Storrs, Connecticut
May 1972

Bahrain, Qatar, and the United Arab Emirates

1 An Overview

Earlier History

Bahrain, Qatar and the seven Trucial states have until only recently remained little known or noticed by the world at large.[1] The obscurity in which these countries remained for so long was largely due to (1) their small size and population; (2) their seeming lack of economic resources; (3) their inaccessible location and inhospitable climate; and (4) their dependence on Great Britain—for more than a century she managed their foreign relations and provided for their protection and security. Since these nine states are quite small and the bulk of the population is concentrated in the capital city in each case, they are in the nature of city states, and they will be referred to frequently in this study as the Gulf city states. This latter term is at times abbreviated as GCS. Until relatively recent discoveries of oil in some of these states, their primary significance has stemmed from the strategic geographic position which eight of them occupy along the coast of the Arabian Gulf, and which the ninth, Fujairah, occupies on the coast of the Gulf of Oman. The Arabian Gulf is also referred to as the Persian Gulf. Iran (Persia), understandably, has fostered the latter name. Since the present study is concerned with nine Arab states which lie along the Gulf, the term "Arabian Gulf" will normally be used here. Their location has given the GCS, historically, an important position in relation to the flow of trade across the Gulf of Persia and other countries to the East, and the passage of shipping through the Gulf and the Strait of Hormuz to the Indian Ocean and the seas beyond. Their potential contemporary geographic importance is measured by the fact that the vast volume of oil shipments by tanker from the major oil-producing countries of the Gulf must flow past them through the narrow Strait of Hormuz on its way to Western Europe and to other countries of the world. This strategic geographic location plus the oil resources discovered in some of them, makes them, as a result of England's withdrawal of its protective shield at the end of 1971, highly valuable pieces in the game of international politics. The map of the Gulf area on the following page shows very clearly the geographic importance of these nine small states. Their strategic significance will be discussed in more detail later, but first it will be helpful to place these states in historical perspective.

1

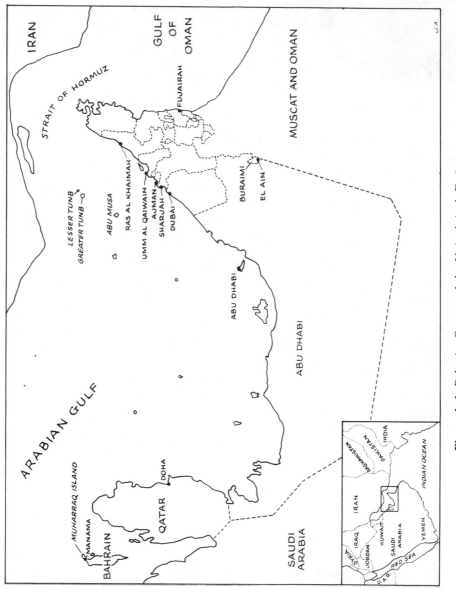

Figure 1-1. Bahrain, Qatar and the United Arab Emirates.

Portuguese Intervention in the Gulf Area

In the very early part of the sixteenth century, the Portuguese gained control of Hormuz on the Strait of Hormuz which is the entrance to the Arabian Gulf from the Indian Ocean. The straight is less than fifty miles wide, and the Portuguese with their naval power were able to close trading with the Gulf states by ships from other countries. England and Persia joined forces against this intervention and succeeded in driving the Portuguese out of Hormuz in 1622.

The Rise of British Influence in the Gulf

England, France and Holland agreed in 1698 to a joint effort in regard to patrolling the Arabian Gulf and maintaining freedom of shipping. Actually, little cooperation seems to have resulted from the agreement, and competition developed between England and Holland for trading predominance in the area. Britain gained the upper hand in the latter half of the eighteenth century and Dutch influence in the area largely disappeared.

The British East India Company which was incorporated in 1600, rather than the British government, actually attempted to regulate trade in the Gulf area. This private trading corporation maintained land and naval forces to protect and extend its economic interests, and it also carried out political negotiations with local rulers in the Gulf area. The success of the Company is indicated by the fact that the Shah of Persia in 1763 designated the British agent of the Company, Governor General for the English nation in the Gulf of Persia.

The Gulf area was politically unstable, however, and in the 18th century France, Holland and Portugal engaged in political intrigue in an effort to gain influence in the region. Similar activities were carried on by France and Russia in the nineteenth century.

Britain's Suppression of Piracy and Its Growing Political Role in the Gulf

The political instability of the area which prevailed in spite of the presence of the East India Company, and the diffusion of political authority among a number of sheiks, each exercising authority over only a relatively small geographic area, resulted in a power vacuum in which piracy began to flourish with greater than usual vigor in the eighteenth century. The waters around the small coastal settlements provided a protective refuge for pirate ships, and though piracy had been practiced for centuries, piratical activities became particularly serious in the eighteenth and the first half of the nineteenth century.

Individual pirate fleets became strong enough to range widely and the Indian coast, itself, became subject to their sweeps.

Expeditions of the East India Company against the Pirates

The pirates operating from Sharjah, later to become one of the Trucial states, were particularly disruptive of trade; and a British punitive expedition from Bombay was sent to attack their home base in 1809. The impact of this expedition lasted only briefly, and depredations of the pirates were soon as serious and extensive as before. In 1819, the East India Company sent a second expedition to attack the pirate lairs. Ras al-Khaimah was the first of the pirate towns to be defeated, and the pirate ships and land fortifications here were destroyed. The expedition then moved on to attack other strongholds.

As a result of the punitive actions of this expedition, the sheiks of the various coastal settlements, including the Sheik of Bahrain, signed a treaty of peace under which they agreed to cooperate in ending piracy activities at sea. This treaty did not intrude in the internal affairs of the sheikdoms and these were left to carry on their rivalries and feuds without interference.

In 1835, the sheiks of the coast were pressured to agree to a truce in sea fighting among themselves during the six-month annual pearling season. Pearl-diving was an important source of income for the area at the time, and the sheiks agreed to continue this annual period of truce.

The Perpetual Truce

A perpetual treaty of peace to be supervised and, if necessary, maintained by force by the British governmental staff in India, was signed by the coastal sheiks in 1853. Under this treaty, the sheiks agreed to refrain from acts of piracy and from engaging in warfare against one another at sea. They were left free under the terms of the treaty to carry on their feuds, but could only resort to actual attacks on one another on land. As a result of this treaty of peace establishing a permanent truce at sea in the area, the small city states which were included in the treaty became known as the Trucial states. This name has continued to the present time, and the seven states involved are currently known as Abu Dhabi, Dubai, Sharjah, Ajman, Umm al-Qaiwain, Ras al-Khaimah and Fujairah.

Further Agreements with the Trucial States

Administrative and political dealings with the Trucial states were carried on, with the blessing of the British government, through the British East India

Company from 1853 to 1858; by the government of Bombay from 1858 to 1873; by the government of British India from 1873 to 1947; and from the granting of independence to India to the end of 1971, by the Foreign Office of the British government.

The sheiks of the Trucial coast signed an agreement with Britain in 1869, which provided that they would not make any concessions to or conclude any agreements with other governments without Britain's consent. Later, as a result of a treaty concluded in 1892, the British government assumed full responsibility for the conduct of the external affairs of the Trucial states.

Bahrain

The islands constituting Bahrain, after a long period of independence, were subjugated by the Portuguese during the first quarter of the sixteenth century. They remained under Portuguese domination until 1602, when Portugal's control was replaced by that of Persia. In 1783, an Arabian tribe from the adjacent mainland, led by the Al-Khalifa family, overthrew the Persian occupiers; and this tribe has continued in control of the 33 islands comprising the Bahrain Archipelago ever since.

During the nineteenth century, Great Britain was also concerned about the acts of piracy committed in the Arabian Gulf area by ships from Bahrain and by the disruptive effects on pearl-fishing of the naval warfare conducted by rival tribes of the Gulf coast and island settlements. Partly as a result of territorial claims and threats by Iran and Turkey, the ruler of Bahrain negotiated an agreement with Britain in 1861, under which it was agreed that Bahrain would not engage in naval warfare, piracy, or slave-trading at sea, in exchange for protection by Britain from countries directing their territorial ambitions against the islands constituting Bahrain. Under a further agreement with Great Britain in the latter part of the nineteenth century, the ruler of Bahrain agreed not to undertake any political relations with foreign governments except with Britain's consent. British control of Bahrain's foreign policy continued to 1971, when this state became fully independent and gained membership in the United Nations (U.N.).

As Britain was preparing to relinquish its control of Bahrain's defense and foreign affairs, Iran reasserted its old claim to the islands. The U.N. agreed to send a mission to Bahrain to determine the wishes of the Bahraini people; and Iran, to its credit, stated that it would abide by the results. The mission reported to the U.N. that the overwhelming sentiment of the inhabitants was for independence rather than for union with Iran, and this is the status that Bahrain has achieved.

In the latter part of 1971, however, Iran's occupation of the three small islands of Abu Musa and Greater and Minor Tunb as soon as the British personnel withdrew was viewed with great concern by a number of the Gulf city states, as well as by some of the other Arab states in the area. Abu Musa was claimed, traditionally, by Sharjah and the other two islands by Ras al-Khaimah. This action by Iran was considered by many other states in the area to be a clear indication of that country's ambition to replace Britain's influence and control in the Gulf city states. There was speculation, indeed, that Britain and the United States were sympathetic with the idea of Iran's filling at least part of the vacuum left by Britain's withdrawal from the Gulf. Be that as it may, one Gulf country, namely Iraq, was moved to break diplomatic relations with both countries by what it considered to be Iran's aggressive action and Britain's complicity in this occupation of the three islands.

Qatar

Qatar is only some fifteen miles from the nearest of the islands comprising Bahrain. It occupies a peninsula which extends some 90 miles into the Arabian Gulf and it has common borders with both Saudi Arabia and Abu Dhabi. The extreme scarcity of water inhibited agricultural development, and fishing, pearl-diving and some nomadic sheep-raising and goat-raising constituted the major economic activities until the discovery of oil during the late 1930s.

The ruling sheik concluded an agreement with Britain in 1916, which defined a special relationship under which Great Britain assumed the responsibility of protecting Qatar from attack by water and also promised to extend its good offices should an external assault on the country be made by land. In addition to assigning the conduct of its foreign affairs to Britain, the agreement also constrained Qatar from assigning or selling any of its land area to another power.

This agreement was terminated in 1971, when Britain relinquished its former special status in the Gulf area, and Qatar became a fully independent state.

The Nature of the British Presence in the GCS

To administer the foreign affairs of Bahrain, Qatar, and the seven Trucial states, Britain stationed a political resident for the area in Bahrain and political officers or agents were assigned to several of the individual states. Britain's presence in the area, though kept relatively low key, was, nonetheless, quite effective in maintaining a protective buffer against the territorial ambitions and desires for political control which other countries had at one time or another. The political vacuum in which these coastal states found themselves, historically, by virtue of their small size and population had served as a natural attraction for a series of outside states until England became dominant in the area in the nineteenth century.

The Discovery of Oil among the Gulf City States

Oil Discoveries in Bahrain and Qatar

In addition to the strategic geographic location of the Gulf city states in relation to shipping in the Arabian Gulf, the discovery of oil in some of them has increased the attraction which they hold for outside powers. Among these states, oil was found first in Bahrain in 1932. Though the output potential of its oil fields is relatively modest in comparison with some of the rich oil fields in the Middle East, the income from its oil resources has so far provided a major source of financing for its development.

The discovery of oil in Qatar occurred just prior to World War II, but actual exports of oil began in 1949. Its fields are much richer in reserves than those of Bahrain, and oil revenues have been the principal source of financing for the country's development over the past twenty years.

Oil Explorations in the Trucial States

In 1936, a company known as Petroleum Development Trucial States Ltd., which was a subsidiary of a subsidiary company of the Iraq Petroleum Company, began to purchase oil exploration and production rights from ruling sheiks in the Trucial states. Agreements were concluded in 1938 with the sheiks of Dubai, Sharjah and Ras al-Khaimah which called for annual concession payments in exchange for the rights granted the company. The following year, a similar agreement was signed with Sheik Shakhbout of Abu Dhabi.

Oil exploration efforts in the area were interrupted by World War II, and after the war, the attention of the oil companies was directed for a time primarily to the rich fields which were being tapped in Kuwait and Qatar. It was not until 1960, when oil was found in commercial quantities in Abu Dhabi, that extensive exploration efforts were undertaken in the Trucial states. After its rich find in Abu Dhabi, Petroleum Development Trucial States decided to concentrate its efforts in this one state, and it gave up its other concessions among the Trucial states. Following this, a number of other companies have acquired either onshore or offshore concessions, or both. Table 1-1 provides a chronological listing of oil discoveries in these states.

Continental Shelf Claims

An interesting new interpretation of sovereign territory emerged in 1945, when the United States stated its claim to ownership of its offshore continental shelf. This action by the United States was quickly duplicated by a number of other

Table 1-1

Dates of Oil Concessions, Discoveries and First Shipments among the GCS

Country	Date of Concession	Date of Discovery of Oil	Date of First Shipment
Bahrain	1928	1932	1934
Qatar	1935	1939	1949
Abu Dhabi	1953	1958	1962
Dubai	1952	1966	1969

Source: Middle East Economic Digest and Arab Report and Record Survey, *Bahrain 1969*, December 1969, p. 10;

Middle East Economic Digest and Arab Report and Record Survey, *Qatar 1969*, October 1969, p. xii;

Arab Report and Record, *Abu Dhabi*, June 1, 1969, p. 226;

Middle East Economic Digest and Arab Report and Record Survey, *Dubai 1969*, July 1969, pp. x-xi.

For further details on concessions in the various countries in the Middle East, see Arabian American Oil Company, *Aramco Handbook: Oil and the Middle East* (Dhahran, 1969), pp. 89-92.

countries and the principle of continental shelf ownership seems to have become established.

Since the bed of the entire Arabian Gulf is of the structure of a continental shelf because the water is nowhere deeper than some 600 feet and only in a few places is deeper than 300 feet, the ruling sheiks of the Trucial states proclaimed ownership of their underwater shelf out to the midpoint of the Gulf opposite their shores. The remaining shelf width was assumed to belong to the countries on the opposite shore.

When various ones of the Gulf city states announced claims to the ownership of the continental shelf off their shores, this gave rise to a serious legal question concerning oil-exploration rights. Companies which had signed exclusive agreements for oil exploration with individual states before these states announced their claims to the underwater continental shelf, now held that their agreements should also entitle them to the exclusive right to explore the shelf areas as well. The states involved rejected this claim and held that they were free to sell concessions to this new area. In the case of both Qatar and Abu Dhabi, the issue was brought to arbitration, and the decision in both instances was favorable to the states and against the claims of the companies. The principle was established that concessions purchased by the oil companies applied only to the land areas claimed by the states granting concessions at the time the agreements were concluded.

Oil Discoveries in Dubai and Sharjah

Dubai was the second of the Trucial states in which oil was discovered. The find occurred in 1966, some fifty kilometers offshore in the continental shelf. By

1967, it was evident that substantial quantities of oil were present in the field and commercial exploitation began. The inflow of oil revenues, though still relatively modest, has more recently helped Dubai finance its developmental efforts.

More recently, oil has also been discovered in Sharjah's continental shelf. Since Dubai and Sharjah are adjacent to each other, it is quite possible that disputes about continental shelf boundaries may arise. Delineating borders a number of kilometers at sea and out of sight of land poses unusual surveying and boundary-marking problems. Doubtless over the course of time ways will be found to solve these satisfactorily.

Possibilities of Oil Discoveries in Other Trucial States

Though at this time, oil has still not been discovered in Ras al-Khaimah, it is anticipated that it soon will be, since geological assessments there are quite favorable. It is also possible that oil will be discovered in some of the other Trucial states in the future, but at the present time, the prospects seem more remote.

**International Politics in the Gulf Area since the
Latter Part of the Nineteenth Century**

To return now to the matter of international politics in relation to the Gulf area in general and to the nine states being considered here in particular, it is interesting to note that during the closing years of the nineteenth and the early part of the twentieth century, efforts were made by some European countries to gain footholds along the Gulf coast and thus to encroach upon England's domination of the area. This was well before the discovery of the vast oil resources in the region, and it indicates the regard for the strategic importance of the Gulf even in the absence of this valuable resource. The later immensely valuable oil discoveries have simply compounded many times the international political significance of the area. Again, it will be helpful to have some historical perspective.

Russia's Efforts

Near the end of the nineteenth century, Russia exerted strong efforts to acquire a concession for the construction of a railroad stretching from the Mediterranean Sea to the Arabian Gulf. Had it succeeded, this would have been an important step toward the development of Russian influence in the part of the Gulf area through which the line would have passed, namely Kuwait. Britain moved to block the intrusion by this outside large power, and succeeded in doing so by concluding in 1899 a formal arrangement with Sheik Mubarak ibn Sabah. Under the agreement, Kuwait was to receive the protection of Great Britain in exchange for refraining from making concessions to or concluding agreements with any other governments. Turkey's effort to occupy Kuwait in 1898, against which England issued a strong protest, doubtless encouraged Sheik Sabah to place his sheikdom under British protection.

Germany's Efforts

At the beginning of the twentieth century, Germany tried to develop an economic and political position in the northern end of the Gulf; and in 1903, it acquired rights to push the Berlin-Baghdad railroad beyond Baghdad to Basra on the Gulf, after failing to work out arrangements to terminate it in Kuwait instead. England was able to blunt this intrusion by acquiring, through an agreement with Turkey in 1913, the power to determine and control any continuation of the railroad southward beyond Basra. As a further part of this agreement, the Turkish government recognized the special agreements which Britain had with the ruling sheiks of Kuwait, Bahrain, Qatar and the seven Trucial states.

The Emergence of Saudi Arabia

One further minor threat to Britain's dominance in the Gulf area prior to World War I should be noted in passing. This resulted from the success which Abdul-Aziz ibn Saud had in forcing a Turkish withdrawal from al-Hasa in 1913, over which Turkey had exercised loose control since 1870. With his consolidation of control, a new political entity thus came into being along the Gulf coast. In fact, Saudi Arabia's strategic location bordering Kuwait, Bahrain, Qatar and the Trucial states, made it a potential threat to Britain's dominance over these areas. Britain clearly indicated that it would not permit Saudi Arabia to change the special relationship which it had with Kuwait and the Gulf city states, and in a later treaty, Abdul-Azziz formally agreed not to interfere with these neighboring sheikdoms.

In spite of these as well as other efforts by various countries to gain a political and economic position in the Arabian Gulf area during the nineteenth and the early part of the twentieth century, England was successful in preventing significant encroachment upon the dominant position which it had acquired through various agreements and treaties. The efforts made by other countries is evidence, however, of recognition of the political significance of the area in the pre-World War I period, which, as mentioned before, was well before major oil discoveries had been made there.

The Period since World War I

The effect of World War I was to reduce potential threats to Britain's position in the Gulf, and it continued its special relationship with the Gulf sheikdoms through the interwar period, as well as during the years following World War II. Major shifts in the realm of international politics which are of potentially great importance for the Gulf area have occurred in the interval since World War II, however. These relate to (1) the decline in Britain's position as a world power; (2) the development of Russia as an economic and political power of the first order; and (3) the growing interest of the United States in the area.

The Political Vacuum Created by Britain's Withdrawal from the Gulf

Britain's shrinking position on the world scene is reflected in the fact that economic considerations forced it to the decision to withdraw its military presence east of the Suez Canal by the end of 1971. This withdrawal has left a political vacuum which is a source of major direct concern for the countries of Western Europe, and of some direct and much indirect concern for the United States.

The Interests of Western Europe and the United States

Western Europe depends upon the Middle East, and particularly the countries of the Arabian Gulf area, for a major part of its oil supplies. The United States also has substantial oil interests in the area through the extensive participation of American oil companies in the exploitation of oil resources which they have helped to discover. Though American oil companies have large investments in their Middle East oil operations, oil imports to the United States from this area represent only a very small percentage of this country's annual oil consumption. England's withdrawal of its protective shield from the Gulf states has been a source of concern for the government of the United States, both with regard to the future protection of the investments of United States oil companies and the continuation of Middle East oil flows to the nations of Western Europe. In addition, the southern end of the Arabian peninsula is strategically located in relation to the trade with India and the Far East which flows through the Suez Canal when it is in operation.

Growing Russian Interests in the Middle East

The Soviet Union has shown by its actions in the past few years that it has an intense interest in developing strong economic, military and political ties in the

Middle East. Though communism is a system which runs counter to the basic spirit and attitude of the Arabs, political policies of the West, and particularly those of the United States with respect to Israel in the period since 1948, have provided Russia with the opportunity to gain important influence among Arab countries of the Middle East. As a result of Russia's heavy military support of Egypt, its political relations with some of the other Arab countries in the Mediterranean area, and the major naval force which it is now able to maintain in this sea, this country has become a strong economic, military and political rival of the West in this strategically highly important area. Already concern is being expressed among the N.A.T.O. nations about the extent to which the Soviet Union appears to be flanking Western Europe to the south.

Recent evidence suggests that Russia's ambitions do not end with the extent of its present penetration in the Middle East. It has already begun to show a naval presence in the Indian Ocean, and it seems logical to conclude that it will make a determined effort to fill as much of the vacuum created by Britain's withdrawal from the Gulf area as it can. The reopening of the Suez Canal would enable Russia to increase the size of the naval force which it can maintain in areas adjacent to the Arabian Gulf.

China, in view of its increasing interest in international politics, may also exert serious efforts to gain influence among the GCS in the years immediately ahead.

Problems of Federation Faced by the Gulf City States

Strength to be Gained from Federation

As a result of the military and economic support which it has provided to Egypt, Syria and Iraq, Russia has been able to pose as a friend of the Arab nations in their confrontation with Israel. Now, with Britain's withdrawal from the Gulf, Russia can be expected to make a determined effort to fill as much of the political vacuum as possible. Unless Bahrain, Qatar and the Trucial states, or some major grouping of these states such as the current United Arab Emirates, can maintain some form of stable political union, the chances of competing world powers' developing major new political and economic relationships in the area will be that much greater. It would be much easier for other powerful countries to find ways of winning over the ruling sheik of one or more of these tiny states and to gain concessions, than would be the case if they had to deal with one overall sovereign entity which had the responsibility of speaking for all of these states, collectively.

Formation of the United Arab Emirates (U.A.E.)

The formation of the United Arab Emirates on December 2, 1971, is an encouraging move. This union was originally composed of six Trucial states: Abu

Dhabi, Dubai, Sharjah, Ajman, Fujairah and Umm al-Qaiwain. Ras al-Khaimah also became a member in early 1972. It is too early to tell how stable this new union will be; but it is to be hoped that it will prove to be durable and that it will soon attract the two remaining Gulf city states to membership as well. The political, economic, administrative and social advantages to be gained from the broadest possible union of these Gulf city states are indeed great. The potential advantages of joining together in one political and economic unit are considered in detail in various parts of this study.

Difficulties in Forming a Federation or Other Union

Experience in other areas of the world has shown that it tends to be extremely difficult for a group of independent states to form a meaningful political federation or other form of union. Attempts to do so in the past have often foundered on the reluctance of individual states to surrender the degree of political sovereignty that is required for the establishment of even a weak political federation. It is apparently considerably easier for nations to form economic than political unions or federations.

Though this subject will be discussed in detail in a later chapter, it should be noted here that the problem of forming a political federation is a difficult one for these nine Gulf city states to solve, in spite of the urgency for doing so which stems from their individual weakness in meeting the various outside political pressures which confront them. Their difficulty in federating is compounded by the tribal differences and rivalries which have existed among some of them for generations. It should be remembered that Britain during its long period of domination in the area only assumed control of the relations of these small sheikdoms with outside countries, and that they were left free to carry on their own relationships among themselves. As a result, old feuds have tended to continue over the years and these are clearly remembered. Britain was able through its good offices and through the internal native police force which it developed under the command of British officials to keep overt fighting among rival tribes fairly well suppressed. Feelings of suspicion, distrust and hostility among some of the tribes continued to percolate over the years and surfaced during the efforts to establish a meaningful political federation.

Loyalty Patterns in the Arab Society

To understand the problem which tribal differences and rivalries can pose to the establishment of a meaningful federation among these nine small city states, one must have an appreciation of the loyalty patterns which have prevailed historically in Arab society. First of all, family ties are extremely strong among the Arabs, and the concept of family here is a very broad one which encompasses even quite remote cousins. The tribe, in turn, represents an extension of family loyalty in the form of sworn loyalty and allegiance to the sheik of the ruling family of the tribe. Given the hostile physical environment of much of the Middle East and the nomadic existence which this required when domestic animals were the foundation of economic life, tribal units formed the basis for physical protection from attack and plunder by outsiders and for the preservation of claims to particular grazing areas and water sources. Though the pastoral, nomadic pattern of life has been largely replaced by settled agriculture and growing urbanization in the Middle East, the old tribal ties and loyalties, as well as intertribal rivalries and differences have remained quite strong. It is important to keep this in mind in assessing the possibilities for the further political development of the area.

The Statesmanship Shown in Forming the U.A.E.

Given the kinds of problems referred to above, it is a tribute to the statesmanship of the leaders of the seven countries which have joined together in forming the United Arab Emirates that they have been able to place the common good of this group of countries above individual parochial interests. It is to be hoped that the other two Gulf city states may be inspired by the example of the seven, and that they, too, may soon join in full membership in the union.

Tribal Rivalries in Relation to Penetration by Outside
Countries

It is the kind of tribal rivalries that make the formation of a meaningful political federation difficult which also provide a greater opportunity for outside nations to gain influence in the area. Though outside competing powers can, of course, be expected to try to take full advantage of the opportunity to get a foothold in these small city states (as a first step in an attempt to acquire as much influence in the Gulf area as they can), some of the larger states in the Gulf area have also been attracted by the political vacuum left by Britain's withdrawal.[2]

Efforts by rival powers to develop economic and political relations with Gulf states are naturally of great concern to the United States and its western European allies. They can be expected to make every effort to counter the attempts of other nations to penetrate the area, for the international economic and political stakes are extremely high.

The foregoing discussion has attempted to show why these nine tiny, remote city states have suddenly become of great significance on the world scene. It will be helpful at this point to consider briefly the physical and population characteristics of these states in relation to their prospects for development.

Area and Population

As can be seen from Table 1-2, the nine Gulf city states have a total population of 510,000 persons which is spread over a total area of 34,300 square miles; and their average population density is 15 persons per square mile. It can be seen from Table 1-3 that this is much less than that of Iraq (30 persons per square mile), Jordan (35 persons per square mile), Kuwait (50 persons per square mile), and Lebanon (374 persons per square mile); but it is five times that of Saudi Arabia (3 persons per square mile). The relatively low population density of these states as a whole conceals the variety of demographic variations, however.

At one extreme, there is Abu Dhabi which comprises an area of 26,000 square miles and has a total population of 60,000 persons. This area is 75.9% of the total area of the Gulf city states, but the population is only 11.8% of the total for the group. Abu Dhabi is the most sparsely populated country with a density of slightly over two persons per square mile. This is only approximately 70% of the population density of Saudi Arabia which is the most sparsely populated major country in the Middle East. To make an even broader

Table 1-2
Area and Population by State of the Nine GCS

| State | Approximate Area | | Population | | | |
	Square Miles	% of Total Area	Population Census 1968	Population Est. 1970	% 1970 Est. of Total Population	Population Density Per Sq. Mi.
Bahrain	256	0.7	182,000[1]	205,000	40.2	800
Qatar	4,000	11.7	–	80,000	15.7	20
Abu Dhabi	26,000	75.9	46,500	60,000	11.8	2
Dubai	1,500	4.4	59,000	75,000	14.7	50
Sharjah	1,000	2.9	31,500	40,000	7.8	40
Ajman	100	0.3	4,200	5,500	1.1	55
Umm-al-Qaiwain	300	0.9	3,700	4,500	0.9	15
Ras-al-Khaima	650	1.9	24,500	30,000	5.9	46
Fujairah	450	1.3	9,700	10,000	2.0	22
Totals	34,256 =34,300	100 %		510,000	100[2]	15

[1] 1965 Census.

[2] Column may not add to 100 because of rounding.

Sources: Land area figures for Bahrain and Qatar are from K.G. Fenelon, *The Trucial States*, Beirut, Khayats, 2d. ed., rev., 1969, p. 142;

Land area figures for the Trucial states are from an unpublished report of the Trucial States Council;

Population figures are from census data and official estimates.

Table 1-3
Population Density in Selected Countries in the Middle East, 1966

Country	Persons per Square Mile
Iraq	30
Jordan	35
Kuwait	50
Lebanon	374
Syria	46
Saudi Arabia	3

Source: *United Nations Studies on Selected Development Problems in Various Countries in the Middle East* (New York, 1969), Table 1, p. 49.

comparison, Abu Dhabi's population density is probably one of the lowest in the world.

At the other extreme is Bahrain, which occupies 256 square miles and has a population of some 205,000 persons. Its area is just 0.7% of the total for the nine states and with 800 persons per square mile, it is the most densely populated of the group. More than this, it is the most densely populated country in the Arabian Gulf as well as in the whole Middle East. For example, its density is more than twice that of Lebanon; and it is even comparable with that of populated, developed countries of Europe.

The other seven countries of the group are also characterized by a variety of demographic conditions. The tiny state of Ajman which occupies just 0.3% of the total area, has 1.1% of the total population and a density of 55 persons per square mile. Dubai comprises 4.4% of the total area and has 14.7% of the total population. Its density is 50 persons per square mile comparing closely with that of Syria. Sharjah and Ras al-Khaimah occupy, respectively, 2.9% and 1.9% of the total area and have 7.8% and 5.9% of the total population. This gives a density of 40 persons per square mile for Sharjah and 46 for Ras al-Khaimah. Their densities, too, are similar to Syria's. In the case of the remaining states, Qatar occupies 11.7% of the total area and has 15.7% of the total population, for a density of 20 persons per square mile; Fujairah comprises 1.3% of the total area and has 2% of the total population, which gives a density of 22 persons per square mile; and Umm al-Qaiwain occupies 300 square miles, which is 0.9% of the total area of the Gulf city states, and also, its population is 0.9% of the total, which gives it a density of approximately 15 persons per square mile.

Urban and Rural Population

The nine capital cities of the Gulf city states have a total population of 320,500 persons, or 63% of the total. It can be seen from Table 1-4 that the capital-city

Table 1-4
Estimated Population of Capital Cities of the GCS in 1970

Country	Capital City	Population of Capital City	% of Total Population
Bahrain	Manama	95,000	46.3
Qatar	Doha	70,000	87.5
Abu Dhabi	Abu Dhabi City	30,000	50.0
Dubai	Dubai City	70,000	93.3
Sharjah	Sharjah City	30,000	75.0
Ajman	Ajman City	4,500	81.8
Umm-al-Qaiwain	Umm-al-Qaiwain City	3,500	78.0
Ras-al-Khaima	Ras-al-Khaima City	15,000	50.0
Fujairah	Fujairah City	2,500	25.0
Totals		320,500	63%

Source: Extrapolations based on previous official census data and information supplied by government officials.

population concentration in all of the Gulf city states, except Bahrain and Fujairah, is more than 50% of the total. In most of these states, the population concentration in the capital city is very high, indeed, and in the case of Dubai, it is a remarkable 93.3%.

There are no major cities or towns in the Gulf city states besides the capital cities, except in the case of Bahrain and Abu Dhabi. In Bahrain, there are four towns: Muharaq, with a population of 50,000; Hidd with 20,000 people; and Rifa'a and Sitra with a population of 10,000 each. This makes the total urban population of Bahrain approximately 185,000, which is roughly 90% of the total.

In Abu Dhabi, in addition to the capital, there is one city, El-Ain, which has a population of 20,000. Thus, the two principal cities together have a population of 50,000, which is 83% of the total for the state.

Population Growth in the Capital Cities

All of the capital cities except Manama, the capital city of Bahrain, have recently witnessed an unusual rate of growth. Manama's annual rate of growth between 1965 and 1970, had levelled off at 4%, which is representative of the natural rate of growth of a normal city. Doha, the capital city of Qatar, has been growing at the rate of 12% since 1966; while the rate of annual growth of Abu Dhabi city from 1968 to 1970 was substantial at 17%. As shown in Table 1-5, the rates of annual growth for Dubai city, Sharjah city, Ajman city, Umm al-Qaiwain city, Ras al-Khaimah city, and Fujairah city during the same period, 1968 to 1970,

Table 1-5
Growth of Capital Cities of the GCS in Recent Years

Country and Capital City	Years	Population	% of Total Population	Annual Growth Rate %
Bahrain	1965C	79,100	46.3	4
Manama	1970E	95,000		
Qatar	1966C	45,000	87.5	12
Doha	1970E	70,000		
Abu Dhabi	1968C	22,000	50.0	17
Abu Dhabi City	1970E	30,000		
Dubai	1968C	57,400	93.3	10
Dubai City	1970E	70,000		
Sharjah	1968C	20,600	75.0	21
Sharjah City	1970E	30,000		
Ajman	1968C	3,700	81.8	10
Ajman City	1970E	4,500		
Umm-al-Qaiwain	1968C	2,900	78.0	10
Umm-al-Qaiwain City	1970E	3,500		
Ras-al-Khaima	1968C	8,800	50.0	31
Ras-al-Khaima City	1970E	15,000		
Fujairah	1968C	2,000	25.0	12
Fujairah City	1970E	2,500		

C = Census data.
E = Estimates.
Sources: Compiled on the basis of official census data and information in Table 1-4.

has been 10%, 21%, 10%, 10%, 31% and 12%, respectively. This unusual growth in the case of all of the capital cities of the Gulf city states except Bahrain, is due to the sudden growth of income resulting from the discovery of oil in Qatar and Abu Dhabi, and the prospects of oil finds in other countries. A large number of foreign nationals have been attracted to Qatar, Abu Dhabi and the other countries. In Bahrain, the nonnative population is about 25% of the total, and in the other eight Gulf city states, it constitutes 50% or more of the total.

Some Effects of the Growth in Population

The unusual rate of population growth in the Gulf city states has caused certain difficulties. It has inevitably led to bottlenecks in such facilities as water, electricity, sewage, health services, education, etc. On the other hand, the inflow of people from more developed countries has served to speed development here, for they have brought in new attitudes, new skills, and new technology. These people have influenced significantly the process of economic and social change in these small states. They have broken the walls of isolation which have shielded these states against external influence for years. The extent to which the inflow of foreigners to the GCS will have been beneficial will depend on the ability of these countries to mobilize this key resource toward achieving their developmental goals.

Present Levels of Development

The Gulf city states are usually grouped under developing countries, though their present levels of development show significant differences. In addition, the possibilities for further economic and social progress vary from one country to another. Collectively, they have a very promising potential for achieving further development; and, ideally, they could become politically, economically and socially, a homogeneous progress unit. To attain such unity will require exceptional statesmanship on the part of all of the rulers. Though the problems to be overcome in order to realize it are difficult, the goal of political and economic unity within the framework of a federation or union of all nine of the GCS is well worth pursuing. The joining together, first, of six of the Trucial states to form the United Arab Emirates near the end of 1971, and the further addition of Ras al-Khaimah in early 1972, are very promising first steps.

Per Capita Gross National Product and Economic Development

In terms of national income as measured by per capita Gross National Product (GNP), the Gulf city states exhibit marked differences, with a range in per capita GNP of from less than $150 to approximately $4,000. If they are grouped according to those with higher and those with lower per capita incomes, the former category would include Qatar, Abu Dhabi, and Dubai which have an estimated per capita GNP, respectively, of $3,490, $4,000 and $1,000. Per capita GNP figures for these states are summarized in Table 1-6. From these figures, it can be seen that Abu Dhabi has a per capita GNP which is roughly ten times that of Bahrain. It would be natural to conclude from these figures that Bahrain is underdeveloped in comparison with Abu Dhabi. Indeed, if per capita GNP is used as the criterion to determine whether a country is developed or not, Abu Dhabi could claim to be the most developed country in the world. Both Dubai and Qatar would also be considered developed countries compared to Bahrain; and they could claim, further, to be advanced countries on the basis of the arbitrary per capita GNP level of $1,000 which is usually accepted as a dividing line between advanced and underdeveloped countries. Per capita GNP

Table 1-6
Per Capita GNP by State for the GCS, 1968

Country	Per Capita G.N.P. (in U.S. $)
Bahrain	390
Qatar	3,490
Abu Dhabi	4,000(E)
Dubai, Sharjah, Ajman, Umm al-Qaiwain, Ras al-Khaimah and Fujairah[1]	600

[1]The figure for just Dubai would be much higher than this, probably over $1,000, but an exact figure for this country alone is not available. Its G.N.P. figure pulls up the per capita G.N.P. for this group to $600. If Dubai were excluded, the figure for the remaining five relatively poor states would be much lower.

E = Estimate

Sources: *An-Nahar*, Economic and Financial Supplement, Nov. 29, 1970, p. 8;

Middle East Development Division, British Embassy, Beirut, *An Economic Survey of the Northern Trucial States*, Vol. 1, p. 21 (unpublished).

figures are not an adequate measure of overall development, however, and actually Bahrain is the most developed country among the Gulf city states. If development is assessed as an integrated whole comprising political, economic, social and administrative aspects, the nine Gulf city states could be listed from the most developed to the least developed as follows: Bahrain, Qatar, Dubai, Abu Dhabi, and the remaining Trucial states. It is difficult to make a meaningful further ordering.

The Common Background of the GCS

The Gulf city states, though they have now achieved various levels of development, started equally. Fifty years ago, the people of all of the Gulf city states lived in extreme poverty and had very little, if anything, to contribute either to their own well-being or to the world community. These Gulf communities were located in and around oases and coastal centers. The lands were, as they are today, arid, with a climate noted for its extreme heat and high humidity. These small sheikdoms had no developed political institutions. The family was the basic social unit, and the tribe formed the basis of their political, economic and social organizations. Life was simple and consequently the tribal system of government served most of their needs. The sea, not the land, was the means of communication and livelihood; and pearling and pearl-fishing were the backbone of their economy. In the 1930s, the pearling industry was seriously affected by the development of cultured pearls by Japan; and the result was further impoverishment for the coastal towns and villages of the region which had been largely dependent on pearling as the main source of cash income.

The Beginnings of Development

In the early 1950s, all of these nine Gulf communities, except Bahrain, started from a similar very low economic position as they began with different degrees of emphasis and financial availability to move along the path of development. Their towns lacked such facilities as water, electricity, sewage, paved roads, airports, hospitals and clinics, schools, etc. All were under British protection; and their traditional tribal governments confined their roles, with the help and direction of the British political agents, to regulatory matters such as internal security.

Development in Bahrain

Bahrain for long has been a trading center; therefore, it did not need to wait for oil revenues before initiating some developmental activities. It started an impressive education program as early as 1920; and, today, it not only has the most advanced primary and secondary educational system in the Arabian Gulf, but its system compares favorably with the best in the Middle East. In health, Bahrain has also been able to develop reasonably adequate facilities. The towns of Bahrain have a well-paved network of streets and roads, sewage, piped water and telephones; and the state is served by an international airport and a six-berth quay in its seaport. Bahrain also has the most advanced system of telecommunications in the Middle East. This important infrastructural development has not been fully paralleled by a corresponding political development. The patriarchal system of government still prevails, but it has developed beyond the system which existed in the 1950s. The ruler continues to be the head of state and the final authority in almost all matters, but with the recent development of the Council of State and the creation of a number of specialized government departments to carry out the programs of the country, the political picture has improved significantly.

Development in Qatar

Qatar started some developmental activities in the 1950s. The first school was opened in Doha, the capital of Qatar in 1951; and since then increasing attention has been given to infrastructural development. Today, Qatar has a full-scale education and health program, and the government gives particular attention to matters related to water, electricity, streets and roads. It has an international airport and a four-berth quay in its seaport. In Qatar, also, political development has not fully paralleled the economic and social development. The government is essentially a modified version of the tribal system, though recently Qatar has created a Council of Ministers and passed what is called the "Fundamental Law" which is the first legal document defining basic duties, obligations and responsibilities of the various agencies of the government.

Development in Dubai

Dubai, which began to receive oil revenues late in 1969, experienced some improvement in its economy before that date. Since the early 1950s, the country has been a flourishing center for entrepot trade. Presently, Dubai derives the largest portion of its national wealth from this trade, and this will probably continue to be one of the major sources of revenue in the near future. Oil revenues will almost certainly become the most important revenue source within three or four years, however. Dubai is now executing sewage, water and electricity programs; it has an international airport; and it will soon have a fifteen-berth quay in its seaport.

Dubai's political development also has not kept pace with its economic development. The system of government is tribal and the ruler directly supervises the entire business of the state. The municipality of Dubia carries out all the functions and services in the country. Though Dubai has some health and education facilities, these are not provided by the government of Dubai, but rather by Kuwait and Qatar which are providing these services in all the Trucial states except Abu Dhabi.

Development in Abu Dhabi

Abu Dhabi, before it began to enjoy large oil revenues in the 1960s, was an impoverished tribal community. Abu Dhabi city lacked such things as water, electricity, health and educational facilities, streets, roads, etc.; and since it had to start from scratch, the job ahead was enormous. Late in the 1960s, the government decided to launch economic and social developmental programs. Signs of achievements are now evident, for roads and streets are being built, water and electricity are being provided, education and health facilities are well underway, an international airport connects the country with the outside world, and a ten-berth quay in its seaport will soon be ready to receive major ships.

Development in the Other Trucial States

In the other five Trucial states of Sharjah, Ajman, Umm al-Qaiwain, Ras al-Khaimah and Fujairah, some development has taken place, but it falls well below the level which has been achieved by the other Gulf states. In these five states, essentially no political development has taken place and a pure tribal system of government prevails. The municipality in each runs all affairs of the country. With the limited assistance provided by the Trucial States Council and other development funds, they have been able to promote a small amount of urban infrastructural development in their capital cities. Few streets are being built and electricity, water and housing are seriously deficient. Education and health facilities, on a limited scale, are being provided by Kuwait, Qatar and other countries.

All five of these countries are, at the moment, very poor in natural resources. Oil has not been discovered in any of them as yet, though there are encouraging prospects in some of them. Agriculture is limited due to the scarcity of cultivable lands. Fishing is a major occupation, but the yield is very low. Their hopes for further development, in the absence of oil discoveries, seem to rest upon the possibility that an approach can be found for the development of the nine Gulf city states, or at least the seven comprising the U.A.E., as an entity. The discovery and exploitation of oil resources would, of course, greatly enhance their developmental possibilities.

Potential for Further Development

All the countries under review aspire to achieve further progress; but aspiration and reality, unfortunately, do not always coincide. All of them have wanted, in the past, to achieve the status of independent national states. A number of them have recognized, however, that it would be very difficult, if not impossible, to survive as independent political units and to move ahead developmentally if they do not strike oil. For those states without oil revenues, there would seem to be no way in which they could become economically viable independent political entities.

Prospects of the Nonoil-Producing Countries

The tiny communities of Fujairah, Ras al-Khaimah, Umm al-Qaiwain, Ajman and Sharjah are still dependent on agriculture and fishing as the major sources of output for their subsistence economies. The bulk of the inhabitants in these five countries are living in extreme poverty. They can, within limits, achieve some development in agriculture and fishing, and consequently increase production, but this would probably result only in a slight increase in the income of the participants; and it could also lead to a larger surplus of labor, since with increased efficiency, fewer workers would be required to produce the quantities needed to meet the local demand. Thus, modernization in agriculture and fishing could accentuate unemployment problems. The labor force in this sector is illiterate, untrained, and extremely traditional, therefore, the surplus labor cannot easily find employment in the neighboring countries where urban infrastructure is well underway. As a result, growing tension and unrest could easily develop.

Since in the absence of oil revenues they cannot find resources of their own, human or material, to promote their infrastructural development, these poorer states will have to depend on the resources of outside countries to help them initiate, activate and operate programs and projects designed to carry forward their development. By joining with the economically more prosperous countries of Abu Dhabi and Dubai in the U.A.E., these poorer countries can expect developmental assistance from the two wealthier members.

Prospects of the Oil-Producing Countries

The prospects for the future even in the oil-producing countries of Bahrain, Qatar, Abu Dhabi and Dubai are questionable, if each is not willing to adopt the maxim "one for all and all for one." In the absence of some form of meaningful federation or very close cooperation which includes all of them, these countries may find it difficult, if not impossible, to withstand the political pressures from outside larger and more powerful nations to which they are likely to be subjected in the absence of Britain's protective shelter.

Although the four oil-producing countries have been able to promote a reasonable degree of urban infrastructural development, their present stage of development is characterized by lags and imbalances. While all four have experienced a considerable decline in participation of the active population in the traditional occupations in agriculture and fishing as a result of new job opportunities, they have not been able to avoid in these new sectors, the backwardness which characterized the traditional sectors. The shift of workers has simply resulted in the transfer of backward labor from the traditional sectors to the newly created sectors, and their low productivity has carried over into these new activities, which has the effect of seriously slowing the development process. The four oil-producing states have achieved a degree of economic affluence, but poverty still prevails among the bulk of the inhabitants. Extreme wealth and extreme poverty are characteristic of each of these countries. In aggregate terms, economic growth has been achieved; but the distribution of the increases in total wealth leaves much to be desired.

It should also be noted that traditional attitudes and institutions have not been transformed to match the nature and extent of the economic changes which have occurred. Varying modifications of their political systems and institutions have been achieved, but essentially all are still operating under the tribal system. Bahrain's present political system may be labelled a transitional tribal one. Qatar's system would fall more or less under the same classification; but Dubai and Abu Dhabi still have a more traditional tribal system.

Toward Unity

Collectively, these four countries have a promising opportunity to serve as the core of a viable political and economic regional unit. They have the same historical heritage, political background, social-tribal habits, and they also enjoy the advantage of oil receipts. If they can throw their lot together with that of the other five states under sincere, honest leadership, *with a vision for the future*, this bloc could evolve as one unit with adequate economic and social foundations upon which to build a modern progressive nation-state.

To assess this regional potential, it is necessary to examine in detail the economic, political and social problems, as well as the potential for further development, individually and collectively, of the nine GCS. It is to these matters that we now turn our attention.

Economic Foundations

Before the 1930s, all the nine Gulf city states had more or less the same economic foundation; they subsisted as coastal settlements, and looked to the sea for their livelihood and communications. Fishing and pearl-fishing were the backbone of their economies. As was mentioned in Chapter 1, in the 1930s, two major developments took place: the first was the discovery of oil in Bahrain in 1932 and in Qatar in 1939; the second was the mortal blow to pearl-fishing dealt by the development of cultured pearls in Japan. The result of the rapid decline in the pearl-fishing industry caused by the competition of cultured pearls was growing poverty since pearling was the only source of cash income. The subsistence economies of these countries started to take on new dimensions in the 1950s, when both Bahrain and Qatar began to receive substantial oil receipts. In 1959, new horizons were opened for Abu Dhabi as a result of its rich oil finds, and Dubai joined the group of oil countries in 1966, when oil was discovered there. Oil receipts have helped to initiate changes not only in the tribal societies of the four oil-producing countries, but in the tribal societies of the other Gulf city states as well.

In examining the existing economic foundation of the Gulf city states and their potential for further growth, individually and collectively, it will be helpful to consider first the structures and levels of the economically active population in these countries and then to examine their major economic sectors.

Economic Status of the Population

Active and Inactive Population Rates

The economically active population of a country is the portion of the total population available for work which falls within the normal working years of an individual's lifetime. Since in the culture of these nine states, most females remain in the house and do not enter outside employment or occupations, this large segment of the population is included in the inactive rather than the active category in the statistical reporting. This, of course, does not mean that these females are not working in their homes—indeed, most of them are working quite hard. It is simply that the conventions of labor statistics exclude those who remain at home doing their own housework from the economically active population category.

27

It should also be noted that the economically inactive category refers both to females at home, as mentioned above, and to males who are below or beyond the normal working age or who are incapacitated and unable to work. Unemployed persons are not, by this classification, economically inactive. Rather they would be the currently unemployed part of the economically active segment of the population.

Among the nine Gulf city states, there are both striking differences and similarities in regard to their active population percentages and the extent of their economic development. Bahrain is the most developed country in the group and Ajman is one of the most underdeveloped, yet they have similar activity rates; 29% of Bahrain's total population is economically active and 71% inactive, and the figures for these categories are approximately the same for Ajman. Fujairah and Umm al-Qaiwain have similar levels of economic and social development, and they also have indentical ratios of economically active population to total population—32% active and 68% inactive. Ras al-Khaimah and Sharjah have about the same level of development, but they have slightly different activity rates; in Sharjah 34% of the total population is active and 66% inactive, and in Ras al-Khaimah 31% is active and 69% inactive. Abu Dhabi, the richest country in the group, has 63% of its total population economically active and just 37% inactive. Dubai has 41% active and 59% inactive. The foregoing figures show clearly that there is no consistent relationship in these countries between their levels of development and the percentages of their populations which are economically active. For a fuller breakdown of the active-inactive population status of these states, see Table 2-1.

Abu Dhabi, which has the highest economically active population percentage, has the highest proportion of population in the age group, 21-60, i.e., 64.3%, while Dubai has 52% of its total population in the same age group (see Table 2-2). The high concentration of population in this age group in these two countries is the result of an unusual situation. The boom which Abu Dhabi witnessed in 1967 and 1968 as a result of substantial oil receipts, and the prospects of increasing oil receipts in Dubai as a result of confirmed oil finds, caused many foreigners, Pakistanis, Indians, Iranis, Arabs and others, to rush into these countries to find employment, and almost all of them were in the age group, 21-60. In the oil-producing Gulf city-states, except Bahrain, foreigners account for not less than 50% of the total population. In Bahrain, they constitute about 25%.

Economic Status and Sex

In Bahrain, 52% of the males are economically active and 48% inactive, while 2% of the females are active and 98% are inactive, according to the conventional statistical classification. Just 3.8% of the total economically active population

Table 2-1

Economically Active Population by State and Economic Status

Economic Status	Bahrain 1965 No.	%	Qatar No.	%	Abu Dhabi 1968 No.	%	Dubai 1968 No.	%	Sharjah 1968 No.	%	Ajman 1968 No.	%	Umm al-Qaiwain 1968 No.	%	Ras al-Khaimah 1968 No.	%	Fujairah 1968 No.	%	Total* No.	%
Employer	816	2	NA	—	559	2	1,134	5	302	3	82	7	55	5	419	6	81	3	2,632	3
Self-Employed	9,790	18	NA	—	3,133	11	4,516	19	2,436	23	384	31	382	32	2,862	38	1,551	50	15,264	20
Employees	39,248	73	NA	—	23,942	82	17,048	71	7,346	69	654	54	639	54	3,626	48	1,015	33	54,270	70
Unpaid Family Workers	1,081	2	NA	—	407	1	641	3	206	2	24	2	45	4	435	6	413	13	2,171	3
Unemployed	1,775	3	NA	—	1,243	4	675	3	352	3	78	6	59	5	243	3	26	1	2,676	3
Not Stated	564	1	NA	—	—	—	—	—	—	—	—	—	—	—	—	—	—	—	—	—
Total Economically Active Population	53,274	100	NA	—	29,284	100	24,014	100	10,642	100	1,222	100	1,180	100	7,585	100	3,086	100	77,013	100

Economic Status	Bahrain 1965 No.	%	Qatar No.	%	Abu Dhabi 1968 No.	%	Dubai 1968 No.	%	Sharjah 1968 No.	%	Ajman 1968 No.	%	Umm al-Qaiwain 1968 No.	%	Ras al-Khaimah 1968 No.	%	Fujairah 1968 No.	%	Total* No.	%
Total Economically Active	53,274	29	NA	—	29,284	63	24,014	41	10,642	34	1,222	29	1,180	32	7,585	31	3,086	32	77,013	43
Total Economically Inactive	128,929	71	NA	—	17,091	37	34,957	59	21,026	66	3,024	71	2,564	68	16,802	69	6,649	68	102,113	57
Total Population	182,203	100	NA	—	46,375	100	58,971	100	31,668	100	4,246	100	3,744	100	24,387	100	9,735	100	179,126	100

Note:

*Total does not include Bahrain & Qatar

Percent column may not add to 100 because of rounding.

NA = Not Available

Sources: Trucial States Census, 1968, (Unpublished); and

Government of Bahrain, *Statistical Abstract*, 1968.

Table 2-2
Population by State and Age Group

Age Group	Bahrain 1965 No.	Bahrain 1965 % of Total	Qatar NA No.	Qatar NA % of Total	Abu Dhabi 1968 No.	Abu Dhabi 1968 % of Total	Dubai 1968 No.	Dubai 1968 % of Total	Sharjah 1968 No.	Sharjah 1968 % of Total
Under 1	4,800	2.6	NA	–	306	0.7	1,192	2.0	623	2.0
1-5	31,675	17.4	NA	–	4,349	9.4	8,409	14.3	4,865	15.4
6-10	28,312	15.5	NA	–	3,300	7.1	6,718	11.4	4,350	13.7
11-15	18,880	10.4	NA	–	2,430	5.2	4,598	7.8	2,742	8.7
16-20	16,579	9.1	NA	–	5,101	11.0	5,852	9.9	2,748	8.7
21-30	32,839	18.0	NA	–	15,637	33.7	14,207	24.1	6,238	19.7
31-40	23,171	12.7	NA	–	8,681	18.7	9,451	16.0	4,970	15.7
41-50	13,492	7.4	NA	–	3,806	8.2	4,843	8.2	2,879	9.1
51-60	7,082	3.9	NA	–	1,698	3.7	2,178	3.7	1,432	4.5
61-75	4,166	2.3	NA	–	835	1.8	1,187	2.0	662	2.1
76 & over	1,207	0.7	NA	–	232	0.5	336	0.6	159	0.5
Total	182,203	100	NA	–	46,375	100	58,971	100	31,668	100

Age Group	Ajman 1968 No.	Ajman 1968 % of Total	Umm al-Qaiwain 1968 No.	Umm al-Qaiwain 1968 % of Total	Ras al-Khaimah 1968 No.	Ras al-Khaimah 1968 % of Total	Fujairah 1968 No.	Fujairah 1968 % of Total	Total* 1968 No.	Total* 1968 % of Total
Under 1	95	2.2	78	2.1	455	1.9	84	0.9	2,833	1.6
1-5	621	14.6	473	12.6	3,451	14.2	1,602	16.5	23,770	13.3
6-10	578	13.6	468	12.5	3,359	13.8	1,618	16.6	20,391	11.4
11-15	386	9.1	321	8.6	2,292	9.4	804	8.3	13,573	7.6
16-20	378	8.9	294	7.9	2,314	9.5	779	8.0	17,466	9.8
21-30	730	17.2	600	16.0	4,520	18.5	1,750	18.0	43,682	24.4
31-40	645	15.2	633	16.9	3,900	16.0	1,593	16.4	29,873	16.7
41-50	404	9.5	446	11.9	2,354	9.7	914	9.4	15,646	8.7
51-60	225	5.3	233	6.2	988	4.1	421	4.3	7,175	4.0
61-75	118	2.8	148	4.0	599	2.5	143	1.5	3,692	2.1
76 & over	66	1.6	50	1.3	155	0.6	27	0.3	1,025	0.6
Total	4,246	100	3,744	100	24,387	100	9,735	100	179,126	100

Note:
*Totals in last column do not include Bahrain and Qatar.
NA = Not Available.
Percent columns may not add to 100 because of rounding.
Sources: Trucial States Census, 1968 (unpublished);
Government of Bahrain, *Statistical Abstract, 1968.*

are females. In case the reader is puzzled by this and the preceding percentage figure for females, it should be remembered that the total female population is substantially larger than the total economically active population. For the seven Trucial states together, 68% of the males are active and 32% inactive, and as in Bahrain, 2% of the females are economically active and 98% are inactive. Female participation in the economic activities is again limited in the case of the Trucial states; it ranges from 1% to 2.5% of the economically active population. A breakdown of the economic status of the population by sex is presented for Bahrain in Table 2-3, and for the seven Trucial states together in Table 2-4.

Bahrain is the most developed country among the Gulf states and it has the highest level of female participation in the economy. In 1965, there were 2,023 females working outside the home in Bahrain, while in 1968, there were only 1,420 females similarly working in all of the seven Trucial states. Realization of and capitalization on the potentiality of female participation in the economic and social life in these countries would undoubtedly enhance the process of economic and social development. In view of this, the reasons for their limited participation should be carefully examined; to the extent that it is a matter of cultural tradition that females should not accept outside employment, optimum strategies should be designed to change the traditional attitudes; and to the extent that it is a result of lack of training for females, providing the needed

Table 2-3

Population by Economic Status and Sex, Bahrain (1965 Census)

Economic Status	Male No.	%	Female No.	%	Total No.	%
Employers	812	2	4	..	816	2
Self-Employed	9,638	19	152	8	9,790	18
Employees	37,499	73	1,749	86	39,248	73
Unpaid Family Workers	1,031	2	50	2	1,081	2
Unemployed	1,769	3	6	..	1,775	3
Others	502	1	62	3	564	1
Total Economically Active	51,251	100	2,023	100	53,274	100

Economic Status	Male No.	%	Female No.	%	Total No.	%
Economically Active	51,251	52	2,023	2	53,274	29
Economically Inactive	48,133	48	80,796	98	128,929	71
Total	99,384	100	82,819	100	182,203	100

Note: (..) signifies less than 1/2 percent.

Percent columns may not add to 100 because of rounding.

Source: Government of Bahrain, 1965 Census.

Table 2-4

Population by Economic Status and Sex, the Seven Trucial States (1968 Census)

Economic Status	Male		Female		Total	
	No.	%	No.	%	No.	%
Employers	2,614	3	18	1	2,632	3
Self-Employed	15,042	20	222	16	15,264	20
Employees	53,198	70	1,072	75	54,270	70
Unpaid Family Workers	2,081	3	90	6	2,171	3
Unemployed	2,658	4	18	1	2,676	3
Total Economically Active	75,593	100	1,420	100	77,013	100

Economic Status	Male		Female		Total	
	No.	%	No.	%	No.	%
Economically Active Population	75,593	68	1,420	2	77,013	43
Economically Inactive Population	35,213	32	66,900	98	102,113	57
Total Population	110,806	100	68,320	100	179,126	100

Note: Percent columns may not add to 100 because of rounding.
Source: Trucial States, 1968 census data.

facilities for this should be given serious consideration by the leadership in these countries.

The economically active population ratio is unfavorable in the countries reviewed, with the exception of Abu Dhabi, and here the more favorable ratio is the result of the inflow of male immigrants from abroad rather than female participation in the economy. In industrial countries, 60% or more of the total population is economically active. It can be seen from the figures in Table 2-1 that only Abu Dhabi falls in this range, while the figures for the other Gulf city states listed fall well below this.[1] From the figures for these developing countries, one cannot find grounds to support the thesis that the more developed a country is, the higher its activity rate will tend to be; for among the group reviewed here, Bahrain is the most advanced, yet, its activity rate is the lowest.

Employment Distribution of the Economically Active Population

As has been mentioned, until recently, and particularly before some of these countries began to enjoy oil receipts, they subsisted on primitive agriculture and fishing. The oil receipts, to the extent that they have been used to promote urban infrastructure, have created new horizons and new employment opportunities. Many workers have left their traditional occupations and have moved into more promising jobs. Consequently, the decline in the traditional occupations in agriculture and fishing is a useful measure of the extent of progress in these countries. Also, the extent of diversity in employment and the absence of acute concentrations are useful indicators of progress. Of course, labor freed from traditional occupations needs to be trained to enable it to participate effectively in the new opportunities brought about by the process of development. The employment figures which are given below for the various sectors of the economies of the countries under review are the most recent ones available. Though there have been some changes since they were issued, the figures listed are quite indicative of the present employment distribution pattern. Unfortunately, employment figures for different sectors for Qatar are not available.

Employment in Agriculture and Fishing

The agriculture and fishing sector absorbs 8.7% of the economically active population in Bahrain, 7.8% in Abu Dhabi, 6.7% in Dubai, 23.5% in Sharjah, 35.8% in Ajman, 49.3% in Umm al-Qaiwain, 49.3% in Ras al-Khaimah and 77.7% in Fujairah (see Table 2-5). This sector plays a major role in the economy of the less developed countries; and, generally speaking, the higher the level of participation in agriculture and fishing, the less is likely to be the level of development in the country. A high level of labor participation in this area in the case of individual Gulf city states does not necessarily mean a level of production which is proportionate to the number of workers. Agriculture and fishing is the most backward and inefficient sector in all of the countries under review. Traditional agricultural and fishing methods are still predominant and, consequently, the average productivity is very low—throughout the Trucial states average annual productivity per worker was estimated at $600 in 1968.

The average educational level of those employed in agriculture and fishing in the Gulf city states is extremely low. Ninety-eight and one-half percent of those working in agriculture and fishing in Bahrain have no formal education whatsoever, 1.3% have primary education and just one person has university training (see Table 2-6). A similar pattern prevails also in the case of the Trucial states where about 98% of those working in this sector have not received any education, only 2% have primary education, and just two persons have university training (see Table 2-7). One can argue for developing countries in general that there is a significant correlation between the level of education and the level of productivity; and in the case of the countries considered here, low levels of education are definitely related to the low worker productivity.

The use of more modern methods would ultimately lead to higher productiv-

Table 2-5

Economically Active Population of the Gulf City States by Sector of Employment

Industry	Bahrain 1965 No.	% of Total	Qatar 1968 No.	% of Total	Abu Dhabi 1968 No.	% of Total	Dubai 1968 No.	% of Total	Sharjah 1968 No.	% of Total	Ajman 1968 No.	% of Total	Umm al-Qaiwain 1968 No.	% of Total	Ras al-Khaimah 1968 No.	% of Total	Fujairah 1968 No.	% of Total
Agriculture & Fishing	4,654	8.7	NA	–	2,284	7.8	1,601	6.7	2,503	23.5	437	35.8	582	49.3	3,736	49.3	2,398	77.7
Manufacturing, Mining, Quarrying	578	1.1	NA	–	880	3.0	1,546	6.4	392	3.7	25	2.0	22	1.9	153	2.0	11	0.4
Construction	8,328	15.6	NA	–	11,731	40.1	4,029	16.8	2,530	23.8	183	15.0	142	12.0	939	12.4	320	10.4
Oil Industry	6,940	13.0	NA	–	2,428	8.3	410	1.7	162	1.5	16	1.3	4	0.3	40	0.5	2	0.1
Retail & Wholesale Trade	7,386	13.9	NA	–	1,787	6.1	4,434	18.5	1,006	9.5	150	12.3	114	9.7	469	6.2	68	2.2
Banking	354	0.7	NA	–	153	0.5	483	2.0	76	0.7	2	0.2	–	–	15	0.2	1	0.0
Transport & Communication	5,494	10.3	NA	–	2,073	7.1	4,153	17.3	1,359	12.8	98	8.0	82	6.9	704	9.3	65	2.1
Government Services	10,394	19.5	NA	–	4,536	15.5	3,658	15.2	1,818	17.1	218	17.8	141	11.9	1,111	14.6	143	4.6
Other Services	9,146	17.2	NA	–	3,412	11.7	3,700	15.4	796	7.5	93	7.6	93	7.9	418	5.5	78	2.5
Total	53,274	100	NA		29,284	100	24,014	100	10,642	100	1,222	100	1,180	100	7,585	100	3,086	100
of which:																		
Male	51,251	96.2	NA		28,981	99.0	23,412	97.5	10,412	97.8	1,190	97.4	1,149	97.4	7,397	97.5	3,052	98.9
Female	2,023	3.8	NA		303	1.0	602	2.5	230	2.2	32	2.6	31	2.6	188	2.5	34	1.1

Note: Percent columns may not add to 100 because of rounding.

NA = Not Available

Sources: Trucial States Census, 1968 (Unpublished); and

Government of Bahrain, *Statistical Abstract*, 1968.

Table 2-6
Economically Active Population of Bahrain by Industry and Level of Education (1965 Census)

| Industry | Level of Education | | | | | | | | Total in Industry |
| | None | | Primary | | Technical & Secondary | | University | | |
	Number	% of Total in Industry	Number	% of Total in Industry	Number	% of Total in Industry	Number	% of Total in Industry	
Agriculture & Fishing	4,585	98.5	61	1.3	7	0.2	1	0.0	4,654
Manufacturing, Mining & Quarrying	463	80.1	91	15.7	20	3.5	4	0.7	578
Construction	7,630	91.6	497	6.0	152	1.8	49	0.6	8,328
Oil Industry	3,718	53.6	1,400	20.2	1,402	20.2	420	6.1	6,940
Retail and Wholesale Trade	5,266	71.3	1,249	16.9	694	9.4	177	2.4	7,386
Banking	82	23.2	103	29.1	131	37.0	38	10.7	354
Transport and Communication	4,102	74.7	678	12.3	469	8.5	245	4.8	5,494
Government Services	6,218	59.8	1,642	15.8	1,979	19.0	555	5.3	10,394
Other Services	7,115	77.8	1,161	12.7	604	6.6	266	2.9	9,146
Total	39,179	73.5	6,882	12.9	5,458	10.2	1,755	3.3	53,274

Note: Addition of percent rows may not add to 100 because of rounding.
Source: Government of Bahrain, 1965 Census.

Table 2-7

Economically Active Population by Industry and Level of Education in the Trucial States, except Abu Dhabi (1968 Census)

Industry	None		Primary		Secondary		Technical		University		Total
	Number	% of Total in Industry	Number	% of Total in Industry	Number	% of Total in Industry	Number	% of Total in Industry	Number	% of Total in Industry	Total
Agriculture & Fishing	11,023	97.9	220	2.0	12	0.1	–	–	2	0.0	11,257
Manufacture, Mining & Quarrying	1,402	65.2	503	23.4	208	9.7	13	0.6	23	1.1	2,149
Construction	6,466	79.4	898	11.0	556	6.8	22	0.3	201	2.5	8,143
Oil Industry	432	68.1	93	14.7	66	10.4	4	0.6	39	6.2	634
Retail and Wholesale	3,435	55.0	1,592	25.6	995	15.9	5	0.1	214	3.4	6,241
Banking	160	27.7	103	17.9	213	36.9	1	0.2	100	17.3	577
Transport and Communication	5,391	83.4	690	10.7	296	4.6	9	0.1	75	1.2	6,461
Government Services	4,652	65.6	1,032	14.6	955	13.5	27	0.4	423	6.0	7,089
Other Services	3,841	74.2	924	17.8	314	6.1	12	0.2	87	1.7	5,178
Total	36,802	77.1	6,055	12.7	3,615	7.6	93	0.2	1,164	2.4	47,729

Note: Percent rows may not add to 100 because of rounding.

Source: Trucial States Census, 1968 (Unpublished).

ity; but in order to be able to use modern methods and techniques, the participants must be trained. The provision of such training depends on the ability and the will of the country to reallocate the necessary resources to training and education in order to develop more productive labor. A labor force trained in modern methods of agriculture and fishing would give higher productivity which would mean that a smaller number of workers would be needed to meet the needs of the community. This would give rise to the question of how to employ the surplus labor. Even in the absence of an interest in raising productivity, to reduce the excessive number of persons employed in agriculture and fishing would involve the channeling of surplus labor to other jobs; and this would necessitate the creation of new job opportunities. Whether this would be possible or not would depend, among other things, on the ability of these countries to finance new projects; but it does not necessarily follow that surplus labor from the agricultural and fishing sector would be qualified to undertake the new jobs created. These laborers are untrained and traditional and it is unlikely that it would be possible to place them easily in other jobs if appropriate productivity standards are to be maintained. In view of this, the choice of technology should not overlook the manpower situation prevailing.

Employment in Manufacturing

Manufacturing is of relatively little significance in all of the countries under review. This sector employs roughly 1.1% of the economically active population in Bahrain, 1.3% in Abu Dhabi, 6.4% in Dubai, 3.7% in Sharjah, 2.0% in Ajman and Ras al-Khaimah, and just 0.4% in Fujairah (see Table 2-5). It is more developed than agriculture and fishing as is reflected in the fact that 23.4% of those employed in industry in the Trucial states have a primary education, 9.7% have had secondary schooling, and about 1% have had university training (see Table 2-7). Similarly, in Bahrain, 15.7% of the industrial workers have primary, 3.5% technical, and 0.7% university education (see Table 2-6).

Employment in Construction

Construction seems to occupy a major role in all of the countries reviewed, since approximately 15.6% of the labor force in Bahrain is employed in this sector, 40.1% in Abu Dhabi, 16.8% in Dubai, 23.8% in Sharjah, 15.0% in Ajman, 12.0% in Umm al-Qaiwain, 12.4% in Ras al-Khaimah and 10.4% in Fujairah (see Table 2-5). All of these countries, in varying degrees, are promoting urban infrastructural development, and they are building roads, streets, private houses, government buildings, etc. Relatively speaking, there is a boom in this sector. The exceptionally high level of employment in construction in Abu Dhabi, 40.1% of the economically active population, is due to the launching by the government in 1967 and 1968 of major construction projects. These projects were made possible by the large volume of oil receipts.

Employment in the Oil Industry

The oil industry plays a significant employment role in the oil-producing countries. Thirteen percent of the active population is employed in this sector in Bahrain, 8.3% in Abu Dhabi and 1.7%, 1.5%, 1.3%, 0.3%, 0.5% and 0.1% in Dubai, Sharjah, Ajman, Umm al-Qaiwain, Ras al-Khaimah and Fujairah, respectively (see Table 2-5). Limited worker participation in the oil sector, except in Bahrain and Abu Dhabi, is due to the fact that six of the remaining seven states have not yet had confirmed oil strikes, and the seventh, Dubai, did not make its first shipment until 1969. The latest figure for employment in the oil sector for Dubai was for 1968, and the figure has undoubtedly risen significantly since then. The smaller relative employment participation in Abu Dhabi compared with Bahrain, 8.5% versus 13.0%, may seem surprising at first glance since the level of production in Abu Dhabi is much higher than that in Bahrain. Actually, the difference stems from the fact that Bahrain has a large refinery which handles local output as well as some oil piped from Saudi Arabia. About 5,000 Bahraini work in this refinery. Should Abu Dhabi decide to refine its production, or part of it, locally and to build a refinery, additional jobs would be created.

The educational level of those employed in the oil industry is not very high. Sixty-eight percent of the oil workers in the Trucial states have no formal education, 14.7% have a primary education, 10.4% have a secondary education and 6.2% have had university training (see Table 2-7). In Bahrain, 53.6% have no formal education, 20.2% have a primary education, 20.2% have a technical and secondary, and 6.1% have had university training (see Table 2-6). The oil industry in Bahrain is more advanced than it is in the other countries, because it has had longer experience in this field.

Employment in Trade

Trade is a major occupation in all of the countries under review. Thirteen and nine-tenths percent, 6.1%, 18.5%, 9.5%, 12.3%, 6.2%, 2.2%, and 9.7% of the economically active population is employed in this sector in Bahrain, Abu Dhabi, Dubai, Sharjah, Ajman, Ras al-Khaimah, Fujairah, and Umm al-Qaiwain, respectively (see Table 2-5). The relatively high level of participation in the case of Bahrain and Dubai is due to the fact that both have an entrepot trade to other

Gulf and non-Gulf countries. The relatively limited participation in the case of Fujairah is a result of its being the only country in the group which has no coast on the Gulf. In Bahrain, 71.3% of the participants in the trade sector have had no formal education, 16.9% have a primary education, 9.4% have a secondary or technical education, and 2.4% have had university training (see Table 2-6). In the Trucial states, 55.0% in this sector have no formal education, 25.6% have a primary education, 15.9% have a secondary education, and 3.4% have had university training (see Table 2-7). Though the educational level in the trade sector is relatively low in comparison with that in developed countries, it is more advanced than that for such sectors as fishing, agriculture and construction in the Gulf city states.

Employment in Banking

Banking is a booming activity in most of the countries reviewed, and it is the most advanced sector because the majority of the workers in the banks are foreigners. In Bahrain, there are eight banks and 0.7% of the economically active population is engaged in the banking sector; in Abu Dhabi, there are five banks and 0.5% of the active population is employed by this sector; in Dubai, there are eight banks, with 2% engaged in banking; in Sharjah, there are six banks and 0.7% of the active population works in this sector; Ajman has one bank with 0.2% employed in this field; and Ras al-Khaimah has six banks with 0.2% of the active population working in the banking sector (see Table 2-5). For a summary listing of the banks operating in these Gulf states, see Table 2-8.

Employment in the Transportation and Communications Sector

Transportation and communications absorb a significant ratio of the active population in all of the countries under review. The figures are 10.3%, 7.1%, 17.3%, 12.8%, 8.0%, 6.9%, 9.3%, and 2.1% for Bahrain, Abu Dhabi, Dubai, Sharjah, Ajman, Umm al-Qaiwain, Ras al-Khaimah and Fujairah, respectively (see Table 2-5). As would be expected, in all of these countries where the level of participation in trade is high, it is also high in transportation and communications. Generally speaking, this sector is also backward. In Bahrain, 74.7% of those in this sector have no education, 12.3% have a primary education, 8.5% have a secondary or technical education, and 4.8% have university training (see Table 2-6). In the Trucial states, 83.4% of those employed in transportation and communications have no education, 10.7% have a primary education, 4.6% have a secondary or technical education, and 1.2% have university training (see Table 2-7).

Table 2-8

Banks Operating in the Gulf City States as of January 1971

	Bahrain	Qatar	Abu Dhabi	Dubai	Sharjah	Ajman	Umm al-Qaiwain	Ras al-Khaimah	Fujairah
1. Bank of Bahrain (Bahrain)	X								
2. Arab Bank, Ltd. (Amman, Jordan)	X	X						X	
3. British Bank of M.E. (London)	X	X	X	X	X			X	
4. The Eastern Bank, Ltd. (London)	X	X	X		X				
5. First National City Bank (New York)	X			X					
6. Habib Bank Overseas, Ltd. (Karachi)	X			X	X			X	
7. Ratidain Bank (Baghdad)	X								
8. Union Bank (Karachi)	X								
9. Qatar National Bank, S.A.		X							
10. Intra Bank, Ltd. (Beirut)		X							
11. Ottoman Bank, Ltd. (London)		X							
12. Bank of Oman, Ltd.			X	X				X	
13. National and Grindlays Bank (London)		X	X		X				
14. National Bank of Abu Dhabi			X						
15. National Bank of Dubai				X					
16. United Bank, Ltd.					X				
17. The Commercial Bank of Dubai				X	X			X	
18. Mille Iran Bank (Iran)				X	X				
19. Bank Saderat Iran (Iran)				X		X		X	
Total	8	7	5	8	7	1	N.A.	6	N.A.

Source: Authors' survey.

Employment in Government

Government services play a major role in the economic activities of these countries. In Bahrain, 19.5% of the active population is employed by the government, which is the highest participation among all the sectors; in Abu Dhabi, 15.5% of the active population works for the government; and for the other states, the figures are 15.2% in Dubai; 17.1% in Sharjah; 17.8% in Ajman; 11.9% in Umm al-Qaiwain; 14.6% in Ras al-Khaimah; and 4.6% in Fujairah (see Table 2-5). The different percentages of employment in this sector indicate the extent of the variation in government participation in the economic and social life of these countries. These differences stem not from different political ideologies, but rather they reflect, in part, the financial situation of the governments concerned.

Although the more developed countries in the group have greater diversity in occupations, this diversity does not necessarily indicate higher levels of performance. Almost all of the sectors are relatively backward as measured by the level of education of the participants. Originally, the traditional sector of agriculture and fishing was predominant in all of the GCS. As a result of promoting urban economic and social infrastructural development, new job opportunities were created and some of the laborers who had been working in traditional occupations were attracted to new sectors. In the process, they carried their lack of training to the new jobs. This suggests that as these communities attempt to modernize the traditional sector of agriculture and fishing by utilizing modern methods and equipment, and to shift the surplus labor to new job opportunities, they will be tending to transfer workers with little training from one place to another. Appropriate planning to ascertain training needs and to develop appropriate training programs and facilities is urgently needed for the upgrading of the labor force which will be required for effective economic, political and social development in these countries. More specific comments on the kinds of training programs that would be desirable will be presented in a later chapter. A summary of the educational pattern for the various states is presented in Table 2-9.

The Economic Importance of Oil

Four Gulf city states, Bahrain, Qatar, Abu Dhabi and Dubai, are presently receiving revenues from oil production; and the other five have oil concessions granted to interested oil companies, though no oil finds in any of them have been confirmed as yet. This means that these nine states can appropriately be grouped into two major categories: oil-producing countries (financially better-off countries) and nonoil-producing countries (poor countries). The total population of the oil-producing countries, Bahrain, Qatar, Abu Dhabi, and

Table 2-9

Economically Active Population of the Gulf City States by Level of Education

Level of Education	Bahrain 1965		Abu Dhabi 1968		Dubai 1968		Sharjah 1968		Ajman 1968		Umm al-Qaiwain 1968		Ras al-Khaimah 1968		Fujairah 1968		Qatar NA	
	No.	% of total	No.	% of total	No.	% of total	No.	% of total	No.	% of total	No.	% of total	No.	% of total	No.	% of total	No.	% of total
None	39,179	73.5	22,827	78.0	15,912	66.3	8,908	83.7	1,114	90.2	1,039	88.1	6,835	90.1	2,994	97.0	NA	—
Primary	6,882	12.9	3,127	10.7	4,475	18.6	949	8.9	48	3.9	106	9.0	413	5.4	64	2.1	NA	—
Secondary	5,458	10.2	2,305	7.9	2,699	11.2	590	5.5	33	2.7	26	2.2	240	3.2	27	0.9	NA	—
Technical			256	0.9	51	0.2	19	0.2	11	0.9	1	0.1	11	0.1	–	–	NA	—
University	1,755	3.3	769	2.6	877	3.7	176	1.7	16	1.3	8	0.7	86	1.1	1	0.0	NA	—
Total	53,274	100	29,284	100	24,014	100	10,642	100	1,222	100	1,180	100	7,585	100	3,086	100	NA	—

Note: Percent columns may not add to 100 because of rounding.

Sources: Trucial States Census, 1968 (Unpublished);
Government of Bahrain, *Statistical Abstract*, 1968.

Dubai, according to the 1970 estimates, is 420,000; and the total population of the other five countries is only 90,000. Thus, more than 80% of the total population of the Gulf city states is located in oil-producing countries. It should be noted that those living in the nonoil countries have benefited from the growing economies of their oil-producing neighbors. The day may come when much of the other 20%, if oil is not discovered in their countries, will have moved to and settled in the rich oil-producing countries in the area.

Although all of the oil countries receiving oil revenues are economically better off than any of those with no oil output, there are substantial differences in output levels among the active producers. Crude oil production estimates in 1970 were 80,000 US barrels per day in Bahrain, 370,000 b/d in Qatar, 695,000 b/d in Abu Dhabi and 100,000 b/d in Dubai (see Table 2-10). The average per capita barrel output per day is 0.4 in Bahrain, 4.6 in Qatar, 11.6 in Abu Dhabi and 1.3 in Dubai (see Table 2-11). According to this measure, Abu Dhabi is the richest of these states, followed by Qatar, Dubai and then Bahrain. On the basis of present knowledge of its oil reserves, Bahrain does not stand a good chance of increasing its production much beyond the present level. In 1950, its average output was 30,000 b/d, and by 1970 it had only reached 80,000 b/d. It cannot increase its production beyond this level if it wishes to maintain this resource for the coming twenty years or so.

Qatar's production in 1950 was 33,000 b/d and by 1970, it had risen to 370,000 b/d. As of 1967, its proven reserves were 3.75 billion US barrels. Abu Dhabi's production in 1962 averaged 15,000 b/d, and in 1970, it was 695,000 b/d. Its proven reserves, as of 1967, were two billion metric tons (14.8 billion US barrels). Dubai's production in 1970 was estimated at 100,000 b/d, and it is expected to double this in five years. A summary of the oil output of the four oil-producing states is presented in Tables 2-10 and 2-11.

Given the known reserve situation, Bahrain cannot hope to finance a greater rate of development from oil receipts, while Qatar and Abu Dhabi have promising further potentialities based upon revenues from the exploitation of this resource. Dubai is in a unique position. Although oil finds were not confirmed in this country until 1966, it has been able for some years, as mentioned previously, to promote a significant amount of infrastructural development financed by entrepot trade. As will be seen in the later discussion of foreign trade, Dubai has served as a major trading center in the area. The new oil revenues which it has been receiving since late 1969, have opened new horizons and promising opportunities for further growth and change in its economic and social fabric as well as in that of the nearby tiny city states of Sharjah, Umm al-Qaiwain, Ajman, Ras al-Khaimah and Fujairah.

Most of the economic and social developments which have been achieved in the oil and in the nonoil Gulf city states have been made possible by oil receipts. Without oil, all these countries had limited coastal economies centered around fishing, though Dubai also had an entrepot trade. Oil receipts have provided the

Table 2-10
Crude Oil Production in the Gulf City States (Thousand U.S. Barrels per Day)

Year	Bahrain	Qatar	Abu Dhabi	Dubai
1950	30	33	–	–
1951	30	49	–	–
1952	30	69	–	–
1953	30	85	–	–
1954	30	100	–	–
1955	30	115	–	–
1956	30	123	–	–
1957	32	140	–	–
1958	41	174	–	–
1959	45	169	–	–
1960	45	175	–	–
1961	45	175	–	–
1962	45	190	15	–
1963	50	195	55	–
1964	60	215	185	–
1965	65	235	280	–
1966	75	290	360	–
1967	75	320	380	–
1968	70	340	500	–
1969	80E	355	600	–
1970	80E	370	695	100E

Note: E = Estimated.
Sources: *Aramco Handbook*, 1966;
Statistical Abstract, Bahrain, 1969;
Arab Report and Record, Abu Dhabi, 1969;
British Petroleum Company, *World Petroleum Statistical Review*, 1970.

means for financing urgently needed economic and social infrastructural development; and they have led to a flourishing trade activity in the oil-producing countries themselves and in the other Gulf city states. Without the oil receipts, any development which has been achieved so far, except in the case of Dubai, would not have been possible; and any further progress would have been beyond hope. Before ending these comments on the vital role which oil has played in setting the base for transforming the traditional tribal communities of the Gulf, a point which bears heavily on the service oil can render in the process of further development should be emphasized. It is true that much weight must be given to the quantity of oil produced by, and the reserves of, these countries as an indicator of their potential for further growth; but this must be accepted with some strong qualifications.

Table 2-11

Estimated Population and Daily per Capita Barrels of Oil Output in the Gulf City States, 1970

Country	1970 Estimated Population[1]	1970 Estimated Crude Oil Production, Barrels per Day	Per Capita Barrels per Day
Bahrain	205,000	80,000	0.4
Qatar	80,000	357,000	4.6
Abu Dhabi	60,000	575,000	11.6
Dubai	75,000	100,000	1.3
Sharjah	40,000	–	–
Ajman	5,500	–	–
Umm al-Qaiwain	4,500	–	–
Ras al-Khaimah	30,000	–	–
Fujairah	10,000	–	–
Total	510,000	1,245,000	2.44

Note: [1] Estimate includes both foreign and local population.

Sources: Compiled on basis of Tables 1-2 and 2-10.

The levels of oil production are indicative of the revenues accruing from this resource, and the amount of these receipts determines the ability of the recipient countries to buy goods and services—more specifically, they determine their ability to import goods from other countries, since they must import foodstuffs, consumer goods and capital goods. At this point, some important questions arise. First, will these receipts be used and distributed equitably? Second, what will be the proportion of these receipts devoted to expenditures on capital goods? No matter how large the receipts are, these countries have unlimited potential demands, and since their resources are limited, efficient use must be made of them if a favorable rate of progress is to be achieved. It is of interest to note, for example, that although Qatar and Bahrain essentially started from the same base before the discovery of oil, and while the oil revenues which have been available to Qatar are several times those of Bahrain, the level of development which Bahrain has achieved so far is substantially higher than that of Qatar. This illustrates the fact that it is not just the money but what is done with it, and how, that counts in development. It is the policies of those who receive the revenues and are entrusted with spending them on behalf of the society that are of crucial importance. If these leaders are conscientious and have a vision for the future, they will allocate available resources according to a scale of priorities which will enhance the development of their societies.

Agriculture and Fishing

Agriculture in the Gulf city states is limited by the scarcity of water. Rainfall is very scanty in the area, and lands suitable for cultivation are confined to some favored localities and oases.

In Bahrain, there are some 6,100 hectares under cultivation which is about 9% of the total area.[2] This cultivable area percentage is much below that of Iraq or Syria, for example, but it compares favorably with the percentages for Kuwait, Southern Yemen and Lebanon. In Qatar, there are about 3,400 hectares under cultivation, or approximately 0.23% of the total area. In the six states of Dubai, Sharjah, Ajman, Umm al-Qaiwain, Ras al-Khaimah and Fujairah, there is a total of some 3,500 hectares under cultivation which is 0.35% of their total land area, while in Abu Dhabi, alone, there are 9,000 hectares under cultivation, or 0.14% of its total area. Summary figures on arable land areas are given in Tables 2-12 and 2-13.

The average amount of cultivable land per capita is .03 hectares in Bahrain, .04 hectares in Qatar, .15 hectares in Abu Dhabi, and .02 hectares per head in the remaining six Trucial States. The overall average for the nine countries is .04. The world average of arable land was 0.4 hectares per head in 1967, so this means that the average in these countries is just one-tenth of the world average. Not only are arable lands limited in these countries, but the problem is further compounded by the fact that most of the arable land in the area is devoted to palm trees, 67% in the case of Bahrain, and 71% in six of the northern Trucial States (see Table 2-14). The gross annual returns from palm trees are estimated at only about $200 per hectare, which is quite low. The rest of the cultivable land is planted with vegetables and summer crops which are not highly productive. The average return from vegetables is estimated at about $800 per hectare which, relatively, also represents a very low productivity.

Table 2-12

Distribution of Arable Land among the Gulf City States

Country	Arable Area (Hectares)	Hectares per Capita	% of Arable Area to Total Area
Bahrain, 1968	6,100	0.03	9
Qatar, 1968	3,400	0.04	0.34
Dubai, Sharjah Ajman, Umm al-Qaiwain, Ras al-Khaimah, Fujairah, 1968	3,500	0.02	0.35
Abu Dhabi	9,000	0.15	0.14
Total	22,000	0.04	0.24

Sources: Report of Bahrain to the Food and Agriculture Organization, 4th Session of the Near East Commission on Agriculture Planning, Baghdad, 23 March to 2 April, 1968;

An-Nahar Survey, *Qatar*, September 1970, p. 41;

Survey conducted by the British Ministry of Overseas Development covering the Northern Trucial States, 1968, Vol. II, p. 21 (unpublished);

Department of Information, Government of Abu Dhabi, *Abu Dhabi: Yesterday and Today*, n.d., pp. 171-173 (in Arabic).

Table 2-13

Percentage Distribution of Agricultural Population and Arable Land in Selected Countries of the Middle East

Country	Arable Land (Percentage)	Agricultural Population (Percentage)
Iraq (1964)	46.2	30.9
Jordan (1965)	7.0	5.1
Kuwait (1964)	—	0.3
Lebanon (1964)	1.8	8.8
Saudi Arabia (1964)	2.3	25.0
Southern Yemen (1964)	1.6	6.9
Syria (1964)	41.1	23.0
	100.0%	100.0%

Source: United Nations, *Selected Development Problems in Various Countries in the Middle East*, 1969, Table 3, p. 50.

Not only is land productivity quite low, but labor productivity in agriculture is also very low, for average annual per capita productivity ranges between $200 and $240. The low level of productivity of both agricultural land and labor can be viewed from another perspective.

Efforts to achieve agricultural development in the area could be directed toward (1) extensive development, or increasing the cultivable area; (2) intensive development, that is, increasing the productivity of both land and labor. As a

Table 2-14

Percentage of Arable Land under Palm Trees and Other Cultivation in Selected Gulf City States

Country	Area under Palm Trees	Area under Other Annual Crops	Total
Bahrain	67	33	100
Qatar	12	88*	100
Abdu Dhabi	NA	NA	100
The Other Trucial States	71	29	100

Note: *Sixty percent of this area is under animal fodder and 28% under vegetables.

Sources: Report of Bahrain to the Food and Agriculture Organization, 4th Session of the Near East Commisssion on Agriculture Planning, Baghdad, 23 March to 2 April, 1968;

An-Nahar Survey, *Qatar*, September 1970, p. 41;

Department of Information, Government of Abu Dhabi, *Abu Dhabi: Yesterday and Today*, n.d., pp. 171-173 (in Arabic);

Survey conducted by the British Ministry of Overseas Development covering the Northern Trucial States, 1968, Vol. II, p. 22 (unpublished).

result of the limited amount of soil suitable for cultivation and the scarcity of water available for irrigation, these countries will probably have to concentrate on intensive development. Modern equipment and methods of cultivation, fertilizers, etc., properly applied, would certainly help to increase land productivity. Again, if workers were trained in modern methods and techniques, the number of persons required to cultivate the land would be smaller and total output, as well as output per worker, would be greater.

There is another opportunity to increase land productivity. Since most of the cultivable land is under palm trees and the productivity of these trees is very low, serious consideration should be given to the feasibility of more intensive land use which will produce high yields of high-value crops. To conclude, it can be said that the area as a whole has little prospect for major agricultural development, and plans to develop available natural resources should take this into consideration.

Fishing for long has been a major economic activity throughout the area. As mentioned previously, fishing was the backbone of the economies of all of these countries before oil discoveries and it still is in almost all the countries which have had no oil finds so far. In Sharjah, there are 1,604 persons working in fishing, or more than 15% of the total economically active population; and in Ajman, 338 persons, or some 30% of the total economically active population are so employed. For other Gulf states, the figures for employment in fishing are 440 persons, or more than 40% in Umm al-Qaiwain; 1,205 persons, or some 15% in Ras al-Khaimah; and 1,590 persons, or more than 50% in Fujairah.[3]

These figures show that fishing holds an important position in the economies of these countries. Again, as in the case of agriculture, productivity in this sector is very low. The average annual per capita productivity in fishing is $840 which, though rather low, is still roughly four times that of agriculture. This sector has a promising potential for development. The introduction of modern fishing craft and equipment and the training of fishermen to use modern equipment will undoubtedly increase productivity in this sector. Saying that this sector has the potential for development does not necessarily mean that it is now desirable to modernize it. Fishermen are uneducated, illiterate and untrained. If steps are taken to increase their productivity without at the same time expanding marketing possibilities, a surplus labor situation could arise in this industry. Surplus labor from this sector is very difficult to absorb into other areas, and if it is not placed, unemployment, with its attendant rising tensions and growing seeds of dissatisfaction, would tend to generate ripples of political and social unrest. Modernizing this sector is possible and would give good returns, but it is important that the development of markets keep pace with increases in productivity. Careful planning and plan execution which take into consideration the relevant political, economic and social factors are needed to achieve an optimum trend of development in this sector.

Foreign Trade

Oil receipts accruing to the oil producing countries have provided the financing for a number of economic activities in them as well as in the other nonoil-producing Gulf city states. In varying degrees, oil receipts have been used to finance imports which include a wide range of products, both consumer and capital goods, since the Gulf city states need to import almost everything except fish. Although Bahrain, Qatar, and Dubai export some dried fish and frozen shrimp, oil is the only export of any significance.

Imports

All of the Gulf city states experienced relatively high and growing levels of imports in the late 1960s; and some indication of this is provided by Table 2-15. Bahrain, Qatar, Abu Dhabi and Dubai are the main centers of foreign trade for the GCS. Bahrain's imports rose from BD 38.7 million in 1965 to BD 57.95 in 1969, which is an increase of roughly 50% over this short time span. Oil production rose by 40% during the same period, and exports and reexports rose by more than 80%. As shown in Table 2-15, Qatar's imports rose during the same period from BD 12.29 million to BD 23 million, or by 80%. Abu Dhabi's imports increased from BD 18.6 million in 1968, to BD 57 million in 1969, which is a jump of more than 200%; and Dubai's imports rose from BD 31.13 in 1966, to BD 76.11 million in 1968, a rise of 144%.

Total imports of Bahrain, Qatar, Abu Dhabi and Dubai in 1969, amounted to at least BD 214 million.[4] Since total oil receipts of the four countries in the same year were approximately BD 150 million, and total exports and reexports amounted to approximately BD 30 million for Bahrain and Dubai combined, the two main reexporting centers, the deficit must have been financed by the gold trade in the area. Qatar is not a reexporting center and its only nonoil export is shrimp. Since 1968, when the Qatar National Fishing Company began to process shrimp, about 260 tons of frozen shrimp have been exported to Europe, Japan and the United States.

Bahrain's imports in 1969 were almost equal to those of Abu Dhabi and were about 80% of Dubai's imports for 1968. As a further comparison, they are roughly 250% of those of Qatar. In per capita import terms, these countries fall into two categories. Both Dubai's and Abu Dhabi's imports are approximately BD 950 per capita, and those for Bahrain and Qatar are roughly BD 290 per capita. The high per capita level of imports in the case of Dubai is indicative of its relative prosperity and is, in part, a result of its prominence in entrepot trade. Though its economy has been based primarily on trade, its oil receipts are becoming of increasing importance. The high levels of imports in Bahrain, Qatar,

Table 2-15
Total Imports of Selected Gulf City States (Million B.D.)

Country	1960	1961	1962	1963	1964	1965	1966	1967	1968	1969	% Change
Bahrain	NA	NA	NA	NA	NA	38.75	42.03	45.45	52.02	57.95	+ 50 (1965-69)
Qatar	13.29	10.95	13.80	11.52	11.74	12.29	12.27	13.55	19.98	23	+ 73 (1960-69)
Abu Dhabi	NA	NA	NA	NA	NA	NA	NA	NA	18.6	57	+210 (1968-69)
Dubai	NA	NA	NA	NA	NA	NA	31.13	47.69	76.11	NA	+140 (1966-68)

Note: NA = not available.

Sources: MEED & ARR Survey, *Bahrain 1969*, December 1969;

MEED & ARR Survey, *Qatar 1969*, October 1969;

An-Nahar Survey, *Qatar*, September 6, 1970;

MEED & ARR Survey, *Dubai 1969*, July 1969;

Financial Times Survey, Abu Dhabi, February 25, 1970;

Government of Bahrain, *Statistical Abstract*, 1970.

Abu Dhabi and Dubai are ascribed to the high rates of growth of their economies. These countries are building their economic and social infrastructures and their levels of income are rising; consequently, this has led to an increased demand for both consumer and capital goods.

The high level of imports in the case of Abu Dhabi is particularly due to the sudden growth of its oil revenue receipts and is indicative of its increasing prosperity and affluence. In the case of Bahrain, the growth of imports indicates growing prosperity; but it is also linked to the prominence of Bahrain as a transshipment center for the imports of other Gulf countries. The growth of imports in the case of Qatar is due to increased oil revenue and the increasing affluence which these have brought.

Whether the rising level of imports in these countries will be beneficial and conducive of further development in the long run will depend partly on the structure of the imports. No details on import structure are available for Qatar and Abu Dhabi, which are both oil-rich countries. Data presented in Table 2-16 on the imports of Bahrain show that consumer goods constitute a significant share of the total, for they comprised 40.2%, 42.3% and 47.7% of all imports in 1966, 1967 and 1968, respectively. There was a slight drop in consumer goods in 1969, when their share fell to roughly 37.5% of total imports. The extent of imports of consumer goods reflects the rising standard of living; but it also suggests that planning of imports may be advisable in order to encourage the inflow of capital goods and industrial supplies needed for a favorable rate of development.

In the case of Dubai, also, consumer goods represent the largest share of total imports, and they constituted, as shown in Table 2-16, 59.8%, 57.2% and 51.5% of the total in 1966, 1967, and 1968, respectively. In contrast with Bahrain, Dubai's proportion of consumer goods imports to total imports has been declining for several years, and machinery, transport and construction goods imports have risen from some 20.4% in 1966 to 32.9% in 1968 (see Table 2-16). Dubai could also benefit from import planning which would help to accelerate its rate of development.

The imports of Bahrain, Qatar, Dubai and Abu Dhabi come from almost all parts of the world, as can be seen from Table 2-17. Their major suppliers are the United Kingdom, Japan, the U.S.A., India, Pakistan, China, West Germany, Hong Kong, the Netherlands, Italy, France, Australia, Belgium, and Switzerland. At the top of the list of the suppliers of Bahrain are Britain, Japan, the United States, China (Peoples Republic), India, West Germany, Pakistan, and Hong Kong. Britain, Japan, the United States, China and West Germany, alone, supply more than 60% of its total imports. Britain again leads in the case of Qatar and Dubai, while Japan, the United States and West Germany are also of major importance among exporters to these two countries. Interestingly, Japan is the leading exporter to Dubai, while Britain, the United States, Pakistan, Switzerland and India are also important suppliers.

Table 2-16

Total Imports by Commodity in Bahrain and Dubai, 1966-69 (Thousand B.D.)

	Bahrain								Dubai							
	1966		1967		1968		1969		1966		1967		1968		1969	
Commodities	Value	% of total	Value	% of total	Value	% of total	Value	% of total	Value	% of total	Value	% of total	Value	% of total	Value	% of total
Foodstuffs	10,241	24.4	10,271	22.6	10,473	20.1	11,772	20.3	6,100	19.6	6,800	14.3	11,760	15.5	NA	–
Consumer Goods	16,894	40.2	19,227	42.3	24,810	47.7	21,715	37.5	18,620	59.8	27,300	57.2	39,170	51.5	NA	–
Machinery, transport & Construction Goods	7,790	18.5	8,028	17.7	8,738	16.8	10,729	18.5	6,350	20.4	13,480	28.3	25,040	32.9	NA	–
Unclassified Goods	7,109	16.9	7,927	17.4	8,000	15.4	13,723	23.7	60	0.2	110	0.2	140	0.2	NA	–
Total	42,034	100	45,453	100	52,021	100	57,939	100	31,130	100	47,690	100	76,110	100	NA	–

Note: Columns may not add to totals because of rounding.

Sources: Government of Bahrain, *Statistical Abstract*, 1970;

MEED & ARR Survey, *Bahrain 1969*, December 1969;

MEED & ARR Survey, *Dubai 1969*, July 1969.

Table 2-17

Total Imports by Country and Main Suppliers for Selected Gulf City States (Percentages)

No.	Supplier[1]	Bahrain 1969	Qatar 1969	Abu Dhabi 1969	Dubai 1968
1.	U.K.	24.6	22.6	31.9	16.4
2.	U.S.A.	10.7	12.5	18.4	9.4
3.	Japan	14.3	7.7	2.7	17.1
4.	India	4.9	4.5	1.9	4.7
5.	Pakistan	3.9	1.6	1.5	7.0
6.	China	6.6	2.3	–	3.8
7.	W. Germany	4.1	7.0	5.9	3.5
8.	Hong Kong	3.9	1.4	–	3.1
9.	Netherlands	2.9	3.3	3.9	2.3
10.	Italy	2.2	2.2	4.1	1.6
11.	France	1.6	3.6	2.9	1.6
12.	Iran	1.6	3.7	–	–
13.	Iraq	1.1	1.0	–	–
14.	Bahrain	–	4.3	–	–
15.	Lebanon	–	6.1	3.4	–
16.	Dubai	–	2.5	6.9	–
17.	U.A.R.	–	0.7	1.4	–
18.	Saudi Arabia	–	0.8	1.5	–
19.	Australia	–	2.3	1.1	–
20.	Belgium	–	2.1	1.0	–
21.	Switzerland	–	–	–	11.8
22.	Other Countries	17.7	7.8	11.5	17.7
–	Total	100	100	100	100

Notes: [1] Some of the suppliers for which figures are not available might have been included with other countries.

Percent columns may not add to 100 because of rounding.

Sources: Same sources as sources (1), (4), (5) and (6) of Table 2-15;

Government of Qatar, Customs Department, *Summary Bulletin of Statistics*, 1969.

Exports and Reexports

The rising level of imports of some of the Gulf city states in the late 1960s was accompanied by a rising level of exports, as can be seen from Table 2-18. The exports and reexports of Bahrain, excluding oil and its refined products, increased from BD 10.7 million in 1965 to BD 19.9 in 1969. This represented an increase of 86% in comparison with an increase of 50% in its imports during the same period. In absolute terms, nonoil exports were 28% of total imports in

Table 2-18

Total Exports and Reexports, Excluding Oil and Its Refined Products, in Value and as a Percent of Imports for Bahrain and Dubai, 1965-70 (Thousand B.D.)

Country	1965 Amount of Exports & Reexports	1965 % of Imports	1966 Amount of Exports & Reexports	1966 % of Imports	1967 Amount of Exports & Reexports	1967 % of Imports	1968 Amount of Exports & Reexports	1968 % of Imports	1969 Amount of Exports & Reexports	1969 % of Imports	1970 Amount of Exports & Reexports	1970 % of Imports
Bahrain	10,740	28	12,595	30	14,690	32	18,494	36	19,874	34	NA	NA
Dubai	NA	–	NA	–	5,948	13	9,572*	13	NA	–	NA	–

Notes: *Exports figure includes B.D. 5,680 of dried fish of which B.D. 4,383 were shipped to Ceylon.

NA = Not Available

Sources: Government of Bahrain, *Statistical Abstract*, 1970;

Government of Dubai, Port and Customs Department, *Statistics Report*, 1968, p. 146.

1965, and they had climbed to 34% by 1969. This trend is encouraging, and Bahrain should plan still further improvement in its trade balance.

Dubai's exports and reexports, again excluding oil and its refined products, increased by 60% between 1967 and 1968, in comparison with a 58% increase in total imports during the same period. In spite of this, nonoil exports and reexports were only 13% of total imports in 1967 and the same ratio continued in 1968. Dubai, also, should seek ways to increase its exports and reexports in order to achieve a better trade balance and to rely less heavily on oil exports to close the gap. Nonoil export and reexport figures for both Qatar and Abu Dhabi are not available; however, they are insignificant.

Fifty percent of the total export and reexport trade of Bahrain in 1969 was to Saudi Arabia, 33% was to other Gulf Arab countries, and 17% was to all other countries. Dubai sends 3.5% of its exports and reexports to Saudi Arabia, roughly 76% to the other Gulf states, and the remainder go to countries outside the Gulf area. A more detailed distribution by countries of the export trade of Bahrain and Dubai is presented in Table 2-19.

Whether or not further growth in their export trade can be achieved will depend largely on the demand for imports in the Gulf area, since the bulk of their reexporting is to the Gulf countries. Since the Gulf city states have a promising potential for further development, this can be expected to lead to

Table 2-19
Percentage Distribution of Exports and Reexports of Bahrain and Dubai by Country of Destination

Destination	Bahrain 1969 %	Dubai 1968 %
Saudi Arabia	49.9	3.5
Qatar	11.6	—[1]
Abu Dhabi	4.9	4.1
Dubai	6.3	—
Kuwait	8.7	—
Iran	3.3	—
Other Gulf States	1.7	71.6
Far East Countries	2.4	20.1
Other Countries	11.2[2]	0.7
Total	100 %	100 %

Notes: [1]Countries for which percentages are not entered may have been included under "Other Gulf States."
[2]Includes ships' stores
Sources: Government of Dubai, *Statistics Report*, 1968, p. 146;
Government of Bahrain, *Statistical Abstract*, 1970, p. 47.

more imports of both consumer and capital goods. It is doubtful, however, that Bahrain and Dubai will be able to increase their rate of reexports, or even maintain it, in the face of growing competition from Abu Dhabi and Qatar. Though Bahrain has recently enhanced its position as a trading center by the completion of the six-berth quay seaport, Mina Sulman, and a fifteen-berth quay is now in operation in Dubai, Abu Dhabi is constructing a ten-berth quay, and Qatar has already completed its four-berth quay. Actually, all four of these countries are shooting for first-class seaport status; and excess port capacity is likely to result. To the extent that it does, an unfortunate waste of developmental resources will have occurred which could have been avoided by greater regional planning and cooperation. While the overall import trend in the Gulf area may continue upward, reexport declines in the case of Bahrain and Dubai can be expected as a result of the development of deep-water seaports in other Gulf city states.

Since roughly 50% of Bahrain's exports and reexports are to Saudi Arabia and over 70% of Dubai's export trade is with the group, "Other Gulf States," they are both vulnerable to adverse changes in the political climate. If Saudi Arabia, for some reason, should decide to decrease sharply, or even curtail altogether, its imports from Bahrain, the impact on the latter country would be extremely serious. Dubai would be similarly adversely affected if the "Other Gulf States" should reduce substantially their imports from it.

It is interesting to note that Bahrain, Dubai, Abu Dhabi and Qatar have all developed international airport facilities. Here again, there has probably been some wasteful duplication which could have been avoided through regional planning.

Import Duties

All of these four countries, which together comprise the four major importers, impose duties on imports. Bahrain collects 5% on foodstuffs and building materials, 10% on electrical appliances, machinery and equipment, 15% on cigarettes and tobacco, 50% on spirits, and it has a gasoline tax of 14%. Qatar has a general duty of 2.5%, except for cigarettes and records on which the duty is 10 to 15%. Abu Dhabi has a flat rate of 2.5%, except on cigarettes which are subject to a 15% tax and on spirits which have a 20% tax rate. Dubai has a flat rate of 4.625%, except on rice, flour, sugar and wheat for which the tax is just 2%. Duties and other charges on imports and reexports have been a major source of state revenue for both Bahrain and Dubai. They are second to oil receipts in Bahrain and have long held first place among revenue sources in Dubai. Oil receipts amounted to approximately 70% of total state revenue in Bahrain in 1969, and customs duties were nearly 18%. A further breakdown of Bahrain's public revenue sources is presented in Table 2-20; and a similar breakdown for Dubai is presented in Table 2-21.

Table 2-20

Sources of Government Revenue for Bahrain, 1968 and 1969 (Thousand B.D.)

Source	1968	% of Total	1969	% of Total
Oil Receipts	8,000	69.7	8,870	69.6
Custom Duties	2,250	19.6	2,250	17.6
Rents, Leases, etc.	750	6.5	750	5.9
Other Revenue	480	4.2	880	6.9
Total	11,480	100	12,750	100

Source: M.E. Economic and Arab Report and Record Survey, *Bahrain 1969*, p. 9.

Table 2-21

Sources of Government Revenue for Dubai, 1966-68 (Thousand B.D.)

Source	1966	% of Total	1967	% of Total	1968	% of Total
Oil Concession	190	12	310	13	310	8
Duties	1,100	69	1,600	69	2,800	75
Municipal Revenue	210	13	280	12	450	12
Stamps & Misc.	100	6	130	6	170	5
Total	1,600	100	2,320	100	3,730	100

Source: M.E. Development Division, British Embassy, Beiruit, "An Economic Survey of the Northern Trucial States," 1969 (unpublished), Vol. 1, p. 9.

Imports and reexports of Dubai more than doubled between 1966 and 1968, and receipts from duties increased correspondingly from BD 1.1 to BD 2.8 million during the same period. In this latter year, duties accounted for 75% of Dubai's total public revenue.

Customs duties in the case of Qatar and Abu Dhabi are small in absolute terms and insignificant in relative terms, since these are oil rich countries. Figures for Abu Dhabi are presented in Table 2-22.

Table 2-22

Sources of Government Revenue for Abu Dhabi, 1967-1968 (Thousand B.D.)

Source	1967	% of Total	1968	% of Total
Petroleum Royalties & Taxes	49,593	93.6	71,608	97.1
Custom Duties	276	0.5	534	0.7
Other	3,125	5.9	1,625	2.2
Total	52,994	100	73,767	100

Source: Government of Abu Dhabi, *Statistical Abstract*, Vol. 1, p. 47, 1969.

Both Bahrain and Dubai have so far depended to a substantial extent on receipts from imports and reexports. Maintenance of the current levels of these receipts (and raising them if possible) is important, especially for Bahrain which has very limited prospects for additional revenue sources at the present time. In the case of Dubai, a decline in imports and reexports and the attendant cut in customs duties could be offset by the increasing trend in oil receipts which the country has been enjoying since late 1969.

Since these Gulf city states are interested in further development, they need a suitable revenue structure. Their existing taxation and tariff systems should be carefully reviewed and modified as may be appropriate. Though they should have relatively low tax rates on the essentials, their existing customs systems seem to leave much to be desired. With careful readjustments, they could increase the state revenue receipts and at the same time tighten their control over imports in order to achieve a larger inflow of goods needed for development.

Need for Economic Cooperation

For optimum progress, it is necessary for the Gulf city states to appreciate the realities of their economic situation. They form a geographic unit and a rather natural economic unit as well. They should strive to take advantage of the opportunities which they have for economic cooperation in various areas, since this will enable them to make the best use of developmental resources. In the case of seaport and airport facilities, coordination would have avoided a substantial amount of duplication of investment and have freed resources urgently needed for other developmental projects.

Industry

To avoid complete dependence on oil, to develop a sounder economic infrastructure, to provide new sources of income and to provide more jobs, the oil-producing countries, Bahrain, Qatar, Abu Dhabi and Dubai, are giving serious thought to diversifying their economies. The other five Gulf city states cannot consider, as yet, such ambitious programs; for in the absence of oil strikes, they will be hard-pressed to find the resources needed to carry forward their limited possibilities for development.

Aside from the potentialities for developing oil-related industries and fisheries, the Gulf city states do not have much promise for substantial industrial development. Of the nine city states under review, the tiny communities of Sharjah, Ajman, Umm al-Qaiwain, Ras al-Khaimah and Fujairah may have the good fortune to strike oil in the not too distant future, but in the meantime, they will need to find the means of financing their economic and social infrastructural development before they can hope to move on to the stage of some industrialization. Their resources are very limited and the majority of the inhabitants still subsist from agriculture and fishing. It would be extremely difficult, if not impossible, for them to raise resources for financing major development projects in the absence of oil income, and even if these countries had the necessary financial resources for industrialization, they could not market the products of large-scale industrial plants since their populations are so small.

The same marketing problem exists for the oil-producing members of the group whose potential for marketing the production of large-scale industries is also rather slim. This means that it is very much in the interest of these countries to plan their industrial expansion together. By doing so, they can avoid overproduction and marketing problems. At the same time, in case of industries with capacities in excess of the region's requirements, they would be better equipped to handle the problem of marketing outside their own area, and benefits would accrue to all of them. So far, it does not appear that these countries have considered adequately the idea of integrating their industrial plans and efforts to avoid inefficient use of vital resources. It will be helpful at this point to survey quickly the industries which have been established or are expected soon to be established in the different countries.

Bahrain

Several projects are already in operation in Bahrain. An oil refinery which processes crude oil has been in operation since 1936. It currently employs about 5,000 workers and supplies large quantities of various oil products to India, Pakistan, East Africa and the Far East. This refinery handles crude oil produced locally as well as crude oil piped from the Dammam field in Saudi Arabia. Its capacity is approximately 200,000 barrels a day, and since the output of Bahrain's wells is only about 80,000 b/d, the balance of its crude oil comes from Saudi Arabia.

In 1966, the Bahrain Fishing Co. was established with an authorized capital of $840,000. This company processes shrimp and has flourishing markets in Japan, Europe and the U.S.A. This industry is a joint venture between local and foreign interests. The Ross Group of Grimsby, a British firm, has a 40% interest, and local shareholders have the remaining 60%.

The Gulf Aviation Company is another example of cooperation between foreign and local interests. The participants in this business are the BOAC, the Bahraini government and local commercial interests. The company provides air services and links almost all of the Gulf States with each other and with Saudi Arabia by regular flights.

In addition to these firms, several other businesses are in the process of being established. In 1969, the Bahraini government gave a $960,000 contract to a British firm, Thomas Robinson and Sons, for the construction of a flour mill. The mill has a scheduled output capacity of 100 tons per day.

In 1969, Bahrain decided to exploit its natural gas to power an aluminum smelter costing $72 million. The smelter is scheduled to go into operation in 1972, and will have a capacity of 90,000 tons per year. During its construction phase, some 2,500 Bahrainis were employed to build the plant, and some 450 skilled and semiskilled workers will be required to operate it. Aside from the foregoing major industrial projects, Bahrain also has a number of small industries such as soft drinks, tiles and data processing.

Qatar

Qatar has several projects that are already, or soon will be, in operation. In 1965, The Qatar National Cement Factory was formed with an authorized capital of $6 million. The government's share was 30%, 30% is held by Qatari public, 10% was subscribed to by the Dubai government, and the remaining shares are privately held by those outside of Qatar. Work on the site started early in 1967, and the project was completed in May 1969. This factory produces 100,000 tons per year, and since Qatar's estimated need is roughly 70,000 tons per year, this leaves an annual surplus of some 30,000 tons which the company must try to export.

In 1968, the Qatar National Company entered into a joint venture in the fishing industry with the Ross Group. The authorized capital is $735,000, and 60% of the shares are Qatari held while the remaining 40% are foreign owned. The company exports processed shrimp to Japan and the United States.

A fully automated flour mill at Umm Said is scheduled to go into operation in 1972. It will have a daily output of 50 tons and a storage capacity of 800 tons of grain. Qatar's full flour needs are expected to be met by this mill, and it will have a surplus which it will hope to export to other Gulf countries.

In 1969, an agreement was entered into between the Deputy Ruler of Qatar and a syndicate of six British banks in connection with the construction of an ammonia and urea fertilizer plant for the Qatar Fertilizer Company. The total cost of the plant is estimated at $62 million, and it will have production capacity of 990 tons of ammonia and 1,100 tons of urea a day when it is in full operation.

A small refinery has been purchased by the government from the Qatar Petroleum Company (Q.P.C.) which refines crude oil and meets some of the local need for gasoline, kerosene and diesel oil. Its capacity is 1,700 gallons per day.

Abu Dhabi

There are no major industries in operation in Abu Dhabi so far but plans are being considered for setting up a refinery, a petrochemical plant and a cement factory.

Dubai

Dubai also has no major industries, but a cement factory has been under construction. When it goes into full operation, it will have a capacity of 500,000 tons a year, which appears to be in excess of the total requirement of all nine of the Gulf city states. Another small industrial project which is underway in Dubai is an aluminum factory for producing household items.

Ras al-Khaimah

A cement factory has been considered, and if it is completed as planned, it, also, will have a capacity of 500,000 tons a year. This production capacity is not only far more than the needs of the country, but again it is greater than the total need of all the Gulf city states taken together.

Concluding Comments

The survey of the economic characteristics of the Gulf city states presented in this chapter shows clearly the extent to which their present stage of development and their future prospects are linked to their existing and potential oil resources. Developmental possibilities in agriculture and fishing are quite limited. Though a few of these states have an extensive entrepot trade, wasteful excess capacity seems to be present in seaport and airport facilities as they now exist or are in process of construction.

Industrial development, except for petroleum-related industries, also seems to have only limited prospects. The tendency to construct redundant capacity in various countries in an industry such as cement is unfortunate, since it results in a waste of scarce developmental capital. This tendency to establish plants that are uneconomically large is frequently present in developing countries. Unfortunately, it all too often results from the efforts of sales engineers from firms in developed countries to get as large a contract for machinery delivery as possible. The purchasing firms in developing countries frequently lack the engineering know-how to judge the optimum capacity needed and tend to rely instead on the "friendly" advice of the sales engineers trying to attract their orders. The advice received tends too often to be more "costly" than "friendly," in the long run. Firms in developing countries which lack adequate engineering staffs would do well to employ the services of reputable, independent consulting firms to help them decide on the most appropriate capacity and types of machinery for new industrial plants.

The conclusion which emerges with greatest clarity from the discussion developed in this chapter, is that the nine Gulf city states must find ways of cooperating in order to coordinate their economic development efforts. Already too much waste from unnecessary duplication of various facilities has occurred. As yet, it is too early to tell how successful the seven states comprising the United Arab Emirates will be in avoiding further wasteful duplication in the future. Finding ways to cooperate in this regard would be a useful first step toward overcoming various obstacles which have impeded development in the past.

In the next chapter, the discussion turns to the matter of social development in the nine Gulf city states. To anticipate, it is evident in this area, also, that important savings of resources are possible through steps to achieve appropriate coordination of efforts.

3 Social Development

The Gulf city states have achieved impressive economic and social development during the past two decades; but social progress would not have been possible without the economic development which they have experienced. At the same time, improvements in their social well-being have contributed to the rate of economic progress which they have been able to achieve. Given the extremely low base from which social development began throughout the whole area, its present level still leaves much to be desired. Education, health, housing and social security need to be given closer attention and their scale of developmental priority should be increased substantially, if at all possible.

Some Major Population Characteristics

Religion

These are predominantly Muslim countries, and the major faith of the inhabitants is Islam. As can be seen from Tables 3-1 and 3-2, in the seven Trucial states and in Bahrain, more than 95% of the total population is Muslim. Though data on the distribution of religious affiliations for Qatar are not available, the percentage of Muslims there would undoubtedly be similarly high. Thus, from the standpoint of religion, the Gulf city states are homogeneous societies and this should make closer integration in the economic, social and political areas easier to attain.

Sex

A second major social feature of the Gulf city states is that they are male societies. In the seven Trucial states, females comprise less than 40% of the total population; and in Bahrain, where the ratio is much better, females still constitute only about 46% of the total population. The preponderance of males in the seven Trucial states is due to the fact that 50% of the population, or more in some cases, is composed of foreigners. These foreigners usually come to work, and many of them leave their families in their home countries. When the male-female ratio of society is abnormal, attendant problems can be expected to arise. Detailed breakdowns of the population of the seven Trucial states and Bahrain by sex and age are presented in Tables 3-3 and 3-4.

63

Table 3-1

Population of the Seven Trucial States, by Religion and Sex (1968 Census)

Religion	Males	Females	Total
Muslim	105,645	66,407	172,052
Christian	2,779	959	3,738
Other Faiths	2,382	954	3,336
Total	110,806	68,320	179,126

Sources: Trucial States Census Figures, 1968 (Unpublished Material); Government of Abu Dhabi, *Statistical Abstract*, Vol. 1, 1969, Table 4, p. 4.

Table 3-2

Population of Bahrain, by Religion and Sex (1965 Census)

Religion	Males	Females	Total
Muslim	NA	NA	173,594
Christian	NA	NA	5,832
Other Faiths	NA	NA	2,777
Total	99,384	82,819	182,203

Source: Government of Bahrain, *Statistical Abstract*, 1968, Table 13, p. 10.

Marital Status

A third major social feature of these states concerns the marital status of their populations. In the seven Trucial states, according to the 1968 census, 28.8% of the males of 21 years of age and over are single, 66.5% are married, 2.5% are widowed and 2.2% are divorced. Females, on the other hand, have a more favorable ratio in marriages. As shown in Table 3-5, just 2.5% are single, while 74.3% are married. Widowed females form a relatively high percentage, 19.0%; and the 4.3% ratio of divorced females is higher than the ratio for males. The high ratio of widowed females compared to males is a result of greater female longevity. For example, only 6.0% of the males are 51 years old and over, while the corresponding figure for females is 7.6%.

Bahrain's 1965 census shows a similar population marital-pattern; 33.8% of the males are single, 62.5% are married, 1.9% are widowed and 1.9% are divorced. Females on the other hand have a pattern of 11.7% single, 70.5% married, 14.6% widowed and 3.2% divorced. Detailed figures for Bahrain are presented in Table 3-6.

Illiteracy

Illiteracy is a serious problem in the Gulf city states, especially among the age group, 15 years and over. In the seven Trucial states, as shown in Table 3-7, 79%

Table 3-3
Population of the Seven Trucial States, by Age Groups and Sex (1968 Census)

Years	Males No.	%	Females No.	%	Total No.	%
Under 1	1,442	1.3	1,391	2.0	2,833	1.6
1	1,984	1.8	1,973	2.9	3,957	2.2
2	2,581	2.3	2,513	3.7	5,094	2.8
3	2,443	2.2	2,582	3.8	5,025	2.8
4	2,590	2.3	2,375	3.5	4,965	2.8
5	2,385	2.2	2,344	3.4	4,729	2.6
6	2,173	2.0	1,958	2.9	4,131	2.3
7	2,523	2.3	2,353	3.4	4,876	2.7
8	2,297	2.1	2,034	3.0	4,331	2.4
9	1,318	1.2	1,300	1.9	2,618	1.5
10	2,533	2.3	1,902	2.8	4,435	2.5
11 – 15	7,935	7.2	5,638	8.2	13,573	7.6
16 – 20	10,962	9.9	6,504	9.5	17,466	9.8
21 – 30	30,237	27.3	13,445	19.7	43,682	24.4
31 – 40	20,446	18.5	9,427	13.8	29,873	16.7
41 – 50	10,249	9.2	5,397	7.9	15,646	8.7
51 – 60	4,186	3.8	2,989	4.4	7,175	4.0
61 – 75	2,035	1.8	1,657	2.4	3,692	2.1
over 75	487	0.4	538	0.8	1,025	0.6
Total	110,806	100	68,320	100	179,126	100

Note: Percent columns may not add to 100 because of rounding.
Sources: Trucial States Census Figures, 1968 (Unpublished Material); Government of Abu Dhabi, *Statistical Abstract*, 1969, Vol. 1, Table 2, p. 2.

of the people are illiterate and just 21% literate. In the same age groups, the illiteracy rate is higher among females than males. This reflects the fact that these tribal societies are not yet free of their traditional discrimination against females; and schooling for males has consequently received greater attention. Illiteracy is also high in Bahrain where education is the best in the Gulf. Here, 71% of the population is illiterate and just 29% literate, as can be seen from Table 3-8. Also in the case of Bahrain, illiteracy is more widespread among females.

The foregoing social problems indicate the extent of social change and improvement that is needed in these countries. If governments are to contribute effectively to solutions, they must develop realistic approaches to these problems; and these solutions will inevitably involve a great expansion in the role of government in the provision of social services.

Table 3-4

Population of Bahrain, by Age Group and Sex (1965 Census)

Years	Males No.	%	Females No.	%	Total No.	%
Under 1	2,360	2.4	2,440	2.9	4,800	2.6
1	2,670	2.7	2,638	3.2	5,308	2.9
2	3,410	3.4	3,395	4.1	6,805	3.7
3	3,207	3.2	3,450	4.2	6,657	3.7
4	3,346	3.4	3,336	4.0	6,682	3.7
5	3,094	3.1	3,129	3.8	6,223	3.4
6	2,865	2.9	2,972	3.6	5,837	3.2
7	3,216	3.2	3,129	3.8	6,345	3.5
8	3,035	3.1	2,971	3.6	6,006	3.3
9	2,347	2.4	2,371	2.9	4,718	2.6
10	2,787	2.8	2,619	3.2	5,406	3.0
11 – 15	9,991	10.1	8,889	10.7	18,880	10.4
16 – 20	9,139	9.2	7,440	9.0	16,579	9.1
21 – 30	19,338	19.5	13,501	16.3	32,839	18.0
31 – 40	13,684	13.8	9,487	11.5	23,171	12.7
41 – 50	8,030	8.1	5,462	6.6	13,492	7.4
51 – 60	4,052	4.1	3,030	3.7	7,082	3.9
61 – 75	2,261	2.3	1,905	2.3	4,166	2.3
Over 75	552	0.6	655	0.8	1,207	0.7
Total	99,384	100	82,819	100	182,203	100

Note: Percent columns may not add to 100 because of rounding.
Source: Government of Bahrain, *Statistical Abstract,* 1968, Table 10, p. 8.

Table 3-5

Population of the Seven Trucial States, 21 Years and Over, by Marital Status and Sex (1968 Census)

Sex	Single No.	%	Married No.	%	Widowed No.	%	Divorced No.	%	Total
Males	19,475	28.8	45,012	66.5	1,696	2.5	1,457	2.2	67,640
Females	829	2.5	24,848	74.3	6,353	19.0	1,425	4.3	33,455
Total	20,304	20.1	69,860	69.1	8,049	8.0	2,882	2.9	101,095

Note: Percent rows may not add to 100 because of rounding.
Definitions: Single—Those who have never married.

Widowed—Those who have lost their spouse and have not remarried.

Divorced—Those divorced persons who have not remarried.

Sources: Trucial States Census Figures, 1968 (Unpublished Material); Government of Abu Dhabi, *Statistical Abstract*, 1969, Vol. 1, Table 3, p. 3.

Table 3-6

Population of Bahrain, 15 Years of Age and Over, by Marital Status and Sex (1965 Census)

Sex	Single No.	%	Married No.	%	Widowed No.	%	Divorced No.	%	Total
Males	19,853	33.8	36,728	62.5	1,116	1.9	1,105	1.9	58,802
Females	5,034	11.7	30,310	70.5	6,259	14.6	1,392	3.2	42,995
Total	24,887	24.4	67,038	65.9	7,375	7.2	2,497	2.5	101,797

Note: Percent rows may not add to 100 because of rounding.

Definitions: Single—Those who have never married.

Widowed—Those who have lost their spouse and have not remarried.

Divorced—Those divorced persons who have not remarried.

Source: Government of Bahrain, *Statistical Abstract*, 1968, Table 11, p. 9.

Education

An Overview

Developing countries in general have increasingly come to appreciate the significant role which education plays in the process of economic and social development. Many of them give education high priority in their national budgets; but too often, they seem to lose sight of the importance of organizing and implementing the kind of educational system which is tuned to their developmental needs. In many cases, these countries fail to achieve an appropriate balance in regard to the type of education provided. Often in organizing their systems, too little attention is given to the type of education which is in demand or would be in demand in both the private and the public sectors. This often results in an imbalance between supply and demand for trained personnel. Shortages in supply in too many cases are not the result of low levels of production in the schools—sometimes, they overproduce—but the real problem is usually in the type and quality of production. The Gulf city states have not been able to strike a reasonable educational balance and, hence, they have so far failed to match effectively the supply of and demand for trained personnel. Or to state the point here in somewhat different terms, developing countries which are attempting to reach and pass beyond the take-off stage in their development need to recognize at an early stage of their developmental push the importance of manpower planning and to gear their educational planning to their projected manpower requirements. The Gulf city states have not so far realized the importance of manpower planning as a means of directing their educational development to meet the needs of their societies.

All the countries under review have achieved significant progress in the quantity of education provided, but the type and quality of education leave much to be desired. General education in all of these countries receives more attention than technical, which is in part a reflection of the fact that serious obstacles to technical education are present. One of these is social, for the

Table 3-7
Literacy by Age Group and Sex in the Seven Trucial States (1968 Census)

Age Group	Literate Male No.	% of Age Group	Literate Female No.	% of Age Group	Literate Total No.	% of Age Group	Illiterate Male No.	% of Age Group	Illiterate Female No.	% of Age Group	Illiterate Total No.	% of Age Group	Total Literate and Illiterate Male	Female	Total
15 – 20	4,580	34	1,278	16	5,858	28	8,698	66	6,596	84	15,294	72	13,278	7,874	21,152
21 – 30	9,336	31	1,589	12	10,925	25	20,901	69	11,856	88	32,757	75	30,237	13,445	43,682
31 – 40	4,999	24	558	6	5,557	19	15,447	76	8,869	94	24,316	81	20,446	9,427	29,873
41 – 50	2,069	20	181	3	2,250	14	8,180	80	5,216	97	13,396	86	10,249	5,397	15,646
51 – 60	651	16	57	2	708	10	3,535	84	2,932	98	6,467	90	4,186	2,989	7,175
61 – 75	212	10	10	0.6	222	6	1,823	90	1,647	99.4	3,470	94	2,035	1,657	3,692
over 75	25	5	2	0.4	27	3	462	95	536	99.6	998	97	487	538	1,025
Total	21,872	27	3,675	9	25,547	21	59,046	73	37,652	91	96,698	79	80,918	41,327	122,245

Sources: Trucial States Census Figures, 1968 (Unpublished Material);
Government of Abu Dhabi, *Statistical Abstract*, 1969, Vol. 1, Tables 5 & 6, p. 4.

Table 3-8
Literacy in Bahrain, Persons Age 15 Years and Over (1965 Census)

| | Literate | | | | | | Illiterate | | | | | | Literate and Illiterate | | |
| | Male | | Female | | Total | | Male | | Female | | Total | | Male | Female | Total |
No.	% of Total	No.	% of Total	No.	% of Total	No.	% of Total	No.	% of Total	No.	% of Total	No.			
21,231	36	7,835	18	29,066	29	37,569	64	35,158	82	72,727	71	58,800	42,993	101,793

Source: Government of Bahrain, *Statistical Abstract*, 1968, Table 4, p. 10.

indigenous population has a negative attitude toward vocations in general and consequently, there has been a traditional tendency to avoid training in the crafts and trades. Another obstacle is financial. Since the cost of establishing and operating technical schools is usually high compared to general schools, these governments have not pushed technical education in view of the heavy burden which it imposes on their thin budgets.

The Evolution of Education

In 1969, Bahrain celebrated its fiftieth anniversary and that of the first primary boys' school which was opened in 1919. It was twenty years later before the inauguration of the first secondary boys' school in 1939. In 1928, nine years after the first primary boys' school was started, the first primary school for girls opened; and twenty-three years after that, in 1951, the first secondary girls' school was established. Technical education was initiated in 1936, when the first technical school for boys went into operation, and teacher training colleges for men and for women were not instituted until 1966 and 1967 when the first teacher-training college for men and the first teacher-training college for women, respectively, were opened.

In the case of Qatar, though oil was discovered in commercial quantities in the 1930s, the first school was not opened in Doha until 1950, and the regular system of boys' education went into operation only in 1956, and that for girls in 1957.

Abu Dhabi opened the first primary boys' school in 1958, but it was closed after four months. It was reopened in 1960; and in 1967, the first intermediate school was started. A year later, the first secondary school and adult education were initiated.

Starting in 1953, the city states of Dubai, Sharjah, Ajman, Umm al-Qaiwain, Ras al-Khaimah and Fujairah began to have schools which were organized, financed and managed by Kuwait. To a lesser extent, the U.A.R., Qatar and Abu Dhabi have also contributed to the development of education in this group of countries.

The Structure of Education

In all of the Gulf city states, except Bahrain, education is restricted to the three stages, primary, intermediate and secondary. Only in Bahrain has some limited higher education been instituted.

The primary stage extends over a period of six years in Bahrain, and Abu Dhabi, and over four years in the other countries. The intermediate stage comprises two years in Bahrain, three in Qatar and Abu Dhabi, and four years in all the rest. The secondary stage extends over three years in Bahrain, Qatar and

Abu Dhabi, and four years in all of the others. Thus, the complete cycle of these three levels is eleven years in Bahrain and twelve in the remainder of these Gulf city states.

General versus Technical Education

As mentioned earlier, technical education in the Gulf city states has not received the attention it deserves in comparison with general education. In Bahrain, the first and only technical school for boys was formally started in 1936. From then until 1958, the school underwent a number of attempts at improving the quality and variety of technical education provided. During its early period of operation, it had sections for carpentry, pipe-fitting and blacksmithing. Later, a number of trade and craft sections were added. But on the whole, the number of trainees remained limited. During the academic year, 1968-1969, the number of classes in the school was six each at the intermediate and secondary levels, with a total of 348 and 196 trainees, respectively. The figures in Table 3-9 show the development of the school from 1948 through 1968. During this period, a total of 225 trainees graduated from the intermediate and the secondary sections of the school. At the present time, the school accepts applicants who have completed their primary education. Those admitted spend two years at the school for their training at the intermediate level. Those who wish and are eligible for further training are admitted to the secondary section of the school where they receive training for three more years.

Some commercial training was started in Bahrain in 1952, when a commercial section was added to the secondary boys' school. Students who complete their intermediate education are eligible to go to the commercial section where they spend three years taking commercial courses in secretarial studies, record-keeping, purchasing, advertisement, distribution and other courses. Table 3-10 shows the extent of participation in this kind of training from its inception in 1952 to 1958.

Also in the case of Qatar, technical training has not received close attention in comparison with general education. Here, there are just two technical schools—one is industrial and the other is a commercial school. The intake of the industrial school in 1969-70 was 170 spread over the various trades and crafts, and the intake of the commercial school during the same year was 74 trainees. The industrial school has 34 vocational training instructors and the commercial school has 10 instructors.

In the seven Trucial states, the only three trade schools are in Dubai, Sharjah and Ras al-Khaimah. The construction of the first trade school in the Trucial states was started in 1958 in Sharjah. It was established to train artisans; and it began with a class of 18 trainees and a curriculum of two years. The intake of the school was increased in 1961 to 30 trainees in carpentry and motor vehicle maintenance. The school has no particular requirements for admission.

Table 3-9

General Statistics on Bahrain's Secondary Technical School (1948-1968)

| Academic Year | No. of Teachers | | | No. of Classes | No. of Students and No. of Graduates According to Specialty | | | | | | | | | General Total |
	Bahraini	Non-Bah.	Total		Blacksmith	Welding	Electricity	Radio & T.V.	Machinery	Vehicles	Carpentry	Refrigeration and Air Cond.	General	
1948-'49	8	3	11	4	—	—	—	—	18	—	17	—	30	65
					—	—	—	—	7	—	3	—	—	10
1949-'50	7	4	11	4	9	—	—	—	10	—	10	—	31	60
					—	—	—	—	2	—	3	—	—	5
1950-'51	3	4	7	4	10	—	—	—	10	—	10	—	35	65
					—	—	—	—	6	—	—	—	—	6
1951-'52	4	4	8	4	14	—	—	—	14	—	10	—	29	67
					—	—	—	—	2	—	2	—	—	4
1952-'53	4	5	9	4	10	—	—	—	17	—	7	—	53	87
					—	—	—	—	4	—	2	—	—	6
1953-'54	4	5	9	3	12	—	—	—	11	—	8	—	32	63
					4	—	—	—	10	—	1	—	—	15
1954-'55	5	5	10	3	10	—	—	—	10	—	8	—	45	73
					—	—	—	—	—	—	—	—	—	—
1955-'56	4	5	9	4	7	—	—	—	20	—	13	—	34	74
					0	—	—	—	6	—	1	—	—	7
1956-'57	6	5	11	4	11	—	9	—	21	—	15	—	40	96
					1	—	—	—	7	—	1	—	—	9
1957-'58	7	7	14	4	9	—	12	—	22	10	17	—	31	101
					3	—	—	—	6	—	3	—	—	12
1958-'59	7	7	14	4	9	—	12	—	22	10	17	—	31	101
					2	—	2	—	3	—	6	—	—	13
1959-'60	12	8	20	5	3	—	8	—	12	13	11	—	38	85
					1	—	3	—	5	—	4	—	—	13

Year														
1960-'61	15	8	23	5	4	–	7	–	10	15	7	–	80	123
					–	–	2	–	3	8	1	–	–	14
1961-'62	16	10	26	6	7	5	13	–	12	14	9	–	90	150
					–	–	2	–	2	3	4	–	–	11
1962-'63	16	12	28	6	12	5	16	–	15	16	8	–	71	143
					3	–	3	–	3	2	1	–	–	12
1963-'64	21	15	36	8	16	7	18	6	26	28	13	–	152	266
					–	–	–	–	–	–	–	–	–	–
1964-'65	26	18	44	12	37	13	30	12	41	45	25	–	258	461
					1	2	4	2	1	2	2	–	–	14
1965-'66	26	22	48	12	48	16	40	14	60	62	44	–	138	422
					3	2	2	4	6	5	1	–	–	23
1966-'67	28	26	54	12	36	13	43	18	55	59	35	–	136	395
					1	–	4	3	10	7	3	–	–	28
1967-'68	30	27	57	12	44	19	43	20	42	53	28	4	134	387
					4	2	5	5	1	2	–	–	–	19

Source: Government of Bahrain, Education Department (Unpublished material, 1968).

Table 3-10
Development of Commercial Education in Bahrain (1952-1969)

Academic Year	No. of Students 1st Sec.	No. of Students 2nd Sec.	No. of Students 3rd Sec.	Total
1952-'53	13	–	–	13
1953-'54	14	10	–	24
1954-'55	16	13	–	29
1955-'56	22	15	–	37
1956-'57	28	22	–	50
1957-'58	29	27	–	56
1958-'59	34	27	–	61
1959-'60	39	31	–	70
1960-'61	26	36	–	62
1961-'62	45	19	–	64
1962-'63	122	32	–	154
1963-'64	117	96	–	213
1964-'65	94	93	–	187
1965-'66	107	80	–	187
1966-'67	124	67	37	228
1967-'68	129	59	40	228
1968-'69	191	73	48	312

Source: Government of Bahrain, Education Department (Unpublished material, 1968).

In 1962, construction of the second school in the Trucial states was started in Dubai. In 1964, 36 trainees joined the school for a three-year course in mechanical engineering, carpentry, cabinet-making and electrical installation. This school requires at least three years of primary education for admission.

In 1969, the third trade school in the Trucial states was opened in Ras al-Khaimah.

In the countries under review, there are no agricultural schools, with the exception of a small center in Ras al-Khaimah. Agricultural training is badly needed in the area since cultivable lands are quite limited and it is important to increase land as well as labor productivity in this sector. To do so, it is necessary to increase the supply of technically trained manpower by providing adequate agricultural training facilities. Regional cooperation in developing such facilities would probably be the most economical way of meeting the need for a greater supply of technically trained personnel in the agricultural sector.

Teacher Training

All of the Gulf city states are depending heavily on expatriates to staff their school and training centers; and most of them do not have facilities to train local teachers to replace, in time, those from abroad. So far, only Bahrain and Qatar have established teacher-training institutions. The first teacher-training college for men was opened in Bahrain in 1966, and the following year, a training college for women was also started. Holders of the secondary general certificate are eligible for admission, and they receive training to quality them as teachers.

In Qatar, there is one teacher-training institute for men and one for women. Holders of the general preparatory certificate are admitted, and they receive training for three years to become qualified teachers at the primary level. There are no teacher-training facilities in the other Gulf city states; and the possibility of regional cooperation in establishing and operating a teacher-training facility should be carefully explored.

School Curricula in Bahrain

In Bahrain, students at the primary level take 34 periods per week from the beginning of the first through the sixth year, as shown in Table 3-11. During the first year, they take 9 subjects: Islamic religion, 4 periods; Arabic language, 12 periods; arithmetic, 6 periods; drawing, 2 periods; physical education, 3 periods;

Table 3-11
Weekly Plan of the Syllabus of the Primary Education Level in Bahrain

Subjects	Periods per week					
	1st Year	2nd Year	3rd Year	4th Year	5th Year	6th Year
Islamic religion	4	4	2	2	2	2
Arabic language	12	12	12	10	9	9
English language	–	–	–	6	7	7
Arithmetic	6	6	7	6	6	6
Geometry	–	–	–	–	1	1
History	–	–	1	1	2	2
Geography	–	–	–	2	2	2
Introductory science & hygiene	–	–	2	2	2	2
Drawing	2	2	2	1	1	1
Handicraft	2	2	2	1	1	1
Physical education	3	3	2	2	1	1
School songs	2	2	2	1	–	–
Stories	2	2	2	–	–	–
Nature observation	1	1	–	–	–	–
Total	34	34	34	34	34	34

Source: Government of Bahrain, Education Department (Unpublished material, 1968).

school songs, 2 periods; stories, 2 periods; and nature observation, 1 period. In the second year, they take the same subjects and the same number of periods. During the third year, they take two periods of Islamic religion instead of four, 7 of arithmetic instead of 6, one history period, and two periods of introductory science and hygiene are added. Also in this year, they discontinue nature observation and take two periods of physical education instead of three. Beginning with the fourth year, they begin to take fewer periods of Arabic, with ten periods during the fourth year and nine periods during the fifth and sixth years. The study of English is begun in the fourth year with six periods and continued with seven periods in the fifth and sixth years. One period of geometry is added in the fifth year and this subject is given the same time in the fifth and sixth years. History is increased to two periods in the fifth and sixth years, and geography is also added beginning with the fourth year at the rate of two periods in the fourth, fifth and sixth years.

At the intermediate level, students in Bahrain take 36 periods; but they take ten subjects instead of the fourteen at the primary level. The ten subjects are religious education, Arabic, English, history, geography, mathematics, general sciences and hygiene, art education, physical education and domestic sciences, as shown in Table 3-12.

At the secondary level, students in Bahrain continue to take 36 periods per week during their first, second and third years, but the number of subjects given at this level is nineteen, as compared with ten at the intermediate level. A

Table 3-12
Weekly Plan of the Syllabus of the Intermediate Education Level in Bahrain

| | Periods per week | |
Subjects	First Year	Second Year
Religious education	2	2
Arabic language	8	8
English language	8	8
History	2	2
Geography	2	2
Mathematics	6	6
General science & hygiene	4	4
Art education[x]	2	2
Physical education[x]	2	2
Domestic science*	2	2
Total	36	36

[x]One period only for girls in both years.
*For girls only.
Source: Government of Bahrain, Education Department (Unpublished material, 1968).

Table 3-13
General Academic Weekly Lesson Plan for Secondary Schools for Boys and Girls in Bahrain (1968-69)

Subjects	1st Year		2nd Year				3rd Year			
			Literary		Scientific		Literary		Scientific	
	Boys	Girls	Boys	Girls	Boys	Girls	Boys	Girls	Boys	Girls
Religion	2	2	3	2	2	2	2	2	2	2
Arabic Language	7	6	9	10	5	5	8	10	5	5
English Language	7	6	9	9	8	6	9	9	7	6
Translation	1	1	1	1	1	1	1	1	1	1
Social Studies: History	2	2	4	3	–	–	3	3	–	–
Social Studies: Geography	2	2	3	3	–	–	5	4	–	–
Social Studies: Sociology	–	–	1	1	–	–	–	–	–	–
Social Studies: Philosophy & Psy.	–	–	–	–	–	–	4	3	–	–
Social Studies: Economics	–	–	1	1	–	–	–	–	–	–
Cultural Studies	–	–	–	–	1	1	–	–	–	–
Mathematics	6	6	–	–	7	8	–	–	9	9
Physics	2	2	–	–	3	3	–	–	4	3
Chemistry	2	2	–	–	3	3	–	–	3	3
Natural History	2	2	–	–	3	3	–	–	3	3
Art Education	1	*	2	1	2	*	1	1	–	1
Physical Education	2	1	2	1	1	1	2	1	2	1
Domestic Science	–	2	–	2	–	2	–	–	–	–
Library	–	2	–	2	–	1	–	2	–	2
General Activities	–	–	1	–	–	–	1	–	–	–
Total	36	36	36	36	36	36	36	36	36	36

*One period every fortnight.

Source: Government of Bahrain, Education Department, Curriculum of the Secondary School (1968-1969) (unpublished).

breakdown of the subjects in the secondary-level curriculum is given in Table 3-13. Beginning with the second year, there are differences between the curriculum for arts students and that for science students. Those in arts take more periods of Arabic and English, while science studies do not take history, geography and sociology. Art students, on the other hand, do not take mathematics, physics and chemistry.

School Curricula in Qatar

In Qatar, students at the primary level take 30 periods per week during their first, second and third year, 34 periods during the fourth and fifth year and 36 during the sixth year, as shown in Table 3-14. They take fewer periods than

Table 3-14

Weekly Plan of the Syllabus of the Primary Education Level in Qatar

Subject	1st		2nd		3rd		4th		5th		6th	
	Boys	Girls	Boys	Girls	Boys	Girls	Boys	Girls	Boys	Girls	Boys	Girls
Religious Education	6	6	6	6	6	6	6	7	8	8	7	7
Arabic Language	12	12	12	12	10	10	11	10	9	9	8	8
English Language	–	–	–	–	–	–	–	–	–	–	4	4
Mathematics	5	5	5	5	5	5	6	6	6	6	6	6
General Science & Hygiene	1	1	1	1	2	2	3	3	3	3	3	3
Social Studies	–	–	–	–	1	1	2	2	4	4	4	4
Art Education*	3	3	3	3	3	3	3	3	2	2	2	2
Physical Education	3	3	3	3	3	3	3	3	2	2	2	2
Total	30	30	30	30	30	30	34	34	34	34	36	36

*Includes domestic science for girls.

Source: Government of Qatar, Ministry of Education (Unpublished material).

Bahraini students during the first three years, and the same number of periods during the last three years. There is a much heavier emphasis on Islamic religion in Qatar, since its students take six periods in the first three years and seven to eight periods in the last three years, as contrasted with four periods in the first year and two periods in the last four years in the case of Bahrain. Primary schools in the two countries give almost the same attention to the Arabic language; but Bahrain places greater emphasis on English with six periods in the fourth year and seven periods in the fifth and sixth years, while English in Qatar's schools begins only in the last primary year and at the rate of only four periods per week.

At the intermediate level, students in Qatar take 36 periods per week in this three-year curriculum. Essentially, the subjects taken at this level are a carry-over of the subjects taken at the primary level, but the number of weekly periods varies. As shown in Table 3-15, intermediate-level students here take five periods of religious education, seven of Arabic, six of English, five of mathematics, four of general science, four of social science and three periods of art education. The same weekly distribution is carried throughout the three years. The appropriateness of this curriculum is open to serious question, since three subjects, religious education, Arabic and English, are given a total of 18 periods out of the total weekly load of 36 periods. With 50% of the total time given to these three subjects, it would seem desirable to review the existing pattern to ascertain how

Table 3-15
Weekly Plan of the Syllabus of the Intermediate Education Level in Qatar

Subject	1st Boys	1st Girls	2nd Boys	2nd Girls	3rd Boys	3rd Girls
Religious Education	5	5	5	5	5	5
Arabic Language	7	7	7	7	7	7
English Language	6	6	6	6	6	6
Mathematics	5	5	5	5	5	5
General Science & Hygiene	4	3	4	3	4	3
Social Studies	4	4	4	4	4	4
Art Education & Handicraft	3	2	3	2	3	2
Physical Education	2	1	2	1	2	1
Domestic Science & Child Welfare	–	3	–	3	–	3
Total	36	36	36	36	36	36

Source: Government of Qatar, Ministry of Education (Unpublished material).

it could advantageously be revised. Bahrain's pattern of distribution could be used as a guide since this state has had longer experience in designing school curricula.

At the secondary level, students in Qatar also take 36 periods per week, as shown in Table 3-16. The subjects given are essentially a carry-over of those included at the intermediate level. Religious education and Arabic continue to receive special attention. As is also the case in Bahrain, beginning with the second year, students branch out into two major groups, the arts and the sciences. Arts and science students both take the same number of periods in religious education; but science students take fewer periods in Arabic and English, and more in science, while arts students devote more time to social studies.

School Curricula in Abu Dhabi

In Abu Dhabi, as shown in Table 3-17, students at the primary level take 29 periods in the first year, 30 in the second, 36 in the third, 35 in the fourth, and 36 periods in the fifth and sixth year. The subjects taken at this level are similar to those given in both Bahrain and Qatar, but the pattern of distribution differs somewhat from the patterns of the other two countries. For example, math in Abu Dhabi's primary-level curriculum is given at the rate of five periods in the first year, six in the second and third years, and is decreased to five periods during the remaining three years. General sciences are given at the rate of two periods per week during the first three years and this is increased to four periods

Table 3-16
Weekly Plan of the Syllabus of the Secondary Education Level in Qatar

Subjects	1st Sec.		2nd Secondary				3rd Secondary			
			Literary		Scientific		Literary		Scientific	
	Boys	Girls	Boys	Girls	Boys	Girls	Boys	Girls	Boys	Girls
Religious Education	5	5	4	4	4	4	3	3	3	3
Arabic Lang. & Lit.	6	6	9	9	6	6	9	9	6	6
English Language	6	6	8	7	6	6	8	8	6	6
Mathematics	4	4	2	2	8	7	2	2	8	8
Physics	2	2	–	–	3	3	–	–	4	3
Chemistry	2	2	2	2	3	3	3	2	3	3
Biology	2	2	–	–	3	3	–	–	3	3
History	2	2	3	3	–	–	3	3	–	–
Geography	2	2	3	3	–	1	3	3	–	1
The Society	1	1	1	1	1	–	–	–	1	–
Sociology	–	–	2	2	–	–	–	–	–	–
Philosophy & Psy.	–	–	–	–	–	–	3	3	–	–
Art Education	2	1	1	1	1	1	1	1	1	1
Physical Education	2	1	1	1	1	1	1	1	1	1
Domestic Science	–	2	–	2	–	2	–	2	–	2
Total	36	36	36	37	36	37	36	37	36	37

(Subjects Physics through Philosophy & Psy. are grouped under "Social Studies Sciences".)

Source: Government of Qatar, Ministry of Education (Unpublished material).

in the fourth year and decreased to three periods during the remaining two years. Religious education, too, has a distinctive pattern, since students are given three periods in the first year, two in the second year, three in the third and fourth year, and then four periods in the fifth and sixth years.

At the intermediate level, students in Abu Dhabi take 36 periods in the first and second year, and 38 periods in the third year, as shown by Table 3-18. The same pattern of distribution prevails during the three years, except in the case of mathematics and social sciences in which one more period of each is taken in the third year than in the first and second year. Arabic receives seven periods, as in the case of Qatar, which is one less period than is given in Bahrain. Religious education receives three periods, two less than in Qatar, and two more than in Bahrain. English receives six periods, as in Qatar, which is two periods less than in Bahrain. The syllabus of the secondary level in Abu Dhabi reveals some unique features when compared with those of Bahrain or Qatar. Generally speaking, the load is heavier since it involves 38 periods per week. Also, the variety of subjects is extensive, for as many as twenty different subjects are given. The subjects offered in Abu Dhabi at this level and which are not offered elsewhere are: French, biology, geology, human culture, political economy and

Table 3-17
Weekly Plan of the Syllabus of the Primary Education Level in Abu Dhabi

Subject	1st Boys	1st Girls	2nd Boys	2nd Girls	3rd Boys	3rd Girls	4th Boys	4th Girls	5th Boys	5th Girls	6th Boys	6th Girls
Religion	3	3	2	2	3	3	3	3	4	4	4	4
Arabic Language	10	10	11	11	10	10	10	10	8	8	8	8
Mathematics	5	5	6	6	6	6	5	5	5	5	5	5
English Language	–	–	–	–	–	–	–	–	6	6	6	6
General Science	2	2	2	2	2	2	4	4	3	3	3	3
Social Studies	2	2	2	2	2	2	3	3	3	3	3	3
Art Education	2	2	2	2	2	2	2	2	2	2	2	2
Physical Education	3	3	3	3	3	3	3	2	3	2	3	2
School Songs	2	2	2	2	2	2	1	1	1	1	1	1
General Activities	–	–	–	–	2	2	2	1	1	–	1	–
Preparation	–	–	–	–	4	4	2	2	–	–	–	–
Domestic Science	–	–	–	–	–	–	–	2	–	2	–	2
Total	29	29	30	30	36	36	35	35	36	36	36	36

Source: Government of Abu Dhabi, Education Department (Unpublished material).

society. The pattern of distribution of the weekly load for boys at this level exhibits significant differences, as can be seen from Table 3-19.

The authors lack detailed information about the systems adopted in the other six Trucial states of Dubai, Sharjah, Umm al-Qaiwain, Ajman, Ras al-Khaimah and Fujairah; but these doubtless have been modeled after the Kuwaiti pattern since Kuwait organizes, finances and manages education in these countries. Of course, there are probably some differences in the weekly load, the varieties of subjects offered and the pattern of distribution of the various subjects in the weekly load.

Conclusions on Curricula

On the basis of this brief survey of the educational curricula of three of the Gulf city states, two tentative conclusions can appropriately be drawn. First, there is a need to reconsider general education versus technical education. These countries are embarking on their development and vocational training graduates are badly needed. So far, vocational training has been seriously underemphasized.

And second, the fact that these states have different educational patterns

Table 3-18
Weekly Plan of the Syllabus of the Intermediate Education Level in Abu Dhabi

Subject	1st		2nd		3rd	
	Boys	Girls	Boys	Girls	Boys	Girls
Religious Education	3	3	3	3	3	3
Arabic Language	7	7	7	7	7	7
English Language	6	6	6	6	6	6
Social Studies	3	3	3	3	4	4
Mathematics	5	5	5	5	6	6
General Science	4	4	4	4	4	4
Technical, Agric., Commercial	5	–	5	–	5	–
Domestic Science	–	3	–	3	–	,3
Art Education	–	2	–	2	–	2
Music & School Songs	1	1	1	1	1	1
Physical Education	2	2	2	2	2	2
Total	36	36	36	36	38	38

Source: Government of Abu Dhabi, Education Department (Unpublished material).

does not mean their educational systems have been geared to their needs. Since these states have more in common than they have in differences, it would seem logical that they should have more nearly identical educational systems. Their peoples speak the same language and they have similar political, social and economic foundations. Thus, if these states are really serious about developing cooperation on a regional basis, they definitely could make a good start in the area of education.

The Availability of Education

General Growth

Table 3-20 shows the development of education in Bahrain between the academic years 1945-46 and 1969-70. The total number of schools in 1945-46 was 18, 13 for males and 5 for females. By 1969-70, the number of schools had increased to 107, 62 for males and 45 for females. Aside from the increase in the absolute number of the schools, another significant development has been the relative growth in the number of schools for females from about 28% of the total number of schools in 1945-46 to 42% in 1969-70. The number of students, both males and females, in 1945-46 was 2,889 and it had risen to 47,666 in 1969-70.

Table 3-19
Weekly Plan of the Syllabus of the Secondary Education Level in Abu Dhabi

Subject	1st Sec.	2nd Sec.		3rd Sec.	
		Scientific	Literary	Scientific	Literary
Religious Education	2	2	2	1	1
Arabic Language	7	6	8	6	8
English Language	8	7	8	7	8
French Language	–	–	5	–	6
Chemistry	2	4	–	4	–
Biology	2	3	–	4	–
Physics	2	4	–	4	–
Geology	1	1	–	1	–
History	2	–	3	–	4
Geography	2	–	3	–	3
Surveying & Geology	–	–	–	–	2
Humanities	–	1	–	–	–
Political Economy	–	–	1	–	–
Philosophy	–	–	–	–	3
Mathematics	5	8	2	8	–
Art Education	2	–	–	–	–
Physical Education	2	2	2	2	2
Elementary Sociology	1	–	2	1	1
General Science	–	–	2	–	–
Domestic Science*	2	2	2	2	2
Total	38 boys	38 boys	38 boys	38 boys	38 boys
	40 girls	40 girls	40 girls	40 girls	40 girls

*For girls only.
Source: Government of Abu Dhabi, Education Department (Unpublished material).

The number of teachers in 1945-46 was 133 and it had increased to 2,313 in 1969-70. The number of Bahraini teachers in 1945-46 was 105, and the remaining 28 were from other countries. Thus, non-Bahrainis accounted for some 21% of the total, and by 1969-70, in spite of the much larger total number of teachers, non-Bahrainis still represented only about 22% of the total. This is an impressive record which indicates that Bahrain has been able to develop native teachers to meet the expanding educational needs.

Despite the considerable increase in educational facilities in Bahrain over the past twenty-five years, there is much room for further expansion. Table 3-21 shows school attendance by ages. The figures in the table indicate that if Bahrain aspires to provide school facilities for potential students in the age range of 7 to 19, it needs to plan an ambitious program of expansion. In view of the fact that

Table 3-20

Development of Education in Bahrain, 1945-1970

Academic Year	Number of Schools			Number of Students			Number of Teachers						
							Bahrainis			Non-Bahrainis			
	Males	Females	Total	Males	Females	Total	Males	Females	Total	Males	Females	Total	Total
45-46	13	5	18	1750	1139	2889	59	46	105	23	5	28	133
46-47	13	5	18	2084	1310	3394	65	51	116	24	6	30	146
47-48	14	5	19	2387	1283	3670	64	51	115	32	6	38	153
48-49	15	6	21	2785	1285	4070	80	57	137	40	7	47	184
49-50	15	6	21	3206	1356	4562	97	49	146	33	9	42	188
50-51	15	6	21	3792	1763	5555	102	55	157	54	11	65	222
51-52	16	6	22	3970	1963	5933	131	59	190	39	16	55	245
52-53	19	9	28	4580	2267	6847	136	65	201	68	18	86	287
53-54	22	9	31	5460	2313	7773	189	63	252	93	21	114	366
54-55	25	9	34	6544	2640	9184	204	72	276	94	28	122	398
55-56	25	12	37	7374	3313	10687	211	80	291	103	39	142	433
56-57	28	13	41	8506	3941	12447	233	90	323	144	47	191	514
57-58	31	13	44	9767	4591	14358	258	105	363	165	59	224	587
58-59	31	15	46	11094	5019	16113	304	121	425	132	59	191	216
59-60	34	16	50	12364	5467	17831	355	130	485	115	72	187	672
60-61	36	19	55	13923	6486	20409	409	172	581	138	80	281	799
61-62	38	22	60	15556	7764	23320	466	219	685	156	110	266	951
62-63	43	24	67	18426	9699	28125	560	253	813	160	146	306	1119

63-64	46	28	74	20630	11920	32550	646	311	957	174	199	373	1330
64-65	48	30	78	22442	13273	35715	738	347	1085	221	257	478	1563
65-66	51	31	82	23353	14254	37607	798	362	1160	251	243	494	1654
66-67	55	34	89	25738	15936	41674	873	434	1307	255	248	503	1810
67-68	56	38	94	26957	17898	45392	958	493	1451	255	261	516	1967
68-69	60	42	102	27245	18990	46235	1020	595	1615	258	246	504	2119
69-70	62	45	107	27376	20290	47666	1107	691	1798	262	253	515	2313

Source: Government of Bahrain, Education Department (Unpublished material).

Table 3-21

Number and Percentages of Children Attending School in Bahrain, Ages 7 to 19 (1965)

Age	Males		Females		Total	
	No.	%[1]	No.	%[1]	No.	%
Bahrainis						
7	1,967	70	1,474	55	3,441	61
8	2,294	85	1,504	58	3,798	72
9	1,861	93	1,255	60	3,116	74
10	2,272	91	1,287	56	3,559	74
11	1,558	97	927	62	2,485	80
12	2,320	93	1,115	56	3,435	76
13	1,481	93	846	60	2,327	78
14	1,370	86	826	49	2,196	67
15-19	4,091	68	1,661	28	5,752	48
Non-Bahrainis						
7	284	72	281	70	565	71
8	291	85	277	79	568	82
9	273	91	203	81	476	87
10	278	89	246	81	524	85
11	186	87	152	82	338	85
12	258	77	187	79	445	78
13	154	80	115	73	269	77
14	118	58	107	66	225	61
15-19	364	22	218	35	582	25

[1] Percent of total population in that age and sex group.

Source: Government of Bahrain, *Statistical Abstract*, 1968, Table 25, p. 17.

Bahrain's financial resources are rather limited, careful planning to develop a realistic program which can be implemented and which will be within the country's financial and other possible constraints is needed.

Qatar has also considerably increased its educational facilities over the past 15 years or so. In 1960, it had 60 schools, 40 for males and 20 for females, and the total number had jumped to 88 by 1969-70, of which 48 schools were for males and 40 for females. The total number of students increased from 1,050 in 1955 to 17,223 in 1970, or at an average annual rate of increase of 49%, which is an excellent record of progress. Comparative figures are shown in Tables 3-22 and 3-23.

Abu Dhabi, which is in a way a newcomer to the business of providing educational facilities for its potential student population, has also achieved a significant growth rate. When it started its regular system of education in 1960-61, one boy's school and one girl's school were added to its facilities,

Table 3-22
Development of Education in Qatar, 1960-1970

Year	No. of Schools			No. of Students		
	Male	Female	Total	Male	Female	Total
1960	40	28	60	4,023	1,942	5,965
1970	48	40	88	10,122	7,101	17,223

Source: Government of Qatar, Ministry of Education (Unpublished material).

Table 3-23
Education Statistics for the Gulf City States, 1969-70

Country	No. of Schools	No. of Classes	No. of Students	No. of Teachers
Bahrain	107	1,313	47,666	2,313
Qatar	88	690	17,223	956
Abu Dhabi	22	193	6,096	320
Dubai	10	142	5,627	231
Sharjah	12	126	4,829	214
Ajman	3	24	796	42
Umm al-Qaiwain	2	17	465	29
Ras al-Khaimah	10	82	2,007	145
Fujairah	2	14	382	22
Total	256	2,601	85,091	4,272

Sources: Government of Bahrain, Education Department (unpublished material);
Government of Qatar, Ministry of Education (unpublished material);
Government of Abu Dhabi, Education Department (unpublished material).

bringing the total number of schools to five. By 1969-70, the number had risen to 22, 14 for males and 8 for females, and the total enrollment in these schools had reached 6,096 students under 320 teachers. Figures on school growth for Abu Dhabi and other countries are presented in Table 3-23.

Abu Dhabi, in spite of the increase in the number of schools, still leaves much to be desired in the area of education. Still more schools and teachers are needed to meet its needs. In 1968, 75% of the age group 5 through 9 were not attending any school; and 71% of the age group 10 through 14, and 95% of the age group 15 through 19 were also not attending, as can be seen from Table 3-24. This means that 81% of the total potential school population in the age group, 5 through 19, was not attending. Thanks to the oil receipts, Abu Dhabi is able to finance the educational development which is needed, but money is not enough. Also required is a careful appraisal of the existing situation and the development of a sound plan which will make it possible to reach appropriate targets for

Table 3-24

School Attendance in the Gulf City States by State and Age Group

Country	5-9 Yrs.					10-14 Yrs.					15-19 Yrs.					Total–5-19 Yrs.				
	Total No.	Attending No.	%	Not Attending No.	%	Total No.	Attending No.	%	Not Attending No.	%	Total No.	Attending No.	%	Not Attending No.	%	Total No.	Attending No.	%	Not Attending No.	%
Bahrain 1965 C	29,129	NA	NA	NA	NA	NA	15,803	NA	NA	NA	NA	3,334	NA	NA	NA	NA	NA	NA	NA	NA
Qatar NA	NA	NA	NA	NA	NA	NA	NA	NA	NA	NA	NA	NA	NA	NA	NA	NA	NA	NA	NA	NA
Abu Dhabi 1968 C	3,458	855	25	2,603	75	2,231	637	29	1,594	71	3,187	166	5	3,021	95	8,876	1,658	19	7,218	81
Dubai 1968 C	6,967	2,197	32	4,770	68	4,759	2,447	51	2,312	49	4,338	821	19	3,517	81	16,064	5,465	34	10,599	66
Sharjah 1968 C	4,341	1,153	27	3,188	73	3,078	1,692	55	1,386	45	2,095	475	23	1,620	77	9,514	3,320	35	6,194	65
Ajman 1968 C	589	242	41	347	59	416	248	60	168	40	307	80	26	227	74	1,312	570	43	742	57
Umm al-Qaiwain 1968 C	446	135	30	311	70	368	211	57	157	43	235	50	21	185	79	1,049	396	38	653	62
Ras al-Khaimah 1968 C	3,305	845	26	2,460	74	2,532	1,279	51	1,253	49	1,799	362	20	1,437	80	7,636	2,486	33	5,150	67
Fujairah 1968 C	1,579	149	9	1,430	91	938	142	15	796	85	580	32	6	548	94	3,097	323	10	2,774	90
Grand Total*	20,685	5,576	27	15,109	73	14,322	6,656	46	7,666	54	12,541	1,986	16	10,555	84	47,548	14,218	30	33,330	70

*Grand Total excludes Bahrain and Qatar.

C = Census, NA = Not Available.

Sources: Government of Bahrain, *The 4th Population Census of Bahrain*, 1965, Table 20, p. 17, 1969.

Government of Abu Dhabi, *Statistical Abstract*, 1969, Vol. 1, Tables 2, 7 and 8, pp. 2 and 5.

Trucial States Census Figures 1968 (unpublished material).

educational development in the years immediately ahead. Among the difficulties to be overcome is the fact that of the total number of 320 teachers in Abu Dhabi, just 4 are Abu Dhabians and the remaining 316 are foreigners, as shown in Table 3-25. Any realistic plan should provide for the elimination of such an imbalance.

In the six most northern Trucial states of Dubai, Sharjah, Ajman, Umm al-Qaiwain, Ras al-Khaimah and Fujairah, educational facilities have increased significantly during the past two decades. Unlike Bahrain, Qatar, and Abu Dhabi, education in these countries has been organized, financed and managed externally, mainly by Kuwait, but also with a small amount of help from Qatar and the U.A.R. Organized education in these countries started on a small scale in 1953, and it has been growing year by year. In 1969-70, there were 10 schools in Dubai, 6 for males and 4 for females, with a total of 5,627 male and female students who were studying under 231 male and female teachers. In Sharjah, there were 12 schools, 6 each for males and females, and a total of 4,829 male and female students who were being taught by 214 male and female teachers. Ajman had two schools for males and one for females, with 796 students enrolled and a total of 42 teachers. In Umm al-Qaiwain, there were two schools, one for males and one for females, with 465 students and 29 teachers. Ras al-Khaimah had 10 schools, 5 for males and 5 for females, 2,007 students and 145 teachers. Fujairah had 2 schools, one for males and one for females, 382 students and 22 teachers. More detailed figures for these countries are presented in Table 3-25.

The existing educational coverage in the Trucial states leaves much to be desired. In Dubai, for the age groups 5-9, 10-14 and 15-19, 68%, 49% and 81%, respectively, were not attending school in 1968; and 66% of the entire age group, 5-19, was not attending. In Sharjah, 73%, 45% and 77% of the corresponding age groups were not attending, and 65% of the age range, 5-19, was not in school. In Ajman, the percentages were 39%, 40% and 74% with 57% of the age group 5-19 not in school. For Umm al-Qaiwain, the figures were 70%, 43% and 79%, with 62% of the age group, 5-19, not attending. In Ras al-Khaimah, 74%, 49% and 80% of the respective age groups were not attending, and the average nonattendance of the age group 5-19, was 67%. Finally, Fujairah is in the worst position with 91%, 85% and 94%, respectively, not attending, and an average of 90% of the age group, 5-19, not in school. The figures for these countries are summarized in Table 3-24.

The problem of education in these six Trucial states is not simply a matter of recognizing the need for increased schools and teachers. Since education in them is supported by external sources, improvements, at least in a number of them, will depend largely on the extent of interest of the helping countries. If these are not prepared to expand their assistance beyond its present level, the picture could be gloomy over the coming years. Except for Dubai, these countries cannot stand on their own and provide more facilities, or take over if the present

Table 3-25
General Educational Statistics for the Gulf City States for the Academic Year, 1969-70

Country	No. of Schools			No. of Students			Number of Teachers						Grand Total
							Local			Foreign			
	Male	Female	Total	Male	Female	Total	Male	Female	Total	Male	Female	Total	
Bahrain	62	45	107	27,376	20,290	47,666	1,107	691	1,798	262	253	515	2,313
Qatar	48	40	88	10,122	7,101	17,223	84	23	107	490	359	849	956
Abu Dhabi*	14	8	22	4,128	1,968	6,096	2	2	4	218	98	316	320
Dubai	6	4	10	3,357	2,270	5,627	3	1	4	145	82	227	231
Sharjah	6	6	12	2,856	1,973	4,829	—	1	1	116	97	213	214
Ajman	2	1	3	483	313	796	—	2	2	29	11	40	42
Umm al-Qaiwain	1	1	2	267	198	465	—	—	—	16	13	29	29
Ras al-Khaimah	5	5	10	1,161	846	2,007	—	—	—	80	65	145	145
Fujairah	1	1	2	265	117	382	—	—	—	13	9	22	22
	145	111	256	50,015	35,076	85,091	1,196	720	1,916	1,369	991	2,360	4,272

Note: Some schools have more than one level.
*Kindergartens were not included.
Sources: Government of Bahrain, Education Department (unpublished material);
Government of Qatar, Ministry of Education (unpublished material);
Government of Abu Dhabi, Education Department (unpublished material);
Kuwait office in Dubai (interview with Education Officer, June 1970, and unpublished material).

Table 3-26
Student and Teacher Data for the Gulf City States, 1969-70

Country	Population*	Male Students		Female Students		Percent of Local to Total Teachers		
		Number	% of Population	Number	% of Population	Male Education	Female Education	Male & Female Education
Bahrain	205,000	27,376	13	20,290	10	80.9	73.2	77.7
Qatar	80,000	10,122	13	7,101	9	14.6	6.0	11.2
Abu Dhabi	60,000	4,128	7	1,968	3	0.9	1.9	1.2
Dubai	75,000	3,357	4	2,270	3	2.0	1.2	1.7
Sharjah	40,000	2,856	7	1,973	5	0	1.0	0.5
Ajman	5,500	483	9	313	6	0	15.4	4.8
Umm al-Qaiwain	4,500	267	6	198	4	0	0	0
Ras al-Khaimah	30,000	1,161	4	846	3	0	0	0
Fujairah	10,000	265	3	117	1	0	0	0
Overall	510,000	50,015	10	35,094	7	46.6	42.1	44.9

*All population figures are estimates for 1970.
Source: Compiled on the basis of data from Tables 1-2, 3-20, 3-22, and 3-25.

helping countries decide for one reason or another to pull out. Dubai, as a result of its recent entry into the family of oil-producing countries, can raise resources to support its educational needs, but in view of its desire to finance many development projects, it probably will not be able to support the level of appropriations for education that would be needed to overcome present deficiencies quickly. The discovery and exploitation of oil in others of these countries would provide financial resources which could be used to quicken the pace of their educational development.

Some further ratios are of interest. In Bahrain, 27,376 male students, or 13% of the population, and 20,290 female students, or 10% of the population, went to school in 1969-70. Or in combined terms, 23% of the total population attended school in that year. Qatar had almost the same situation, with 22% of the total population in school, and with male and female students representing 13% and 9%, respectively, of the population total. The other seven countries have much lower ratios. Ten percent of the total population in Abu Dhabi, 7% in Dubai, 13% in Umm al-Qaiwain, 7% in Ras al-Khaimah and 4% of the population in Fujairah went to school.

The low ratio in the case of the oil-rich country of Abu Dhabi is a reflection of the fact that educational development there is of recent origin. Regular education was initiated in the early 1960s and facilities have not been expanded to meet the needs of the potential student population. The unfavorable ratios in the other countries is a result of the fact that they have not developed educational facilities of their own and the helping countries have not been providing adequate support. The hope for improving this situation rests in the hands of the helping countries in part, but it also depends upon the willingness of the countries themselves to exert greater efforts to expand their educational facilities.

Distribution of Students among Different Levels

Primary Level

From Table 3-27, it can be seen that students at the primary level constituted 73.1%, 79.3%, 90.1%, 67.9%, 66.6%, 76.5%, 68.4%, 69.7% and 66.2% of the total student population in Bahrain, Qatar, Abu Dhabi, Dubai, Sharjah, Ajman, Umm al-Qaiwain, Ras al-Khaimah and Fujairah respectively. In France and the U.S.A. the ratios in 1965 were, in order, 59.5% and 58.5%. In Jordan, Lebanon and Syria, the ratios in the same year were 70.8%, 76.5% and 74.5%, respectively. It is characteristic of developing countries to have a major concentration at the primary level. This is due to the shortage of higher-level facilities on the one hand, and to some environmental conditions on the other. For example, in Dubai it is not unusual for many students to leave school at the

Table 3-27

Ratio of Students in the Gulf City States in Each Level to the Total Number of Students

Country	Male Students				Female Students				Male & Female Students			
	% Primary Level	% Int. Level	% Sec. Level	% Higher Level	% Primary Level	% Int. Level	% Sec. Level	% Higher Level	% Primary Level	% Int. Level	% Sec. Level	% Higher Level
Bahrain	72.6	14.9	12.1	0.4	74.0	13.4	12.0	0.6	73.1	14.3	12.1	0.5
Qatar	75.2	14.2	10.6	–	85.3	10.4	4.3	–	79.3	12.7	8.0	–
Abu Dhabi	87.7	8.6	3.7	–	94.8	4.2	1.0	–	90.1	7.1	2.8	–
Dubai	61.9	28.2	9.9	–	76.8	21.8	1.4	–	67.9	25.6	6.5	–
Sharjah	65.3	27.7	7.0	–	68.5	24.7	6.8	–	66.6	26.5	6.9	–
Ajman	61.3	38.7	–	–	100	–	–	–	76.5	23.5	–	–
Umm al-Qaiwain	64.0	36.0	–	–	74.2	25.8	–	–	68.4	31.6	–	–
Ras al-Khaimah	65.1	29.6	5.3	–	76.1	22.7	1.2	–	69.7	26.7	3.6	–
Fujairah	62.6	37.4	–	–	74.4	25.6	–	–	66.2	33.8	–	–
Overall	72.8	16.7	10.3	0.2	77.5	13.7	8.4	0.4	74.8	15.4	9.5	0.3

Source: Compiled on the basis of data from tables in Chapter 3.

age of 10 because they feel that they can work and earn money in the trade sector. Another observation is that female ratios at the primary level are higher than male ratios. This may be explained in part by the lack of female facilities for further education beyond the primary level, and it is also partly a result of a traditional attitude toward female education in general. After a certain age, parents in these traditional societies prefer to marry their daughters and often feel that when they have grown enough, the daughters should not continue in school and be exposed to the society. This is an attitude which persists in some of these male-dominated societies where women are far from having been accorded recognition as equal partners.

Intermediate Level

As shown in Table 3-27, 14.9%, 14.2%, 8.6%, 28.2%, 27.7%, 38.7%, 36.0%, 29.6% and 37.3% of the total male students attending school in Bahrain, Qatar, Abu Dhabi, Dubai, Sharjah, Ajman, Umm al-Qaiwain, Ras al-Khaimah, and Fujairah were at the intermediate level. The relatively higher ratios in the case of these countries, except Bahrain, Qatar and Abu Dhabi, does not represent a favorable distribution, but rather it stems, in part, from the limited secondary facilities in some of them, and the nonexistence of such facilities in the others. In short, the vast majority of students in these states are in the primary and intermediate levels. With an expansion in secondary school facilities, which is urgently needed, the structure of these ratios would be changed for the better.

Secondary Level

Some of these countries have no secondary schools as yet, and those which have such facilities do not have high ratios of students enrolled in them. As mentioned, this is a result of shortages in secondary school facilities and of certain cultural constraints in these transitional societies. As shown in Table 3-27, 12.1%, 10.6%, 3.7%, 9.9%, 7.0% and 5.3% of the male students are at the secondary level in Bahrain, Qatar, Abu Dhabi, Dubai, Sharjah and Ras al-Khaimah, respectively.

Some Basic Ratios

Students-per-Class Ratios

The countries under review have an overall student per class ratio of 33. Ras al-Khaimah has the most favorable ratio, 24, followed by Qatar at 25, Fujairah at 27, Abu Dhabi at 32, Ajman at 33, Bahrain at 36, Sharjah at 38 and Dubai at

40. These ratios, which are listed in Table 3-28, should be received with some caution. For example, Ras al-Khaimah has the lowest ratio, but it does not follow that its quality of education is the best. We know, for example, that Bahrain has the most developed system among the group, yet its ratio is higher than is the case in a number of the other Gulf city states.

At the intermediate level, students-per-class ratios are about the same as those at the primary level, but at the secondary level, the ratios are generally more favorable.

Students-per-Teacher Ratios

Generally speaking, students-per-teacher ratios in all of these countries compare favorably with ratios in advanced countries. The overall ratio for the nine countries combined is 20, as is shown in Table 3-28; and the individual ratios are 21, 18, 19, 24, 23, 19, 16, 14, and 17 in Bahrain, Qatar, Abu Dhabi, Dubai, Sharjah, Ajman, Umm al-Qaiwain, Ras al-Khaimah and Fujairah, respectively.[1] It would be reasonable to have some increase in these ratios if this would provide an opportunity for more students to attend school.

Ratios of Local to Total Teachers

All countries except Bahrain suffer from shortages of local teachers and depend heavily on imported teachers from the other Arab countries. While 77.7% of the

Table 3-28
Students-per-Class and Students-per-Teacher Ratios for the Three Educational Levels Combined in the Gulf City States, 1969-70

Country	Male		Female		Male & Female	
	Students per Class	Students per Teacher	Students per Class	Students per Teacher	Students per Class	Students per Teacher
Bahrain	35	20	38	21	36	21
Qatar	26	18	23	19	25	18
Abu Dhabi	32	19	31	20	32	19
Dubai	37	23	44	27	40	24
Sharjah	40	25	36	20	38	23
Ajman	30	17	39	24	33	19
Umm al-Qaiwain	30	17	25	15	27	16
Ras al-Khaimah	26	15	22	13	24	14
Fujairah	33	20	20	13	27	17
Overall	33	19	33	21	33	20

Source: Compiled on the basis of data from tables in Chapter 3.

Table 3-29

Students-per-Class Ratios at the Primary Education Level in the Gulf City States, 1969-70

	Students-per-Class Ratios		
Country	Male	Female	Male & Female
Bahrain	36	38	37
Qatar	24	22	23
Abu Dhabi	34	35	34
Dubai	44	46	45
Sharjah	48	48	48
Ajman	37	38	38
Umm al-Qaiwain	34	37	35
Ras al-Khaimah	34	29	32
Fujairah	41	22	32
Overall	34	33	33

Source: Compiled on the basis of data from tables in Chapter 3.

Table 3-30

Students-per-Class and Students-per-Teacher Ratios for Male and Female Students at the Intermediate Education Level in the Gulf City States, 1969-70

	Male		Female		Male & Female	
Country	Students per Class	Students per Teacher	Students per Class	Students per Teacher	Students per Class	Students per Teacher
Bahrain	36	NA	36	NA	36	NA
Qatar	39	20	31	16	36	18
Abu Dhabi	26	NA	18	NA	25	NA
Dubai	34	NA	38	NA	35	NA
Sharjah	32	NA	26	NA	29	NA
Ajman	21	NA	—	—	21	NA
Umm al-Qaiwain	24	NA	13	NA	18	NA
Ras al-Khaimah	19	NA	13	NA	16	NA
Fujairah	25	NA	15	NA	22	NA
Overall	34	NA	33	NA	33	NA

Note: NA = Not Available
Source: Compiled on the basis of data from tables in Chapter 3.

teachers in Bahrain are natives, room certainly still exists for further Bahraini participation in this profession. Local participation in the other eight countries is relatively insignificant. As was shown in Table 3-26, 11.2% of the total teachers in Qatar and just 1.2%, 1.7%, 0.5% and 4.8% of the total teachers in Abu Dhabi,

Table 3-31

Students-per-Class and Students-per-Teacher Ratios for Male and Female Students at the Secondary Education Level in the Gulf City States, 1969-70

Country	Male		Female		Male & Female	
	Students per Class	Students per Teacher	Students per Class	Students per Teacher	Students per Class	Students per Teacher
Bahrain	31	NA	36	NA	33	NA
Qatar	30	NA	30	NA	30	NA
Abu Dhabi	17	NA	7	NA	14	NA
Dubai	22	NA	31	NA	23	NA
Sharjah	28	NA	17	NA	22	NA
Ajman	–	–	–	–	–	–
Umm al-Qaiwain	–	–	–	–	–	–
Ras al-Khaimah	16	NA	10	NA	14	NA
Fujairah	–	–	–	–	–	–
Overall	29	NA	33	NA	30	NA

Note: NA = Not Available

Source: Compiled on the basis of data from tables in Chapter 3.

Dubai, Sharjah, and Ajman, respectively, are locals. Umm al-Qaiwain, Ras al-Khaimah and Fujairah have not been able so far to find local participants, and all the teachers in these three countries are expatriates.

The Cost of Education

Of the nine Gulf city states, only three are financing their education programs themselves. Bahrain, Qatar, and Abu Dhabi are appropriating large amounts for education, and this activity is given top priority among other developmental programs in these countries. Table 3-32 shows the amounts allocated annually for education by Bahrain for the period 1956 through 1969. These allocations are indicative of the importance attached to education by the Bahraini government. The rapid growth in Qatar's expenditures on education is illustrated by the figures presented in Table 3-33. Calculations based on these figures show that though the average annual rate of increase in expenditures over the period 1955 through 1968 was an impressive 31%, the average annual rate of increase in the number of students was still greater at 49%.

Abu Dhabi has followed the efforts of both the Bahraini and Qatari governments to provide favorable educational opportunities for their people by giving special attention to education in its five-year development plan. An impressive total of BD 12,140,000 has been allocated for this area for the years 1968-1972. It should also be noted that the rate of growth in Abu Dhabi's

Table 3-32

Annual Expenditures on Education in Bahrain, 1956-69 (Thousand B.D.)

Year	Expenditure on Education	Total Government Expenditure	Educational Expenditure as Percent of Total
1956	541	2,093	25.8
1957	581	2,707	21.4
1958	711	3,156	22.5
1959	815	4,284	19.0
1960	990	4,184	23.7
1961	1,191	4,638	25.6
1962	1,403	5,066	27.7
1963	1,618	5,697	28.4
1964	1,888	6,631	28.5
1965	2,127	7,312	29.0
1966	2,333	8,505	27.4
1967	2,727	10,151	26.9
1968	2,935	10,931	26.9
1969	3,286	12,473	26.3

Source: Government of Bahrain, *Statistical Abstract*, 1969, p. 15.

Table 3-33

Annual Expenditures on Education in Qatar, 1955-68 (Thousand B.D.)

Year	Expenditure on Education	No. of Students
1955	109	1,050
1956	219	1,510
1957	644	2,331
1958	1,342	3,016
1959	1,639	4,658
1960	2,588	5,965
1961	2,778	7,060
1962	2,635	8,079
1963	2,606	9,526
1964	2,750	10,853
1965	3,254	12,723
1966	3,134	13,706
1967	2,902	14,336
1968	3,498	15,652

Source: Ministry of Education, Qatar (unpublished material).

appropriation for education during the past four years has been quite high, and this, too, is indicative of the high priority given to this sector.

In spite of these favorable expenditure trends, there is need for substantial further increases in educational appropriations in these three countries.

The other six Trucial states do not finance their education programs. Kuwait has been organizing and financing education in these six countries since 1953; and other countries such as Qatar, Abu Dhabi and the U.A.R. now are also providing them with limited assistance in this sector. Though the outside assistance has been generous, the need for additional expenditures on education in these countries is great.

Health

Background

Fifty years ago, none of the nine Gulf city states had any health service. Their subsistence economies and the attendant low levels of living of the people plus the harsh climatic conditions throughout the region contributed to the high incidence of a number of diseases such as malaria, tuberculosis, dysentery, typhoid and trachoma. Coping with such problems in the past was beyond the competence of these countries. They lacked all types of medical staff and health facilities and it was not within their financial means to make any significant attempt at solving such problems. Bahrain had only one doctor in 1925, and he was employed by the government to take care of the entire population. As recently as 1945, only one doctor provided medical services for all of Qatar; and in 1939, the seven Trucial states of Abu Dhabi, Dubai, Sharjah, Ajman, Umm al-Qaiwain, Ras al-Khaimah and Fujairah, together, had only one clinic, stationed in Dubai, under one Indian doctor hired by the British government. Given these facts, it is not very difficult to imagine how acute and distressing the health problems were in the region.

Bahrain and Qatar, thanks to their oil receipts, started to improve their health facilities during the early 1940s. The first hospital went into operation in Bahrain under two medical officers and one matron in 1948; and in Qatar, a small hospital under one resident doctor went into operation in 1945. In 1950, a central hospital to serve the seven Trucial states was opened in Dubai; and in 1959, clinics were established in Sharjah and Umm al-Qaiwain. A clinic was opened in Fujairah in 1960; a 10-bed hospital went into operation in Ras al-Khaimah in 1962; and a clinic was started in Ajman in 1963. Finances for the limited health services in the seven Trucial states were provided by the rulers, mostly by the ruler of Dubai; and after 1954, the British government began to make some allocations as well.

As a result of their income from oil, both Bahrain and Qatar have been able to increase the quality and quantity of available medical services. Abu Dhabi which had but one clinic under one doctor as recently as 1966, has also been able to improve its medical services as a result of substantial oil receipts. The six most northern Trucial states of Dubai, Sharjah, Ajman, Umm al-Qaiwain, Ras al-Khaimah and Fujairah have been able to do but little to develop their health services because of their limited financial resources. Health services which are provided in these countries are supported by Kuwait, whose aid in this field began in 1963. At the present time, if Kuwait should elect to stop its aid in the area of health in these countries, only Dubai would be able to help take up the slack.

Current Health Facilities

At present, there are six government hospitals in Bahrain with a total of 929 beds. In addition, there are three nongovernment hospitals, one for the American mission with 58 beds, one for the Bahrain Petroleum Company (BAPCO) with 32 beds, and the Victoria Memorial Hospital with 10 beds. Qatar has three government hospitals with a total of 621 beds and two private hospitals with a total of 37 beds. Abu Dhabi has 300 beds divided between two government hospitals; and Dubai has two Kuwaiti-managed hospitals with a bed total of 164. Sharjah has a small hospital of 18 beds and Ras al-Khaimah also has a small hospital with 20 beds. Ajman has no government or Kuwaiti-managed hospitals, but it has a 15-bed hospital staffed and financed by Iran. Figures for government hospitals are summarized in Table 3-34, and nongovernment health service data are listed in Table 3-35.

Table 3-34

Government Hospitals and Number of Beds in the Gulf City States, 1970

Country	No. of Hospitals	Total No. of Beds
Bahrain (1)	6	929
Qatar (2)	3	621
Abu Dhabi (3)	2	300
Dubai (4)	2	164
Sharjah (4)	1	18
Ajman (4)	–	–
Umm al-Qaiwain (4)	–	–
Ras al-Khaimah (4)	1	20
Fujairah (4)	–	–

Sources: (1) Government of Bahrain, *Statistical Abstract, 1970*, p. 16;
(2) Government of Qatar, Ministry of Health, 1970 (unpublished material);
(3) Government of Abu Dhabi, Dept. of Health, 1970 (unpublished material);
(4) Kuwait Office in Dubai, July 1970 (unpublished material).

Table 3-35
Nongovernment Health Facilities and Services in the Gulf City States, 1970

Country	No. of Hospitals	No. of Beds	No. of Physicians	No. of Nurses & Assistant Nurses
Bahrain	3	100	38	NA
Qatar	2	37	19	23
Abu Dhabi	NA	NA	NA	NA
Dubai	NA	NA	NA	NA
Sharjah	NA	NA	NA	NA
Ajman	1	15	NA	NA
Umm al-Qaiwain	–	–	–	–
Ras al-Khaimah	–	–	–	–
Fujairah	–	–	–	–

NA: Stands for information not available.
Sources: (1) Government of Bahrain, *Statistical Abstract*, 1970, p. 16;
(2) Government of Qatar, Ministry of Health (unpublished material);
(3) Government of Abu Dhabi, Department of Health (unpublished material);
(4) Kuwait Office in Dubai (unpublished material).

Table 3-36 shows beds in hospitals by treatment category for Bahrain and Qatar. In both countries, obstetrics is given top priority. Medical and surgical beds constitute a significant percentage of the total, and so does the number of beds allocated to chest diseases.

In addition to hospitals, there are clinics in these countries. As shown in Table 3-37, Bahrain has 19 government clinics, Qatar has 5, Dubai has 2, and each of the other Gulf city states has one.

Table 3-38 shows the number of available physicians, nurses and matrons in these countries. Bahrain leads in physicians with 92; Qatar is next with 64; and Abu Dhabi and Dubai follow with 35 and 26 doctors, respectively. Sharjah has three doctors, Ras al-Khaimah has three, and each of the remaining states has but one. Only Bahrain, Qatar, Abu Dhabi and Dubai have dentists.

All of these countries have nurses, both male and female, and orderlies and dressers, but only Bahrain has matrons (senior and most experienced nurses), as shown in Tables 3-38 aand 3-39. Finally, they all have pharmacists except Fujairah. Table 3-40 shows the distribution of dentists and pharmacists.

Some Comparisons with Other Arab Countries

It is interesting to compare the status of the health facilities available in the Gulf city states with those of some of the other Arab states. Table 3-41 shows the population per hospital bed, per physician and per nurse in the Gulf city states; and Table 3-42 shows the same information for Iran, Jordan, Kuwait, Lebanon,

Table 3-36

Beds in Hospitals by Treatment Category in Bahrain and Qatar, 1970

Category	Bahrain		Qatar	
	No. of Beds	% of Total	No. of Beds	% of Total
Medical	104	11.2	90	14.5
Surgical	123[1]	13.2[1]	73	11.8
Obstetrics	256	27.5	150	24.1
Pediatric	74	8.0	50	8.0
Eye Diseases	42	4.5	16	2.6
E.N.T.	12	1.3	18	2.9
Chest Diseases	134	14.4	70	11.3
Geriatric	16	1.7	–	–
Psychiatric	136	14.6	36	5.8
Intensive care unit	8	0.9	35	5.6
Sick Staff	12	1.3	–	–
Police	12	1.3	–	–
Isolation	–	–	30	4.9
Bone Surgery	–	–	39	6.3
Not Classified	–	–	14	2.2
Total	929	100	621	100

[1]Includes bone surgery.

Sources: (1) Bahrain, *Statistical Abstract*, 1970, p. 16;
(2) Qatar, Ministry of Health (unpublished material).

Table 3-37

Clinics in the Gulf City States, 1970

Country	No. of Clinics
Bahrain	19
Qatar	5
Abu Dhabi	NA
Dubai	2
Sharjah	1
Ajman	1
Umm al-Qaiwain	1
Ras al-Khaimah	1
Fujairah	1

Source: Government of Bahrain, *Statistical Abstract*, 1970, p. 16. Others based on authors' survey.

Table 3-38

Physicians, Nurses, and Matrons in the Gulf City States, 1970

Country	Physicians			Nurses			Matrons[1]
	Male	Female	Total	Male	Female	Total	
Bahrain	69	23	92	119	309	428	10
Qatar	–	–	64	11	149	160	NA
Abu Dhabi	26	9	35	24	66	90	NA
Dubai	–	–	26	–	35	35	NA
Sharjah	3	–	3	–	7	7	–
Ajman	1	–	1	–	1	1	–
Umm al-Qaiwain	1	–	1	–	1	1	–
Ras al-Khaimah	2	1	3	–	5	5	–
Fujairah	1	–	1	–	1	1	–

[1] Matrons are senior and most experienced nurses.

Sources: Government of Bahrain, *Statistical Abstract*, 1970, p. 18;
Qatar, Ministry of Health (unpublished material);
Kuwait Office, Dubai (unpublished material);
Abu Dhabi, Department of Health (unpublished material).

Table 3-39

Dressers and Orderlies in the Gulf City States, 1970

Country	Male	Female	Total
Bahrain	120	167	287
Qatar	–	–	31
Abu Dhabi	–	–	67
Dubai	–	–	19
Sharjah	–	–	4
Ajman	–	–	2
Umm al-Qaiwain	–	–	2
Ras al-Khaimah	–	–	2
Fujairah	–	–	2

Sources: Government of Bahrain, *Statistical Abstract*, 1970, p. 18;
Qatar, Ministry of Health (unpublished material);
Health Department, Abu Dhabi (unpublished material);
Kuwait Office, Dubai (unpublished material).

Saudi Arabia and Syria. It can be seen from these tables that Qatar has the most favorable ratio in regard to population per hospital bed, not only in the Gulf states, but in the Middle East. Kuwait holds the second position with a ratio of

Table 3-40

Dentists and Pharmacists in the Gulf City States, 1970

Country	Dentists	Pharmacists
Bahrain	2	41
Qatar	5	16
Abu Dhabi	1	NA
Dubai	1	NA
Sharjah	–	1
Ajman	–	1
Umm al-Qaiwain	–	–
Ras al-Khaimah	–	1
Fujairah	–	–

Sources: Government of Bahrain, *Statistical Abstract*, 1970, p. 18;
Qatar, Ministry of Health (unpublished material);
Dubai, Kuwait office (unpublished material).

Table 3-41

Population per Hospital Bed, Physician and Nurse in the Gulf City States, 1970

Country	Population		
	Per Hospital Bed	Per Physician	Per Nurse
Bahrain	220	2,220	500
Qatar	130	1,250	500
Abu Dhabi	200	1,700	700
Dubai	460	2,900	1,700
Sharjah	2,200	13,300	5,700
Ajman	–	5,500	5,500
Umm al-Qaiwain	–	4,500	4,500
Ras al-Khaimah	1,500	15,000	6,000
Fujairah	–	10,000	10,000

Source: Compiled on the basis of information from previous tables in Chapter 3.

145 to 1, and it is followed by Abu Dhabi with 200 to 1. Bahrain, Qatar, Abu Dhabi and Dubai, if we accept this ratio as a measure of health development, could be considered more developed than a number of other generally more advanced Middle Eastern countries. Also in the case of population per physician, these four states compare favorably with the countries included in Table 3-42, with the exception of Kuwait. Qatar also has the most favorable ratio in this category of any of the Gulf city states. It is followed by Abu Dhabi, Bahrain and

Table 3-42

Some Comparative Data on Health Facilities in Selected Middle Eastern Countries

	Iraq 1964	Jordan 1966	Kuwait 1966	Lebanon 1964	S. Arabia 1967	Syria 1966
Population per physician	4,760	4,077	746	1,390	10,542	5,000
Population per hospital bed	470	597	145	210	1,174	884
Population per nurse	10,640	7,003	NA	2,913	3,905	5,000
Population per mid wife	71,909	11,439	NA	5,330	NA	NA

Source: United Nations, *Studies on Selected Development Problems in Various Countries in the Middle East*, 1969, pp. 98-107.

Dubai, in that order. The ratio of population per nurse is the same in both Qatar and Bahrain and it compares very favorably with other Middle Eastern countries.

Although one might conclude from the available quantity of health services in these countries that, generally, the service is in line with similar services in other countries in the area, in reality this would be an unrealistic conclusion. There is inadequate information on the quality of the hospitals, the level of the services which they can provide, and the types of medical problems which they can attempt to handle. In reviewing the efforts of these countries to achieve a reasonable level of medical services, several points are worth considering.

When all of the Gulf city states began to try to develop their health services, they initially lacked doctors, dressers, pharmacists and even medical orderlies. Though they either had or were given money to build clinics and hospitals and to purchase equipment, they did not have trained manpower. Although reliable information on the exact number of local staff is lacking, it is evident that even now very few local physicians and nurses are available in these countries. Some of them, such as Bahrain and Qatar, have recently begun to appreciate the nature of the problem and the need for training nationals to provide health services. Both of these countries have started nursing schools. The one in Bahrain had a total enrollment of 124 as of 1970, which included 24 male and 100 female students. The nursing school in Qatar was started in October 1969, and it is now helping to supply the need for native medical personnel. In 1970, a total of 55 Bahraini were under special training abroad, including doctors, nurses, lab technicians, etc. Seven Qataris are receiving training in medical service abroad and one doctor has already returned to Qatar to practice. It is not known to the authors if there are any doctors in the seven Trucial states who are native to the area. The broad lack of native medical personnel points to the need for a carefully constructed plan for medical staff development in the Gulf city states.

The size of some of these states does not justify the establishment of general hospitals, and certainly not specialized hospitals. Given the very limited financial resources available to a number of them and the high cost involved in starting and operating hospitals, particularly specialized ones, serious thought should be given to working out some means for regional cooperation in the provision of modern health services. Local facilities to take care of the simple and routine cases should be developed and maintained; but establishing one or more regional health centers to handle difficult and specialized cases would seem to be a reasonable and feasible approach to health development in the area.

The Gulf city states should seek to develop a philosophy of health services appropriate to their particular circumstances which would strike an optimum balance between preventive and curative medicine. Increased emphasis upon preventive programs would reduce the extent of the curative facilities and personnel needed. In attempting to achieve a proper balance between preventive and curative programs, the advice of outstanding outside health experts should be sought and considered.

Housing

Table 3-43 illustrates the level of housing development in the Gulf city states. Bahrain enjoys the most favorable position among the group in regard to the types of houses constructed. As of 1965, that country had a total of 31,061 houses, 90% of which were of stone, 6% of barasti construction, and 4% were made of other materials.[2] Abu Dhabi, which is the richest country of the group, had, in 1968, a total of 9,136 houses, only 26% of which were stone, 43% were barasti, and 31% were of other construction. At the same time, Dubai had 12,193 houses, 51% being of stone, 40% barasti, and 9% of other construction; and Sharjah had 6,778 houses with 56% being of stone, 36% barasti and 8% of other types of construction. Only Fujairah had a smaller percentage of stone houses than Abu Dhabi. The figures in Table 3-43 are easily subject to misinterpretation, however, for except in the case of Bahrain, higher ratios of stone houses do not necessarily reflect higher levels of development. Ras al-Khaimah and Sharjah, for example, have higher percentages of stone houses than the affluent cities of Dubai and Abu Dhabi, but it does not follow that they are more developed. All of the Trucial states witnessed an unusual rate of growth in the late 1960s as a result of the booming oil industry in Abu Dhabi and the prospects of oil finds in Dubai and the other tiny Trucial states. As a result, the building industry flourished in all these countries, and stone houses rather than barasti or other types were built to accommodate the continuous influx of expatriates into these countries. To an extent, growth in stone houses roughly reflects the growth of foreign populations.

The level of housing development should also be viewed from the standpoint of the size of houses. In Bahrain, 26.9% of the houses have one room, 32.9% have two rooms, 20% have three rooms, 10.1% have four rooms, and only 10% have 5 rooms or more. In other words, nearly 60% of all houses are very small.

In Dubai, about 75% of all houses would be classified as small, with two rooms or less; in Sharjah, more than 80% fall in the small category; in Ajman, 78% are small; in Umm al-Qaiwain, the figure is roughly 85%; in Ras al-Khaimah, it is about 78%; and in Fujairah, it is approximately 73%. Table 3-44 gives a summary of data on house size for the nine states.

When size is taken into account, it is reasonable to conclude that in the countries under review, with the exception of Bahrain, housing is backward since a very high percentage of existing houses are of the small type and the average number of persons per room per household is large. The governments of Bahrain, Qatar and Abu Dhabi have begun to take positive steps to develop housing policies which are intended to improve the housing situation. Bahrain has an ambitious housing project known as Isa town which, when completed, will provide modern houses for 35,000 persons. The foundation stone of Isa town was laid by Shaikh Isa Bin Sulman Al-Khalifa on December 16, 1963. This completely new town which is seven miles from Manama, the capital, covers an area of 2-1/2 square miles. The first phase of the project was opened by the ruler on November 13, 1968. A complete range of services has been incorporated in the design, including municipal offices, police and fire stations, mosques, schools for boys and girls, medical clinics, a traffic-free shopping center and a sport stadium. Householders will eventually own their houses. The government will finance the whole project; and only the construction costs will be recovered from householders since the land on which the town is being built was donated by the ruler. The cost varies between BD 1,800 and BD 3,900, according to the standard of the houses. The cost is to be recovered in monthly installments, which include a small interest charge, over a period of 20 years. Installment payments are devoted to financing further expansion of the town.

Qatar passed in 1964, Law Number 1, calling for the creation of regulations for low-cost housing. Under this law, the government provides Qataris who have limited income, the land necessary to build a suitable home and a loan to build a house which is in line with the family's level of income and the number of persons in the family. To benefit from these provisions, an applicant must be a Qatari, his income should be in the range of QDR 300 to 1500, and he should be between 20 and 50 years of age.[3] The loan will be recovered by the government over a period of 25 years if the income of the beneficiary should be less than QDR 300 per month, and if his salary is more than QDR 300 per month, the loan will be recovered over a period of 20 years. From the initiation of this project in 1965 to the end of 1968, 673 applications had been accepted, 340 for large houses and 333 for small ones. A total of 301 houses, 150 large and 151 small ones, had been completed and turned over to the respective applicants by late 1970. Incapacitated and old people are given free houses. By 1968, 66 houses had been built and given to beneficiaries eligible for them.

Abu Dhabi also has ambitious housing plans. The Abu Dhabi Petroleum Company completed a low-cost housing project in 1966. Shaik Zayid, soon

Table 3-43
Housing in the Gulf City States by Type of House and Number of Rooms per Household

No. of Rooms per Household	Bahrain 1965 Census			Qatar NA			Abu Dhabi 1968 Census			Dubai 1968 Census			Sharjah 1968 Census		
	Stone	Barasti	Others	Stone	Barasti	Others	Stone	Barasti	Others	Stone	Barasti	Others	Stone	Barasti	Others
1 room	7,284	799	270	NA	NA	NA	NA	NA	NA	1,835	2,406	875	1,307	1,365	364
2 rooms	9,180	693	336	NA	NA	NA	NA	NA	NA	2,146	1,836	211	1,497	850	134
3 rooms	5,669	215	339	NA	NA	NA	NA	NA	NA	1,138	496	33	648	165	18
4 rooms	2,921	56	153	NA	NA	NA	NA	NA	NA	563	93	12	242	35	8
5 rooms	1,342	13	72	NA	NA	NA	NA	NA	NA	215	27	2	69	8	1
6 rooms	1,685	4	30	NA	NA	NA	NA	NA	NA	292	13	–	61	6	–
Total by Type	28,081	1,780	1,200	NA	NA	NA	2,380	3,968	2,788	6,189	4,871	1,133	3,824	2,429	525
% of total households*	90	6	4	NA	NA	NA	26	43	31	51	40	9	56	36	8
Total Households (All Types)	31,061			NA			9,136			12,193			6,778		

No. of Rooms per Household	Ajman 1968 Census			Umm al-Qaiwain 1968 Census			Ras al-Khaimah 1968 Census			Fujairah 1968 Census			Six Northern Trucial States 1968
	Stone	Barasti	Others	Stone	Barasti	Others	Stone	Barasti	Others	Stone	Barasti	Others	Total[1]
1 room	243	136	26	164	257	85	1,297	786	281	137	535	7	12,106
2 rooms	244	68	24	162	131	34	1,631	552	97	185	850	6	10,658
3 rooms	103	17	8	68	43	6	704	154	16	84	288	3	3,992
4 rooms	42	6	–	12	8	1	226	33	4	41	118	1	1,445
5 rooms	17	–	1	3	2	–	94	5	1	17	30	–	491
6 rooms	5	–	1	2	–	–	43	5	–	18	29	–	475
Total by Type	654	227	59	411	441	126	3,995	1,535	399	482	1,850	17	29,167
% of total households	70	24	6	42	45	13	67	26	7	21	79	1	100
Total Households (All Types)	940			978			5,929			2,349			29,167

[1]These totals do not include Bahrain, Qatar and Abu Dhabi.

*Percent rows may not add to 100 because of rounding.

NA = Not Available.

Sources: Government of Bahrain, *The Fourth Population Census*, 1965, Table 14, p. 11;
Trucial States Census Figures (unpublished material).

Table 3-44

Housing in the Gulf City States by Number of Rooms

Total Households	Bahrain 1965C		Qatar NA		Abu Dhabi 1968C		Dubai 1968C		Sharjah 1968C		Ajman 1968C		Umm al-Qaiwain 1968C		Ras al-Khaimah 1968C		Fujairah 1968C	
	No.	% of Total	No.	% of Total	No.	% of Total	No.	% of Total	No.	% of Total	No.	% of Total	No.	% of Total	No.	% of Total	No.	% of Total
1 room	8,353	26.9*	NA	NA	NA	NA	5,116	42.0	3,036	44.8	405	43.1	506	51.7	2,364	39.9	679	28.9
2 rooms	10,209	32.9	NA	NA	NA	NA	4,193	34.4	2,481	36.6	336	35.7	327	33.4	2,280	38.5	1,041	44.3
3 rooms	6,223	20.0	NA	NA	NA	NA	1,667	13.7	831	12.3	128	13.6	117	12.0	874	14.7	375	16.0
4 rooms	3,130	10.1	NA	NA	NA	NA	668	5.5	285	4.2	48	5.1	21	2.1	263	4.4	160	6.8
5 rooms	1,427	4.6	NA	NA	NA	NA	244	2.0	78	1.2	17	1.8	5	0.5	100	1.7	47	2.0
6 rooms or more	1,719	5.5	NA	NA	NA	NA	305	2.5	67	1.0	6	0.6	2	0.2	48	0.8	47	2.0
Total	31,061	100	NA	100	9,136	100	12,193	100	6,778	100	940	100	978	100	5,929	100	2,349	100

*Percentage columns may not add to 100 because of rounding.

C = Census

NA = Not Available.

Sources: Government of Bahrain, *The Fourth Population Census*, 1965, Table 14, p. 11; Trucial States Census Figures (unpublished material).

after his accession to the rulership, launched other low-cost housing projects. The five-year development plan, 1968-1972, appropriated BD 16,700,000 for housing. Zayid town near Al-Ain, the second largest town in Abu Dhabi, will, when completed, accommodate the inhabitants of Al-Ain and the neighboring oasis villages. Four thousand houses are to be built under the existing plan; and an additional 4,000 new houses will be offered free to citizens of Abu Dhabi. Five hundred villas are being provided for government staff.

Social Security

Social security programs in the Gulf city states, though badly needed, are not yet given the recognition and concern they deserve. Qatar, alone, provides some social security services to its citizens. Law Number 9 of 1963 called for the initiation and organization of social security programs in that country. Widows who have children or have no means of support, divorced women who have no support, orphans, the incapacitated, and old people who have no sources of income are entitled to benefit from the social security program. Social security payments are given in cash to those who meet the conditions prescribed for eligibility; but the amounts of such payments are not determined by the law. Each case is studied on its merit, and the appropriate amount is then determined. Between 1963 and 1968, a total of QDR 9,778,650 was distributed to eligible Qataris.[4] In 1969, 3,831 Qataris received a total of QDR 1,250,000 under the social security programs.[5]

Other countries, especially Abu Dhabi, Dubai and Bahrain which have oil income should consider instituting social security programs. In all of the Gulf city states, extreme poverty persists and if any of those existing in such impoverished circumstances should be cut off from a source of income, their lives would be in real danger. The governments in these countries should be aware of these problems and should try to cope with them as rapidly as they can.

Concluding Comments

It is evident from the discussions of the population characteristics of the Gulf city states and their accomplishments in education, health, housing and social security, that though significant progress has been made, a great deal remains to be done. When it is considered how relatively recently even the more advanced among these states embarked on the path of development, one can only be encouraged about the prospects for the future. It is true, of course, that the states receiving oil revenues have made by far the greatest social progress. But the nonoil-producing states, also, have been able to make a start on their social development. This has been made possible largely by outside financial support for such things as schools and medical facilities.

Particularly in the areas of education and medical facilities, vast savings can be made by the Gulf city states through cooperation and through a close coordination of their development efforts. Teacher-training, for example, can most economically be provided on a regional basis. Also, certain types of specialized medical care are too expensive for each of these small states to provide on its own. Centers to serve the entire area could be financed successfully, however, through joint support. It is to be hoped that such political differences as may exist among these states will not be permitted to interfere with cooperation in those areas of social development in which a joint effort would clearly be the most economical way of proceeding.

The following chapter considers in detail the political structures of the Gulf city states and discusses some of the major political problems.

Political Foundations

Relationships between Types of Government and Developmental Progress

Some Problems of Comparison

To determine whether any particular type of government is more favorable to development than another, in his article "The Politics of Development Administration," Milton Esman developed five models which can be used in seeking an answer.[1] These models are: (1) conservative oligarchies; (2) authoritarian military reformers; (3) dominant mass parties; (4) competitive interest-oriented party systems; and (5) communist totalitarian systems. George Grassmuck adapted and applied the Esman models to thirteen Near Eastern and North African countries. He classified Saudi Arabia, Morocco, Libya and Iran as conservative oligarchies; Syria, Jordan and Iraq as authoritarian military reformers; the U.A.R., Tunisia and Algeria as dominant mass party systems; and Turkey, Lebanon and Israel as competitive interest-oriented party systems. After classifying the thirteen states into the four categories, Grassmuck used some selected indexes of economic and social development to measure the relative suitability of each category for achieving development. The selected indexes of development were revealing to Professor Grassmuck; for he detected correlation between development as measured by these indexes and type of government.[2]

Countries in the competitive interest-oriented party systems category (Turkey, Lebanon and Israel) were at the upper end of the development scale; the conservative oligarchies (Saudi Arabia, Morocco, Libya and Iran) stood at the lower end; and authoritarian military reformers and dominant mass party systems were in between.[3] From Grassmuck's analysis, the conclusion could be drawn that developing countries would enhance their developmental efforts by creating competitive interest-oriented party systems. Before suggesting that the Gulf city states should turn to this form of government as a means of maximizing the rate of their developmental progress, one should examine Professor Grassmuck's criteria carefully to see if they give adequate support to his conclusion. As shown in Table 4-1, G.N.P. per capita, literacy, school enrollment, the percent of labor in agriculture, and the percent of population in cities over 20,000 were selected by Professor Grassmuck to determine possible relationships between type of government and the capacity to achieve development.

113

Table 4-1
Selected Indexes of Social and Economic Development, Near East and North Africa

Country	Total Population (in Thousands)	G.N.P. Per Capita (1957)	Percent Literate (of Population Aged 15 and Over)	Percent In Primary & Secondary School (of Population 5-19)	Students Enrolled Higher Education (Per 100,000 Population)	Percent of Labor Force in Agriculture	Percent of Population in Cities Over 20,000
Conservative Oligarchies							
Saudi Arabia	6,313	$170	2.5	5	6	–	9.5
Morocco	11,925	142	12.5	21	40	71	24.2
Libya	1,216	60	13.0	35	49	–	18.4
Iran	20,678	108	15.0	24	90	80	21.0
Authoritarian Military Reformers							
Syria	4,903	173	27.5	31	223	70	38.8
Jordan	1,690	129	17.5	46	–	–	25.5
Iraq	7,263	156	10.0	37	173	81	23.6
Dominant Mass Party Systems							
U.A.R. (EGYPT)	26,593	142	19.9	33	399	64	29.1
Tunisia	4,254	173	17.5	31	64	68	19.9
Algeria	10,989	178	19.0	23	70	75	14.1
Competitive Interest-Oriented Party Systems							
Turkey	28,602	220	39.0	38	255	77	18.2
Lebanon	1,817	362	47.5	53	345	50	23.0
Israel	2,185	726	93.7	69	668	15	60.9

Source: George Grassmuck, "Polity, Bureaucracy and Interest Groups in the Near East and North Africa," Revised draft, Comparative Administrative Group, American Society for Public Administration (CAG), Occasional Papers, Bloomington, Indiana: Indiana University, June 1965, p. 78.

G.N.P. per capita is usually a key indicator in measuring a country's level of economic well-being. The compilation in Table 4-1 shows G.N.P. per capita for the same thirteen Near East and African countries for both 1957 and 1968. If one takes the absolute figures for 1968, some of the previous conclusions seem to be supported. If the thirteen countries are ranked according to their levels of G.N.P. per capita, they will be in the following order from highest to lowest: Israel, Libya, Lebanon, Saudi Arabia, Turkey and Iran, Jordan and Iraq, Algeria and Tunisia, Morocco and the U.A.R. This new order differs from that of 1957; for only Israel maintains its rank at the upper end. Lebanon fell to third and Turkey to fifth place. But since we are interested in the relative ability of each system to accelerate the pace of development, a more reliable indicator would seem to be the rate of change in per capita G.N.P. between 1957 and 1968. On the basis of this criterion, conservative Libya had the highest rate of change; Iran was next, and was followed, in turn, by Saudi Arabia. Thus, the performance of the so-called conservative oligarchies in this regard was much better than that of the other categories. It can be argued, of course, that these are oil-producing countries and that the relatively high rate of change in their G.N.P. per capita was due more to the trend of oil production than to improved governmental capacity. This may be partly true, but Table 4-2 is also revealing in the case of the second category, authoritarian military reformers. Jordan and Iraq, for

Table 4-2

G.N.P. per Capita in 1957 and 1968, and Its Rate of Growth, for Selected Countries in the Near East and North Africa

Country	G.N.P. per Capita[1] (1957)	G.N.P. per Capita[2] (1968)	Rate of Change %
Saudi Arabia	$170	$ 360	111.76
Morocco	142	190	33.80
Libya	60	1,020	1,600.00
Iran	108	310	187.04
Syria	173	210	21.40
Jordan	129	260	101.55
Iraq	156	260	66.67
U.A.R.	142	170	19.72
Tunisia	173	220	27.17
Algeria	178	220	23.60
Turkey	220	310	40.91
Lebanon	362	560	54.70
Israel	726	1,360	87.33

Source: [1]From Table 4-1.

[2]AN-Nahar, *Economic and Financial Supplement*, November 29, 1970, pp. 8-10.

example, did better than Lebanon and Turkey. Here, at least in the case of Jordan, oil played no part.

The differences in performance among these countries suggests that the G.N.P.-per-capita criterion is not a valid or reliable one for measuring the suitability of various types of government to achieve development. Although the performance of the oligarchies, as measured by this criterion, was superior to that of the others, it cannot be concluded that it is the most appropriate type for development. One must be very careful about generalizations concerning political systems and development, for there are many factors that are not subject to measurement or even to identification.

Table 4-3 reveals that the other indicators also are not reliable. If we take the percentage of population living in cities of over 20,000, we find the highest ratio in some of the most underdeveloped countries where there are tribal governments. In all of the nine Gulf city states, for example, more than 85% of the people live in cities over 20,000; in fact, some 80%, or more, live in the capital cities. Based on this criterion, then, the traditional tribal system of government which has prevailed in the Gulf city states would qualify as more conducive to development than any of the four major patterns of government which are assumed to be found among developing countries. Our conclusion at this point is that development is so complex that measuring it by some selected indexes is not sufficient to justify generalizations. In order to appraise the relative suitability of a certain pattern of government for achieving developmental goals,

Table 4-3
The Percentage of Illiteracy among the Age Group 15 to 24, and the Rate of Growth in Student Enrollment at the Primary and Secondary Levels, for Selected Countries in the Near East and North Africa

Country	% of Illiteracy[1]	Annual Rate of Growth in Enrollment 1960-1967[2]
Saudi Arabia (1960)	99.0	26.3
Morocco (1966)	90.9	22.8
Libya (1964)	88.8	15.7
Syria (1960)	77.0	14.1
Jordan (1966)	57.0	9.9
Iraq (1962)	84.3	8.8
U.A.R. (1960)	84.2	13.1
Tunisia (1961)	90.1	10.4
Algeria (1966)	81.7	4.9
Lebanon (1962)	14.6	13.4

[1]United Nations, *Studies on Selected Development Problems in Various Countries in the Middle East*, 1970, Table 6, p. 79.
[2]Ibid., Table 8, p. 82.

one needs to compare countries which make it possible to identify all relevant variables which relate directly or indirectly to the process of development over a definite period of time. Even then, the findings would not be reassuring except in relation to the countries covered. A pattern of government is no better than the people who happen to operate it; a structure of government, no matter how elaborate and sophisticated, is a lifeless thing; it will never be able to push development an inch without the honest and sincere will and desire of those who influence, shape, design, manage and control its destiny. Since the Gulf city states have achieved varying levels of development, we shall attempt to determine the nature and extent of correlation, if any, between the type of government and development.

To undertake such an investigation, it is necessary to know the type of government and its developmental achievements in each country. As a first step, it is important to see whether governments of the GCS lend themselves to any meaningful classification. Before proceeding to identify the more detailed features of these governments, it will be helpful, first, to identify major elements which they may have in common. Since the government of a country is the product of the political, economic and social environment, we should consider the major factors in these areas which have influenced and shaped the governments of the GCS.

The British Colonial Heritage

The Gulf city states have been exposed to a common colonial influence. For more than a hundred years, Britain was the dominant foreign power in the Gulf and assumed the role of protector, with the result that all of the GCS were British protectorates for a long period. Before the British were able to establish their upper hand in the Gulf and protect their trading links with India and the interests of the East India Company, they had to turn aside first the challenge of the Portuguese and then of the Dutch, as was mentioned in Chapter 1.[4]

Britain's initial contacts with the people of the lower Gulf Coast followed the plunder of two British vessels by a Gulf tribe. To force the pirates of the coast to respect the flag, the British levelled a naval action against them. Following this action, the sheik of the tribe signed in 1820 what is known as the "General Peace Treaty." Fifteen years later, a "Perpetual Maritime Treaty" was entered into between the British and the sheiks of the coast. A third treaty known as the "Perpetual Truce Treaty" was entered into between the British and the sheiks of the coast in 1853, under which the latter pledged to recognize the presence of the British in the lower Gulf coast. The name, "Trucial Coast," was given to the area by the "Perpetual Truce Treaty." The area coming under this treaty included what is known today as the seven Trucial states or the United Arab Emirates. About that time, Bahrain was also brought under British influence.[5]

Al Khalifa, the present ruling family of Bahrain, had won control over the country from the Persians in 1783. In 1861, Sheik Muhammad bin Khalifa, then Ruler of Bahrain, accepted British protection thus initiating close ties and cooperation between Britain and Bahrain.[6] These ties were further strengthened in 1892, when the ruler, Sheik Isa bin Ali, entered into an exclusive agreement with the British government.[7] In accordance with that agreement, the sheik agreed not to enter into any agreement or correspondence with any power other than the British government; not to accept residence of the agent of any government without the assent of the British government; and not to cede, sell, mortgage or otherwise give for occupation any part of his territory, except to the British government. Thus, the exclusive agreement brought Bahrain under tight British control and protection.

Qatar established ties with Britain in 1868, when Sheik Muhammad al-Thani, then ruler of Qatar, entered into an agreement with the British resident in the Gulf. The sheik undertook not to break the peace at sea and to maintain friendly relations with his neighbors.[8] In 1916, Sheik Abdallah bin Jassim al-Thani entered into an agreement with Britain which formed the basis of relations from that point. In accordance with this agreement, Britain pledged itself to protect Qatar, and the ruler, in turn, agreed to give the British the guiding hand in his country.[9]

The rulers of Abu Dhabi and Dubai, Sheik Rashid bin Maktoum and Sheik Zayid bin Khalifa, respectively, also signed exclusive agreements in 1892, in which they placed their countries under tight British control.[10] Thus, the nineteenth century agreements provided legal foundations for Britain as the colonial power in the area. Early in the present century, Britain obtained further rights related to oil concessions from a number of these countries under which they pledged not to grant oil concessions except to the party appointed by the British government. These rights were obtained by virtue of agreements entered into between Britain and Sharjah (February 22, 1922), Ras al-Khaimah (February 22, 1922), Dubai (May 3, 1922), Ajman (May 4, 1922) and Umm al-Qaiwain (May 8, 1922).[11]

It is appropriate at this point to examine the nature of the relationships which the foregoing series of agreements established.

First, it should be noted that the agreements were not between equal sovereign political entities, but were between a strong sovereign state and minor states. In fact, it is very difficult to assume that those tribal communities had qualified as states when they signed the agreements. Because the agreements were not between equal sovereign powers, the stronger party was in a position to dictate the terms.

It is true that the text of the agreements shows that Britain pledged to protect the interests of these proteges, but it is most likely that the rulers' interests prompted their demand for protection. Probably, they were motivated by conditions prevailing in the Gulf and, therefore, a superior power could serve as a buffer and help to maintain the status quo.

Traditional rivalries among the rulers served the interests of the protector, Britain, for they prevented the rulers from dealing with her as a united group. It would probably have been possible for Britain to bring at least some of them together, but its own interests would have tended to prevent the protector country from taking positive actions toward this end. This colonial attitude may also partly explain the fragmented nature of the territories of some of the Trucial states. The often-used colonial policy of divide and rule seems to have been effectively applied in the case of the GCS. It is not our concern here to probe into the motives and strategies of colonial powers. The matter has been mentioned, however, because the effects of colonialism have not been fully overcome; for competition has made more difficult the formation of the United Arab Emirates (U.A.E.), and two of the GCS, Bahrain and Qatar, still have not become members.

Second, though one can argue that the first step toward the political development of the Gulf communities was taken when they fell under Britain's protection, their political advancement in actuality progressed rather slowly beyond that initial step; and their economic and social development have also been, at least until recently for some, relatively slow. As a colonial power, Britain was keen on maintaining an excellent record of internal security in these countries; but, whether by coincidence or design, it did not do much in the way of helping them achieve economic and social development. In the earlier discussions of the economic and social foundations of these countries, it was evident that the role of Britain in pushing the wheels of economic and social development had been quite minor from its early entry into the area until the early 1960s, when it began to show some interest in the development of the GCS.

It should be noted that in these states Britain has helped the ruling families to establish themselves and has also reinforced the separate identity of each of these tiny communities. Furthermore, the rate of development of the GCS over the past one hundred years gives additional support to the thesis that colonial powers in general place strong emphasis upon maintaining the status quo and law and order. With such an emphasis on the status quo, the process of development tends to be very slow during the period of colonial control. Such was indeed the case in the Gulf city states.

Tribalism

The second major element which has influenced and shaped the political development of the GCS is the tribal nature of their societies. Before the discovery of oil, tribesmen of the Gulf roamed the desert in search of water, food and pasturage. Scarcity of the sources of life imposed on the individual and the group a constant mobility. The tribe, as such, was the basis of social organization; it was also a political unit. Tribesmen did not feel that they were subject to a central authority. The tribe as a social and political unit was independent; and its members were tied together by tribal ties based on ancestry. The only authority was the habits and customs of the tribe which provided the only law. The head of the tribe, the sheik, was the father of the tribe and had a moral authority over its members. Identity and loyalty of the members went to the tribe itself which fixed their rights and obligations. The moral authority of the sheik of the tribe was exercised through the consent of its members and through the pressure of habits, customs and traditions which supported his authority.

In other words, the tribal nature of these communities precluded any form of central authority except that of their own tribe; for political authority requires settled life, and mobility is antithetical to centralized political authority. The love of these tribesmen for freedom and their resentment of any action which would check their movement in search of the needs for survival generated in them a basic hostility to any form of authority other than that of the head of the tribe. The concept of Arabs as killers of kings is probably the product of the close attachment of tribesmen to freedom of movement and hostility to central authority.

While life was so simple, the tribal system of government served effectively the needs of the Gulf communities, but more recently, life has begun to take on new dimensions in most of them.

The Impact of Oil Discoveries

Among the forces which have influenced and shaped political systems in the GCS, oil has played a most significant role. Before the discovery of oil, the Gulf people led a simple life in and around oases and coastal centers. They lived largely in extreme poverty and had little to contribute either to their own well-being or to that of the world. Life generally was unpleasant and definitely uninviting except to lovers of the harsh desert life.

Oil receipts have opened new horizons, not only in the oil-producing countries, but also in the neighboring nonoil-producing communities as well. Oil companies brought with them new ways of thinking and new ways of life. They gave concrete evidence to the inhabitants of these countries that the application of science and technology helps man to create better life opportunities. The oil royalties which poured into the pockets of the rulers gave them a new source of power and caused them to consider possible ways of spending the newly acquired funds. The needs of their people were too many to satisfy fully, no matter how large the royalties were. Some have found it appropriate to spend a large portion of their receipts in promoting social change.

Oil royalties provided the initial economic stimulus in the area. New economic activities were created and, consequently, work opportunities were enlarged. Many workers left their traditional occupations in agriculture and fishing and moved to new locations around the oil fields where they could find work either in the oil industry, itself, or in other sectors which were sparked by the oil boom, such as trade, construction, government, etc. This process of mobility worked in two directions. First, it resulted in the depopulation of a number of previously established tribal settlement centers; and, second, it resulted in a larger population concentration in and around the major town in each state where new opportunities had emerged.

Population growth in and around the major town of a state inevitably brought with it new problems to be handled by the machinery of government. More efforts were needed to maintain the traditional functions of law and order as more and more of the tribal population, which had been moving from one place to another in search for water and pasturage, began to settle down. With money available to the rulers, the promotion of urban infrastructures began. The introduction of new functions and services has led to the gradual improvement in the economic and social level of most of these communities; and in some of the states, the beginning of a sense of political awareness has emerged. Some citizens have begun to question the suitability of the tribal system of government in which essentially the whole business of government is highly centralized. Also, a number of the rulers have found they could no longer attend to all matters by themselves. The job of governing has outgrown their capacity to rule single-handedly on a strictly personal basis. Consequently, a number of these rulers have created some functional organizations to provide necessary links. In addition, they have surrounded themselves with a body of chosen advisors, mostly from the ranks of the ruling families, to help them in the profession of government. While economic progress has influenced the political setting and placed in question the adequacy of the traditional tribal system of government, it has not as yet, led to truly radical changes. In fact, the tribal system, in various degrees, is still in operation in all of the nine Gulf city states.

Common Political Aspects of the GCS

It will be useful at this point to attempt to identify common features shared by all of the GCS as well as the distinguishing features of each.

Ruling Families

The ruling family in each country has been ruling for a long period. The Al-Khalifa in Bahrain have been ruling for about two hundred years. From 1782 to the present, ten rulers have succeeded to the rulership of that country. Ahmad al-Khalifa (1782-1796), Abdallah bin Ahmad (1796-1843), Sulman bin Ahmad (1796-1825), Khalifa bin Sulman (1825-1834), Muhammad bin Khalifa

(1843-1867), Ali bin Khalifa (1868-1869), Isa bin Ali (1869-1932), Hamed bin Isa (1932-1942), Sulman bin Hamed (1942-1961) and Isa bin Sulman (1961-   ).[12] The average period of each ruler has been about twenty years.

The ruling family in Qatar, the al-Thani, has been ruling since 1822; and that of Dubai, a branch of the Bani Yas tribe, has been ruling since 1833. The ruling family in Abu Dhabi, also a branch of the Bani Yas tribe, has provided the twelve rulers who have succeeded to the rulership there: Shakhbut bin Dhiyab (1793-1816), Muhammad bin Shakhbout (1816-1818), Tahnoun bin Shakhbout (1818-1833), Khalifa bin Shakhbout (1833-1845), Said bin Tahnoun (1845-1855), Zayid bin Khalifa (1855-1909), Tahnoun bin Zayid (1909-1912), Hamdan bin Zayid (1912-1922), Sultan bin Zayid (1922-1927), Saqr bin Zayid (1927-1928), Shakhbout bin Sultan (1928-1966) and Zayid bin Sultan (1966-   ).[13]

Similarly, the ruling families in other, smaller, states have been providing the tribal leadership. Succession to the rulership in each of the nine GCS has been confined to the male line of the ruling family.[14] Table 4-4 shows the rulers and their apparent heirs. It is interesting to note that only the rulers of Bahrain, Qatar and Sharjah are young, while all the others are above sixty.

Table 4-4
Rulers of the Gulf City States and Their Ages, 1972

Country	Ruler	Date of Accession	Age (1972)	Heir
Bahrain	Sheik Isa bin Sulman al-Khalifa	1961	39	Sheik Hamad bin Isa al-Khalifa
Qatar	Sheik Khalifa bin Hamad al-Thani	1972	37	N.A.
Abu-Dhabi	Sheik Zayid bin Sultan Al-Nahayan	1966	67	Sheik Khalifa bin Zayid
Dubai	Sheik Rashid bin Said al-Maktoum	1958	67	Sheik Maktoum bin Rashid al-Maktoum
Sharjah	Sheik Mohammed bin Sultan	1972	30	N.A.
Ajman	Sheik Rashid al-Na'imi	N.A.	72	Sheik Hamad bin Rashid al-Na'imi
Umm al-Qaiwain	Sheik Ahmad bin Rashid al-Mu'alla	N.A.	82	Sheik Rashid bin Ahmed al-Mu'alla
Ras al-Khaimah	Sheik Sakr bin Mohammed al-Qasimi	N.A.	62	Sheik Khalid bin Sakr al-Qasimi
Fujairah	Sheik Mohammed Ash-Sharki	N.A.	72	N.A.

Source: Authors' survey.

Absolute Power of the Ruler

None of the GCS has a written constitution or any other similarly binding written document.[15] In the absence of such an instrument, the ruler is absolute and his actions are not checked; he is infallible. Sovereignty belongs to him, not to the people. He is the symbol of unity and personifies the state. Political leadership, as such, centers around the ruler. He concentrates, in his own hands, the legislative, the judicial and executive powers. As such, he is the focal point as well as the source of all powers and authorities.

Privileged Groups

Members of the ruling family in each country are privileged groups. They have superior rights compared to the other members of the community and they are exempt from obligations. At the same time, some nonruling families are considered superior to other families; and, consequently, they become closer to the ruler and the ruling families. The privileged groups expect and get favors from the ruler in return for continuous support and unquestioned loyalty and obedience. The system, as such, allows the exaltation of a privileged few; and it does not submit itself to any significant procedure of control by the governed.

Tribal versus National Loyalty

Tribesmen have their loyalty to their tribe. Differences among tribes exist, and some are considered socially superior to others. Even within the tribe itself, some families are considered superior to others. The ruling family is considered superior to other families in its tribe which, in turn, is regarded as superior to other tribes in the country. Tribesmen traditionally have extended their loyalty to the head of their tribe because, in the past, the tribe performed certain economic and social functions; but now the state is performing these various functions and services. Members of tribal societies experience difficulty in transferring their loyalty to a larger entity, the state; for they have been conditioned in the past to submit their loyalty to the ruler, in person, as the head of the superior and ruling family. Loyalty is not attached to the office of the ruler of the state, but rather it belongs to his own person; he is looked to as the father, and hence loyalty in these countries is a personal, rather than a functional loyalty. The people feel that it is due to the paternalism of the ruler that they enjoy certain benefits, and they believe that if it were not for the ruler's fatherly attitude and dedication, such benefits would not be forthcoming.

National Integration

The tribal nature of society in the GCS has precluded the achievement of national integration, which is still only slightly discernible. Table 4-5 shows tribal population by state and by tribe in the Trucial states. Some tribes are small while others are large.

Because of tribal solidarity, affiliation and loyalty, it has not been easy to transfer tribal allegiance and loyalty to the larger entity, the state. The more tribes there are in a country, the greater will be the extent of loyalty conflict and the problem of national integration. As such, tribesmen in the GCS tend to resist the central authority of a modern state, and they do not feel closely attached to a nation. As a result, each of these countries approximates a confederation of tribes.

In order to promote the idea of a nation or the nation state, it is necessary to strengthen the ties of national integration which is most difficult to achieve as long as tribesmen continue to be proud and conscious of their tribal identity. They must become willing to submit themselves to a larger identity, the state. But they do not submit easily to this overall identity unless they are convinced that the larger entity will provide them with better life opportunities. As the state increases its functions and services to touch gradually upon the needs of all members of the society, there will be a better opportunity to extend the idea of a nation state and to promote national loyalty. Since the tribe has been the closest approximation to the state, the major shift to national integration should be promoted gradually, for an evolutionary process can most effectively avoid conflicts and possible setbacks.

Not only must the matter of achieving national integration be viewed in the light of the tribal nature of society in these countries, but it is also to some extent a function of the composition of society in terms of local and foreign population. The foreign population in Bahrain accounts for 25% of the total; and foreigners in the other countries constitute 50% or more of the current population. Foreigners do not feel the same attachment which they have for their own nation, but tend merely to observe that degree of loyalty which is adequate to keep them inside the other country in which they are earning their living. They believe that a day will come when they will leave; and, basically, they feel that they do not belong. Many are interested in the development of their temporary country only to the extent that this will further their own interests. Actually, quite a number of these foreign residents spend many years earning their living in these host countries, and many would consider staying for longer periods or even settling down for good. To encourage them to stay and become assimilated with the indigenous element of the society, however, the cities and towns where they reside would need to be better places for living.

Table 4-5
Tribal Population of the GCS, by State and Tribe, 1968

Tribe	Abu Dhabi	Dubai 1968	Sharjah 1968	Ajman 1968	Umm al-Qaiwain 1968	Ras al-Khaimah 1968	Fujairah 1968	Total 1968
1. Ahbab	319	1	25	–	7	–	–	347
2. Al-ali	60	155	508	85	2,862	1,445	3	5,118
3. Al Awamir	1,721	69	37	7	19	34	5	1,892
4. Biduwat	42	450	–	1	–	–	6	499
5. Dahanimah	9	59	13	7	–	551	94	7,333
6. Dahababiha	3	–	2	6	–	–	8	19
7. Dhawahir	2,844	42	109	41	–	9	57	3,102
8. Ghafalah	96	6	34	5	127	25	–	293
9. Habus-Shihuh-Dhahuriyin	147	74	74	13	–	5,845	244	6,177
10. Bani Jabir	49	8	4	–	5	15	–	81
11. Bani Kaab (inc. Shwaihiyin)	217	16	197	39	–	189	59	717
12. Muhariza	17	–	12	–	–	312	10	351
13. Manasir	3,224	275	49	21	–	38	–	3,607
14. Masafarah	6	–	39	–	7	19	1	72
15. Mazari	1,287	271	293	17	38	1,062	76	3,044
16. Naaim (inc. Khuwatir)	325	171	219	616	25	968	10	2,334
17. Najadat	662	29	5	1	–	11	85	793
18. Nagbiyin	16	–	1,345	–	–	541	3	1,905
19. Qawasim	101	108	3,592	8	3	1,055	14	4,881
20. Bani Qitab	617	156	1,458	21	6	112	–	2,370
21. Quwaid	3	1	162	–	4	19	6	195
22. Shahairah	–	3	1	11	–	69	–	84
23. Al bu Shamis	370	769	689	190	12	408	–	2,438
24. Sharqiyin	80	65	116	69	25	82	8,372	8,809
25. Tunaij	13	2	372	7	–	21	22	437
26. Bani Yas	4,597	3,913	1,424	213	1	290	27	10,465
27. Zaab	22	27	710	7	4	2,455	–	3,225
28. Other	903	1,194	1,280	226	69	2,366	256	6,294
30. Total	17,750	7,864	12,769	1,611	3,209	17,941	9,138	70,282

Note: Statistics are not available for Bahrain and Qatar.
Source: 1968 Trucial States Census (unpublished).

Also, these foreign residents would need some form of assurance that they will not be suddenly surprised and asked to leave the country for one reason or another at some point in the future. Except for Bahrain, where the population density is already quite high, all of the GCS could not only absorb their present foreign populations, but also could take even more, once economic and social development is in high gear.

All of the GCS suffer from shortages of qualified manpower to meet the growing requirements of economic and social development; and they need semiskilled, skilled, technical, professional and administrative personnel. Given these needs they will continue to have to depend in large part on foreigners for their manpower requirements for some time to come. A policy which aims at integrating foreigners in general, and nationals of the Arab states in particular, seems to be most appropriate at this stage of their development.

Imported manpower will play two major roles. First, it will perform functions and services which cannot, or will not, be rendered by the indigenous element of the population; and, second, it will also act as a change agent. New attitudes, new ways of life are usually brought with them by those who come to these countries to work. As encouragement, these foreigners need to have a sense of relative stability. Those who show reasonable interest in acquiring local citizenship should be permitted to do so. In this respect, relaxed naturalization laws would be effective measures. If foreigners are given some form of assurance that they would be welcome to stay, their attitudes toward the country in which they are working and their interest in its national development would be more positive. Their motivations, their way of life and the manner of their dealings and associations with the natives would be improved. If the ties of national loyalties and the ingredients of national integration could be harnessed, the forces for the building of nation states in the area would become stronger and the process would proceed at a much faster rate.

Political Parties, Pressure Groups and the Press

The reader will by now have observed that participation in the political life of these countries is limited. There are no political parties or similar interest groups. Also, the communications media, particularly daily papers, are relatively limited. It is reasonable to say that political maturity and awareness among the governed still have not evolved to any great extent. The people, in general, have had no political experience; and they have not been exposed to any form of secondary organization. All share the same experience as members of a primary organization, the family and the tribe. Secondary organizations would help to cut across tribal boundaries, could grow in significance if permitted to evolve, and could contribute to the growth of political maturity.

Independence

All of the nine Gulf city states were under British protection for a long period. Britain handled their foreign relations and in a way influenced their ties with each other, with other countries in the area, and on the international level. Britain's decision to withdraw from the Gulf area at the end of 1971 evoked in each of them a sense of narrow nationalism. They all aspired to become independent, viable political units; but it is not easy for these states to emerge overnight from isolation to independence since they lack, at present, the necessary ingredients for building progressive, viable, independent political units. Instead of being overly concerned about independence and narrow nationalism, these states would do well to concentrate on possible ways and means to insure their survival by taking common economic and political steps as communities which share the same heritage, culture and problems. The formation of the United Arab Emirates, which since early 1972 has comprised the seven Trucial states, is an important progressive move in this direction.

Having discussed the common political features shared by the GCS, we shall now attempt to capture the distinguishing features of each. A country-by-country approach is most appropriate for this purpose.

Bahrain

Background

Under the leadership of Sheikh Ahmad al-Khalifa (1782-1796), the authority of the al-Khalifa dynasty was established. Aggression, piracy and gun-running were commonplace in the Gulf, and since Bahrain was a trading center, it had special problems.

Before the discovery of oil, Bahrain had subsisted on primitive agriculture, fishing and pearl-fishing; but above all, Bahrain was, as it is today, a trading center. On the whole, resources available to the rulers were very limited and, consequently, very little was provided by them in the form of state-supported economic and social functions and services. Bahrain started its public education program in the early 1920s, but it was not able to finance a more ambitious educational program until it began to enjoy oil receipts. Other social welfare programs were also launched in the early 1950s, on the basis of oil revenues.

During all of this period, the ruler ran the show single-handed and concentrated all the powers of the state in his hands. Heads of government departments derived their authority directly from the ruler who could appoint or dismiss them at his pleasure. None of the rulers was bound by a written constitution, or by any other similarly binding document. The infallibility of the ruler was not challenged until late in 1954, when an eight-member body, the Higher Executive Committee (HEC), which was supported by two shadowy underground organizations, requested certain political reforms. Among other things, the HEC requested "The Establishment of a Legislative Council, the tabling of a labor law, the tabling of civil and criminal codes, the registration of trade unions, and the replacement by trained judges of the members of the ruling family who then presided over courts."[16] To back these demands, strikes were staged by the HEC. In deference to the staged political pressures, Ruler Sulman bin Hamed (1942-1961), took some steps to satisfy the strikers by appointing an advisory committee to draft labor and workmen's compensation laws and by establishing education and health councils.

The hostile attitude toward the government did not come to a halt, however, but continued to simmer. Again in the spring of 1956, the HEC staged antigovernment demonstrations calling for progress and condemning paternalism. For the second time, the ruler could not but bend to the desires of the demonstrators; and he agreed to take any step which would answer their general cry, "Progress." Following the success which the HEC achieved during the first and the second rounds with the government, it renamed itself the Committee of National Union, or CNU.

The Suez Crisis in 1956 gave the Committee of National Union an excuse to organize a protest procession in Manama, the capital city. The marchers wrecked a newspaper office and damaged other buildings. The government sentenced to imprisonment on St. Helena a number of the leaders of the Committee of National Union. They were released in 1961, after application for a writ of habeas corpus. Since the Suez Crisis, Bahrain's political awareness has increased. Bahraini legal jurisdiction replaced that of the British in local courts in 1957, local postage stamps were issued in 1960; and the Bahraini dinar was introduced in 1965.[17]

The Administrative Council

Rule in the Bahrain from the time the al-Khalifa established themselves as masters under the leadership of Sheik Ahmad Al-Khalifa (1782-1796), until 1956, followed the pattern of traditional paternalism.

As a result of growing antigovernment sentiment directed at paternalism, Sheik Sulman bin Hamad (1942-1961), the ninth lineal descendant of the al-Khalifa dynasty and the father of the present ruler, Isa bin Sulman (1961-   ), issued circular No. 19 on March 20, 1956, in which he decreed the creation of the Administrative Council. This council was to be composed of a chairman and six members, with the chairman and three members to be from the al-Khalifa, two members to be from the ranks of the ordinary people, and one member to be a British advisor. The members of the initial council were as follows:[18]

1. Abdalla bin Isa al-Khalifa, Chairman
2. Khalifa bin Hamad bin Isa Al-Khalifa
3. Du'je bin Hamad al-Khalifa
4. Khalid bin Muhammad al-Khalifa
5. J.W.R. Smith
6. Ahmad Omran
7. Yusuf Shirawi

The appointing decree specifically defined the powers and functions of the Administrative Council. It was more of an administrative body; and matters related to finances of the state, foreign relations, or any other political matter fell outside its jurisdiction. It is difficult to consider the creation of the Administrative Council as a major step in the process of political development, though it was meant to be so by the ruler when he established it in response to growing antigovernment feeling. Even granted that the council had some competence within the scope of political matters, it inevitably operated in the shadow of the ruler and the ruling family, since four of its seven members, including the chairman, were from this family. Nonetheless, it did have some political significance. For the first time, members of the ruling family and ordinary people met together as partners, though not equal ones, to discuss problems of common interest. The administrative council apparently served the needs of the rulers until 1970. By then, it had become evident that the council would no longer serve the needs of a more enlightened Bahraini public which had come about as a result of the promotion of economic and social infrastructural development, and which had become more politically minded and more concerned with trends and developments not only in Bahrain, but also in the other Arab countries.

The Council of State

Britain's decision to terminate its presence in and withdraw from the Gulf by 1971, prompted a series of political actions at the local as well as at the international level. The first significant political action in the series was the creation by the ruler of the Council of State. Convinced of the need for reorganizing the government to cope with the needs of the transitional period required to build sound foundations for a modern progressive state, the ruler, Sheikh Isa bin Sulman, issued on January 19, 1970, two decrees. The first created the Council of State, and the second reorganized the administrative set-up of this council.[19]

Composition of the Council of State

The Council of State is composed of a president and twelve members who are appointed and released by a decree. Sheik Khalifa bin Sulman was appointed president, and the presidents of the operating departments of Defense, Finance and National Economy, Public Security, Justice, Development and Engineering Services, Labor and Social Affairs, Municipalities and Agriculture, Foreign Affairs, Information, Education, and Health, were appointed members. Dr. Hussein M. Albaharna has also been appointed as a legal advisor to the Council and a member.

Powers of the Council[20]

The establishing decree vested the executive power in the Council of State. It is responsible for the execution of the overall internal and external policies of the state in accordance with laws, decrees and regulations. In particular, the Council is empowered to organize financial, economic, cultural, health and social matters which would promote the welfare of the people.

Jurisdiction of the Council of State[21]

The Council of State performs the following functions:

1. Directs, coordinates and reviews the work of government departments and agencies;
2. Issues administrative decisions and follows up on their implementation;
3. Proposes drafts of laws, decrees, and regulations to the ruler;
4. Prepares the general budget of the state;
5. Prepares an economic development plan and takes necessary measures for its implementation in accordance with the law;
6. Controls and supervises government departments and agencies;
7. Supervises all semiofficial agencies and organizations which have a public interest;
8. Performs other functions which may be delegated to the Council by a decree.

The President of the Council

The president of the Council is appointed and released by a decree issued by the ruler.[22] He directs the work of the government and presides over the meetings of the Council.[23] The president and members of the Council are collectively responsible to the ruler for the proper execution of the internal and external policies of the state; and they are individually responsible to the ruler for the work of their respective departments or offices.[24]

Quorum, Decisions and Deliberation

An absolute majority constitutes the quorum of the Council; its decisions are taken by a majority vote of the members present; and the president can break a tie vote when such occurs. Deliberations of the Council are secret and are not disclosed, whether its decisions are public or not.

The creation of the Council of State can be considered a first step in positive political modernization in Bahrain. Some may not agree with this evaluation and may view the Council as just a committee composed of the heads of the major operating departments which is entrusted with routine matters, and whose decisions are not final but must be stamped by the approval of the ruler. Some may go farther and see in it a convenient body through which the wishes of top leadership can more conveniently be adopted than before. Those who hold this opinion would not consider members of the Council as political appointees but would view them, instead, as administrative appointees.

The president of the Council is a political appointee appointed by the ruler, since he comes from the ruling family. In addition, four out of the twelve members on the Council come from the ruling family. They are the presidents of Defense, Foreign Affairs, Justice, and Municipalities and Agriculture. This means, in effect, that the influence and the dominance of the ruler's personal interests still extend down the line to the day-to-day routine.

It is true that these Council members are not like ministers in other countries. They do not stand for certain parties, pressure groups or interests; but the fact remains that it is the first time in Bahrain that heads of departments have been called on to consider nationwide issues. The Council opens to them new avenues which hitherto have been tightly closed. From a purely hierarchical point of view, the structure of government in Bahrain is similar to that of many modern governments, except that the ruler is not constrained by a constitution or any other equally binding document. The ruler is at the apex of the hierarchy; and next to him is the Council of State, followed by heads of operating departments. The Council of State in Bahrain is similar in many respects to the Council of Ministers in Saudi Arabia.

The Independence of Bahrain

The second major political development in Bahrain has been its gaining of independence. Britain's decision to withdraw from the Gulf area by the end of 1971, brought to the surface Iran's long-outstanding claim to Bahrain; and Bahrain's plans for the future were influenced by this. The prospects for its joining any union of the Gulf states were directly influenced by what might happen to the Irani claim. Bahrain faced the threat that Iran might not recognize or might refuse to recognize any union which it had joined.

As a result of informal contacts with the permanent representatives at the U.N. of the governments of Iran and the United Kingdom, Secretary General U Thant appointed on March 28, 1970, the Director General of the U.N. office at Geneva to a special mission to ascertain the wishes of the people of Bahrain concerning the future status of their country. On March 30, 1970, Mr. Guicciardi arrived at Bahrain to begin his mission. An office was set up at the Gulf Hotel, and arrangements were made to ensure ready and free access to Mr. Guicciardi who did his best to take every opportunity to meet the people of Bahrain in the capital city and in outlying towns and centers. After he completed his mission, Mr. Guicciardi reported, "The Bahrainis I met were virtually unanimous in wanting a fully independent sovereign state. The great majority added that this should be an Arab State."[25] On May 11, 1970, at 3:00 p.m., the delegates of fifteen nations represented at the fifteen-hundred-and-thirty-sixth meeting of the United Nations Security Council took a unanimous vote in favor of a resolution based on the report of the personal representative of the Secretary General, Mr. Guicciardi.

The decision of the Council has been significant in more than one way. First and foremost it has ended the long-outstanding dispute between Iran and the United Kingdom over Bahrain. Second, it is a credit to the U.N., which probably for the first time has been able to resolve a political conflict through diplomatic efforts in such a manner. The cooperation of the parties concerned in seeking a solution through the United Nations is a successful application of Charter principles to international affairs.

The significance of the decision to Bahrain, however, is more than a matter of resolving an issue or a conflict; for resolving the conflict in such a peaceful manner has given Bahrain a badly needed opportunity to devote its efforts to achieving national development.

Qatar

Background

The Bani Utba tribe, whose main tribal centers were along the coast of al-Hasa in what is today the eastern province of the Kingdom of Saudi Arabia and the country of Kuwait, moved on from these centers to Qatar in the 1790s, and established what was to become the present state of Qatar. During the Wahhabi expansion from al-Hasa at the end of the eighteen century, more of the Bani Utba tribe made their way into Qatar; and by 1822, they were able to establish their main tribal center at al Bida, now part of Doha, the capital city of Qatar.

Sheik Muhammad Al-Thani was the first ruler to establish relations with Britain; and in 1868, he entered into an agreement with the British resident in the Gulf, under the terms of which he pledged not to break the peace at sea and to maintain friendly relations with his neighbors. Soon after the Turks extended their control over al-Hasa in 1871, they established a small outpost at Doha, in Qatar, and appointed ruler, Sheik Jassim Ibn Muhammad al-Thani, governor *(qaimaqam)* in 1876. The Anglo-Ottoman draft treaty in 1913 recognized the independence of Qatar, and the Anglo-Ottoman convention in 1914 confined the Turkish influence to areas west of the Qatari Peninsula. Also, under the convention, Britain was not to interfere in Qatari affairs. Thus the possible friction which was created by the special relationship both with Britain and the Turks was eliminated. When Britain extended its interest in Qatar during the First World War, Sheik Abdallah bin Jassim, then ruler of Qatar, entered into an Anglo-Qatari Agreement which continued until Britain's recent withdrawal from the Gulf. Britain, according to this agreement, pledged itself to protect Qatari interests, and the ruler agreed to give Britain the upper hand in return. When Qatar began to enjoy oil receipts after long years of depression and search for oil, Sheik Abdallah abdicated in 1949, and was succeeded by his son, Sheik Ali bin Abdallah al Thani, who remained in power until 1960, when he abdicated in favor of his son, Sheik Ahmad bin Ali al-Thani. This abdication was agreed upon by the ruling family and by Britain.

Paternalism, apparently, was acceptable to the Qatari people. The regime in Qatar was not exposed to organized pressure such as that which developed in Bahrain in 1954 and 1956; and the Qatari rulers, therefore, did not find it necessary to modify their governance. No attempt was made to create a central administrative body similar to the Administrative Council which was created in Bahrain in 1956. As in Bahrain, so, too, in Qatar, the ruler and the State have been the shadow of the other.

Though these countries maintained patriarchal systems for a long period in the past, new development forces recently have begun to exert pressure on them to modify their systems. Qatar took its first positive step toward political change in April 1970, when the ruler enacted a temporary Fundamental Law defining powers and authorities of the various organs of the state. Some may argue that the Fundamental Law was prompted by the decision of Britain to withdraw from the area after 1971. This may be partly true, but it is also unlikely that the regime could have operated much beyond this time without acknowledging some role for its clientele, the people. Such an acknowledgment was made public upon the promulgation of the Fundamental Law. It is useful to examine the major features of the law which is supposed to have modified paternalism in Qatar.

The Fundamental Law[26]

As for the objectives of the law, the preamble indicates that the need for organizing public authorities and responsibilities and defining rights and obligations of the citizens are among the major reasons which prompted its passage.

The preamble also highlights the role of the law in achieving Qatari goals of national development within the frame of the would-be federation of the Gulf states. Qatar has a firm belief that a union is the most reliable and effective means for ensuring stability and progress for the GCS, collectively and individually.

The law has five chapters comprising 77 articles. Part 1 deals with the form of government. Qatar, according to it, is an independent, democratic Arab sovereign state. It is a member in the Federation of the Arab Emirates; Islam is its religion and a major legislative source; Arabic is its official language; and the Qatari people are an integral part of the Arab nation.

Part 2 outlines the basic principles which govern the policy of the Qatari State in various fields. In the political field, Qatar is to take the necessary steps to maintain and preserve stability and security, and to defend itself against external aggression. As a member in the Federation of the Arab Emirates—not to be confused with the later United Arab Emirates—Qatar is to do its best to establish close ties with other member states. Democracy and a sound administrative system capable of promoting respect for law and order are to receive the closest attention of the state. Qatar, as an Arab Country, believes in the brotherhood of all Arabs; it endeavors to promote cooperation and unity among them; and it supports the Arab league and its goals. As to its foreign policy, Qatar aims at establishing friendly relations with all peace-loving countries in general, and with Islamic countries and people in particular. Principles of the United Nations which support the right to self-determination and promotion of international cooperation for the welfare of all mankind receive its full support. Such are the political prescriptions of the Fundamental Law.

In the economic field, the state guarantees economic freedom within the requirements of public interest. Property, work and capital are individual rights which have a social function regulated by law. Economic development is to be guided by scientific planning and technical cooperation with specialized international organizations.

In the social fields, the Fundamental Law stipulates that the family is the basis of society; principles of Islam are to be observed and supported; and the youth are to receive special state care. Such matters as social security, illness, ignorance and need are also to receive the earnest attention of the Qatari state.

As to the cultural principles incorporated in the Law, the state recognizes education as a basic foundation for the development of the welfare of the society; and, consequently, the Qatari government is to endeavor to enforce free compulsory education.

Part 3 deals with general obligations. Equality is guaranteed without distinction as to race, sex or religion. The accused is innocent until proved guilty, has a right to a fair trial and is entitled to defend himself. Freedom of the press and publication are also guaranteed. Individual as well as collective property is sacred; it cannot be expropriated except in accordance with a law.

Part 4 deals with powers of the state. Section 1 of Part 4 is concerned with general principles. Laws are issued by the ruler upon the recommendation of the Council of Ministers and the advice of the Consultative Council. The executive power is vested in the ruler who is helped by the Council of Ministers. The judicial powers are vested in the courts in accordance with laws issued by the ruler to this effect.

Part 4, Section 2, deals with powers and authorities of the ruler. The ruler is the head of the state; and a viceroy assists the ruler in carrying out the responsibilities of his office. The viceroy exercises all powers and authorities of the ruler during the latter's absence for any reason. Specifically, the ruler represents the state at home and before other states and in all its international relations. He calls the Council of Ministers for session and presides over its meetings when he finds it in the interest of the state to do so. He approves and promulgates laws and decrees which go into effect only after their publication in the Official Gazette; he takes charge and command of the armed forces; and he appoints and releases senior civil and military officers by decrees according to the law.

The Council of Ministers

The viceroy presides over the Council of Ministers and, in cooperation with the Council, undertakes the preparation of a comprehensive plan which aims at the highest rate of economic, social and administrative development in accordance with the basic principles of the state. Such a plan has to be submitted to the ruler for adoption and approval. The viceroy directs the various government departments and ensures the execution of laws and regulations through the Council of Ministers or the respective ministers. He appoints and releases employees who are outside the domain of the ruler.

Section 3 of Part 4 of the Fundamental Law deals with the Council of Ministers. The law stipulates that the number of ministers is defined by law and that the first council should be composed of ten ministers, including the viceroy who is president. Ministers of Finance and Petroleum; Education; Interior; Justice; Health; Public Works; Labor and Social Affairs; Commerce; Industry and Agriculture; Communications, Transport, Electricity and Water, were to form the first council.

Ministers are appointed and released by the ruler upon the recommendation of the president of the Council of Ministers. The president and members of the Council of Ministers each take an oath pledging to carry out the functions of his office in the best interest of the country.

Quorum, Decision and Accountability

Absolute majority constitutes the quorum; and decisions of the Council are taken by majority vote of those present. The president breaks the deadlock in case of a tie. Deliberations of the Council are secret.

The Council is collectively responsible to the ruler for the execution of the overall policy of the state. Every minister is individually responsible to the president of the Council.

The president of the Council presides over its meetings, directs the ministers, coordinates the functions of the various ministries and issues general guiding instructions. He refers recommendations of the Council to the ruler and signs, on behalf of the Council, its decisions.

Jurisdiction of the Council of Ministers

As the highest executive authority, the Council of Ministers administers all internal and external matters of the state. Specifically, the Council

1. Proposes drafts of laws and decrees and refers these to the ruler for approval and promulgation. Drafts of laws are referred to the Consultative Council for advice before their transmittal to the ruler;
2. Supervises the execution of laws, regulations, etc.;
3. Enacts regulations and decisions necessary to put laws into effect;
4. Creates and organizes governmental departments and agencies;
5. Supervises the interests of the state abroad;
6. Manages finances of the state and prepares budget estimates;
7. Enacts general rules required to ensure internal security;
8. Supervises the employees of the state;
9. Prepares an annual report on the major achievements at home and abroad, together with recommendations on the best ways and means for achieving the overall development of the country.

The Council of Ministers in Qatar is a prototype of the Council of State in Bahrain; the only difference is that members of the council in Bahrain are heads of the operating departments. In a sense, the ministers in Qatar are also heads of the operating departments. The difference seems to relate to the name of the major national unit in each country; in Bahrain, it is called "department," while it is called "ministry" in Qatar. The ministers of Qatar, as is the case with members of the Council of State in Bahrain, are not political appointees; for they do not represent political parties or pressure groups and their loyalty and allegiance are solely to the regime. Both in Qatar and Bahrain, the Council derives its authority from the ruler who is the source of all powers. While it is impressive to see Qatar's Fundamental Law discussing and supporting basic issues such as equality, democracy, planning and the like, there is some distance to go before these will have been fully realized in practice.

The first Council of Ministers was formed on May 29, 1970, under the Presidency of Sheik Khalifa bin Hamad al-Thani, Viceroy and heir apparent.[27]

Of the nine ministers, three come from the ranks of the people, and the rest come from the royal family.

The Consultative Council

Part 4, Section 4, of the Fundamental Law deals with the creation of a Consultative Council to help the ruler and the Council of Ministers in the discharge of their responsibilities. Its help is to be in the form of recommendations.

Composition of the Consultative Council

The Consultative Council is composed of twenty elected members plus the ministers. The ruler may appoint a number of councilors, not to exceed three, if he finds it in the public interest. For purposes of election, Qatar is divided into ten constituencies. Each constituency elects four candidates; and the ruler selects two persons from the four elected to be members of the Consultative Council. This technique, in a way, gives the ruler some control; for though four candidates are elected, the ruler screens them and selects the two who he feels would better qualify as members.

Qualifications of members of the Consultative Council include Qatari original citizenship, a minimum age of 24 at the time of election, and a clean conduct record.

A circular announcing the names of the members of the Consultative Council is issued within a week from the date of election. Such circulars are promulgated in the official gazette within a week from the date of announcement by the ruler. The ministers become members in the Council from the date of their appointment as ministers.

During its annual ordinary session, the Consultative Council elects by a secret ballot a president and a vice-president. These elections are by a majority vote. The oldest member presides over its election meeting.

The period of the Council is three years from the date of its first session, but the period may be extended if found in the public interest. Members of the Consultative Council take an oath before they begin their official duties, pledging loyalty, honesty and sincerity in the discharge of their functions to the state, the ruler and the people.

Jurisdiction of the Consultative Council

The Consultative Council deliberates on: (1) laws proposed by the Council of Ministers; (2) the overall political, social and administrative policies of the state;

and (3) major items in the budget estimates. It submits recommendations to the ruler on the results of its deliberations.

Sessions of the Council

The Consultative Council holds an annual ordinary session in the capital, or in any other place designated by the ruler. The duration of the ordinary session is eight months and it must meet monthly during this period. A majority of the members constitutes a quorum; and decisions are taken by the majority vote of the members present. The president breaks the deadlock in case of a tie.

Justice

Part 4, Section 5, deals with justice. Independence of judges is assured in accordance with laws to be enacted to this effect.

Concluding Comments on Qatar's Fundamental Law

The passage of the Fundamental Law and the institutions which were to be created in accordance with it are the first positive step in Qatar toward building a modern progressive state. Qatar for long has been operating under the tribal system of government, and although the law gives supreme authority to the ruler, and makes him the focal point of authority, yet, the recent attempt to define authorities and responsibilities and to recognize the need for the participation of people in the process of government is a healthy sign which deserves credit. It is not realistic, it should be emphasized, to expect to move immediately from the traditional tribal system and its institutions and implications to a completely new modern system in a society where tribal ties and loyalties are still dominant, and where, on the whole, the society lacks political maturity. Therefore, gradual change in a piecemeal approach may serve best the needs of the Qatari society. If the existing tribal model were abolished overnight, it is unlikely that Qatar could operate under a newly devised modern system; it will do much better to follow the maxim, "slow but sure." Probably, the most appropriate label to be attached to the present Qatari political system is tribal transitional, as is the case also in Bahrain.

Abu Dhabi

Background

The Al-Nahayan, the ruling family in Abu Dhabi, is a branch of the Bani Yas tribe which is the largest tribe in Trucial Oman. As shown in Table 4-5, the total number of members of the tribe in 1968 was 10,465, of whom 4,597 lived in Abu Dhabi, 3,913 lived in Dubai, 1,424 lived in Sharjah, and the rest lived in the other four Trucial States. It was in 1761, that tribesmen of the Bani Yas tribe established their first settlement center near a well on the island of Abu Dhabi. Sheik Shakhbout bin Dhiyab was the first ruler of this settlement, and he ruled from 1793 to 1816. The Al-Nahayan family, which had a dominant position in the tribe, led the Bufalasah section of the Bani Yas.

During the rule of the fourth lineal descendant of the ruling family, Sheik Khalifa bin Shakhbout (1833-1845), a section of the Bani Yas tribe, the Bufalasah, became dissatisfied with his rule, migrated, and established a new settlement at Dubai which has been since then a separate center.

Another section of the Bani Yas tribe, two years later and for different reasons, migrated to al-Udaid and established the western limits of Abu Dhabi territory. "During these years and for many decades to come the occupation of Buraimi alternated between the Bani Yas and their allies, the Saudi Arabians; occupations which were to be the basis for claims and counter claims when the Buraimi dispute became an international affair a century later."[28]

During his rule, the sixth ruler of Abu Dhabi, Zayid bin Khalifa (1855-1909), entered in 1892 into an exclusive agreement with Britain, pledging loyalty and cooperation in return for British protection. After the death of Sheik Zayid, family feuds retarded political coherence; and the decline of pearl-fishing deprived thousands of their livelihood. Four sons of Sheik Zayid ruled after his death: Tahnoum (1909-1912), Hamdan (1912-1922), Sultan (1922-1927) and Shakhbout (1928-1966).

Recent Economic and Political Development

As a result of the dying pearl-fishing industry, Abu Dhabi lived in extreme poverty from the 1930s until the discovery of oil only a few years ago. The lot of the rulers during these hard years was hardly better than that of their tribesmen. Poverty did not allow the tribesmen to question adequacy of the patriarchal system of government; and the ruler and the ruled were in the same boat of stricken poverty. When oil receipts began pouring into the pockets of the ruler, Sheik Shakhbout was reluctant to finance development projects. His family was not satisfied with this, and his attitude aroused strong criticism which led to his deposition. His brother, Sheik Zayid, succeeded him to the rulership in August 1966.

The deposition of Sheik Shakhbout represented a landmark in tribal politics. Since he was removed because he was hesitant to introduce development projects designed to transform the tribal society, his successor has been under pressure to adopt the policies and attitudes which his predecessor failed to institute. Thus, being implicitly committed to a policy of modernization, Sheik Zayid has been rushing the country into a new era. He has the money needed for this, but he lacks everything else. For the past four years, he has been pushing the building of the economic and social infrastructure. The system of government, however, has remained basically the same. Sovereignty belongs to ruler as the ultimate source of authority and power.

The enlargement of government as a result of the expansion of its functions and services has led to the creation of many specialized government departments which have accommodated a number of ruling family members; for all departments are headed by sheiks from the ruling family. Sheik Zayid has been doing more for his country than his predecessor. Since the headship of a government department is a position of some power and authority, he is thus sharing some of the power of the political entity with the other members of his family. In a sense, this may be considered political development since the base of participation has been enlarged to include more persons. It seems reasonable to conclude that paternalism has not been modified in Abu Dhabi to the extent that it has in both Bahrain and Qatar, and that the label, "traditional paternalism," is an appropriate one to attach to its government.

Dubai

Background

Some 800 tribesmen of the Butalasah section of the Bani Yas tribe, who originally settled down in Abu Dhabi in 1761, being dissatisfied with the ruler, moved away from Abu Dhabi in 1833, and found shelter for their boats at Dubai. The absence of regular naval forces in the gulf and rivalry among European powers made possible local piracy.

The first intervention on behalf of the British merchants was undertaken by the Royal Navy in 1775; and from 1861, there was a British naval force based in the Gulf. Sheik Maktoum bin Buti, then ruler of Dubai, undertook in 1835 to keep peace at sea; and his brother, Sheik Said bin Buti, signed the Perpetual Truce Treaty of 1853, which acknowledged the British presence in the Gulf. Formal relations with Britain, however, were not established until 1892, when Sheik Rashid bin Maktoum entered into an exclusive agreement with that country which remained the basis of their relationship until Britain's recent withdrawal from the Gulf. A British resident representative was stationed at Dubai in 1948. The present ruler, Sheik Rashid bin Said al-Maktoum, succeeded his father in 1958.

Recent Developments

Paternalism, to date, has been the system of government in Dubai. Until the past fifteen years or so, the ruler and the ruled subsisted on scanty resources; and severe poverty prevailed. After the mid-1950s, economic prosperity in the other

Gulf countries, as well as other developments, opened new horizons in Dubai. Since then, it has been known as the city of traders, and the ruler, himself, is a qualified expert in the trading profession. Duties on imports were the major source of income for the ruler until 1969, when he began to receive some oil revenues. The limited income which the ruler has been receiving, has been used to promote urban infrastructural development.

Trading has brought substantial amounts of wealth to the traders; and a group of entrepreneurs has emerged in Dubai. In order to harness more wealth, many businessmen have pooled their resources and established firms to provide or produce badly needed services or commodities. By this method, a number of development projects have been launched by the private sector which have been government undertakings in other Gulf countries. Electricity, water and telephone service have been promoted in this way. A cement factory will go into operation very soon which has also been financed by the private sector.

Reasonable progress has been achieved in Dubai in promoting economic and social infrastructural development; but the country joined the oil-producing group late in 1969, and, as yet, there has not been sufficient time to determine whether its paternalism will continue to meet the needs of an enlarged and expanded government as increasing oil receipts enable the ruler to undertake more ambitious development programs and projects.

At present, the ruler runs the state through a municipal council chaired by his second son, Sheik Hamdan. His eldest son and heir, Sheik Maktoum, heads a land registration committee; and his third son, Sheik Muhammad, heads the police force. In classifying the political system of Dubai, it is appropriate here, also, to apply the label, "traditional paternalism."

The Other Trucial States

The other five Trucial states—Sharjah, Ajman, Umm al-Qaiwain, Ras al-Khaimah and Fujairah have not, as yet, had oil discoveries. Therefore, they have only indirectly experienced the impact of oil. Through contributions, mostly from the oil-producing countries, they have been able to promote some urban infrastructural development. Governments in these tiny communities have not been enlarged and expanded, since their income can hardly finance the keeping of law and order. Thus, paternalism has not been questioned; and it still serves effectively the needs of these tribal societies. Each of the rulers runs his country, together with his sons and/or brothers, unchecked by anything except the force of habits and customs.

The Governmental Typology of the Gulf City States

It has been indicated that paternalism has been the common element of government among the GCS; but the type of paternalism seems to differ, at least in the case of the larger states of Bahrain and Qatar. None of the GCS would fall under any of the so-called modern forms of government such as federal, federal republic, constitutional monarchy or unitary republic. The larger states of Bahrain, Qatar, Abu Dhabi and Dubai, to a certain extent, perform functions and provide services, although in different degrees, similar to those undertaken by modern governments, particularly in the fields of education, health, housing, social security and law-and-order-keeping. But this is not sufficient to qualify them for inclusion under the modern label. Policy formulation and the process of decision-making in modern governments have upward, downward and lateral channels. The people in countries with modern governments are the ultimate source of power. In the GCS, the people do not participate in policy formulation and decision-making, though the regimes in both Bahrain and Qatar have begun to allow limited participation. This is a step forward along the long path to political modernization.

Although the people do not directly participate in the process of decision-making, the regime in each of the GCS has been introducing changes in the economic and social life of these communities, and therefore, in a sense, all of the rulers have shown interest in the welfare of their people. The degree of this interest and the extent of its sincerity varies, of course, from one to another. All of the rulers, each according to his own resources, have been genuinely interested in economic and social development. But at the same time, all of them have been hesitant to allow political changes. Bahrain and Qatar are the only two countries which have opened narrow doors for political change. Since all of them would fail the test of modernity, it may be revealing to consider their position in comparison with a near-by developing country, namely, Saudi Arabia.

Saudi Arabia has many things in common with these states. Some have labeled its government a conservative oligarchy. Would this label be appropriate for all or some of the GCS? Apparently it would not. Saudi Arabia has been established as a full-fledged political entity for more than forty years; it has promoted many economic and social development programs and projects; but it still lags behind a number of the GCS in some respects. Its system of government is not more advanced than the system in either Bahrain or Qatar. The Council of State in Bahrain is a prototype of the Council of Ministers in Saudi Arabia. Qatar also has a Council of Ministers, and it is ahead of Saudi Arabia in the recent promulgation of its "Fundamental Law" defining powers and authorities of the state and its various organs.

The climate of personal freedom is healthier in any of the GCS than it is in Saudi Arabia. Movies in the GCS, for example, are not banned, and almost all of them have one or more cinemas. Thus, although the rulers of the GCS are cautious reformers because they are keen to ensure their power and authority, they are less conservative than their Saudi Arabian counterparts. Although the conservative oligarchy model applies to the GCS in some respects, it does not apply, by any means, in all respects. Also, the sharp differences which exist among the GCS make it inappropriate to use this label. We need, then, to search for new labels which could properly be attached to each of them.

It will be helpful, first, to determine a common label and then to try to add sublabels, as may be appropriate in each case. It has been shown already that paternalism is the underlying principle of government throughout the GCS. There are, as we have seen, some variations in their individual practices; but such variations are essentially variations of degree within the overall framework of paternalism. If recent modifications in both Bahrain and Qatar are discounted, the differences are relatively insignificant.

The Continuum of Paternalism

Although all of the GCS can be placed under the common label, paternalism, certain distinct paternalistic features in some of them can be identified. If the nine GCS are arranged in a descending order from the most paternalistic to the least, the appropriate sequence would seem to be as follows: Fujairah, Umm al-Qaiwain, Ajman, Ras al-Khaimah, Sharjah, Dubai, Abu Dhabi, Bahrain and Qatar. This order suggests that Fujairah is the most paternalistic among the group while Qatar is the least. Actually, however, it is most difficult to determine the fine differences that warrant categorizing each into a distinct paternalistic pattern; and placing the nine countries along a continuum in this fashion is impressionistic and cannot be scientifically supported.

Based on tangible differences, they can readily be divided into two major groups. The seven Trucial states would form one group, and Qatar and Bahrain would constitute the other. The first group is clearly more paternalistic than the second, and we could say that the Trucial states fall in the classification of traditional paternalism while Bahrain and Qatar are representative of modern paternalism. What are the criteria for establishing this kind of classification? In the case of each of the seven Trucial states, the ruler has not so far institutionalized participation in the process of policy formulation and decision-making; for he continues to run the whole show as a father. Indeed, he runs it as a traditional father manages the affairs of his children who have no voice in what is being decided for them. His philosophy is that, as a father, he, after all, knows best what is good for his people. The people cannot but obey, observe loyalty and extend full trust and confidence in the wisdom of their ruler. The assumption is that the people have not grown enough to know what is good for them, and, consequently, their participation would not lead to the improvement of policy formulation and decision-making.

In the case of both Bahrain and Qatar, the rulers have developed into modern fathers; they are appreciating the potentials of their people. In Bahrain, limited participation has been introduced through the creation of the Council of State; and in Qatar, the Council of Ministers and the Consultative Council have provided vehicles for participation. Within this limited scope, paternalism has been modified in these two countries. This is not meant to suggest, however, that they have introduced the same modifications or have achieved the same level of political development. On the contrary, the two countries, Bahrain and Qatar, while both fitting the category, modern paternalism, have seen different political modifications and have achieved varying levels of development. The pertinent question here is whether economic and social development in each have invoked political modifications, or whether the reverse is true.

The facts of development in the GCS in general, and in Bahrain and Qatar in particular, seem to support the thesis that economic and social development have brought about political modifications; in fact, development has forced such modifications. The forces which have pushed political modifications in Bahrain and Qatar have not matured enough in the other states to bring about similar modifications. The level of economic and social well-being in Bahrain and Qatar has opened new horizons for the average citizen and stimulated speculation about the political process and his role in it. The rulers, therefore, could not ignore rising expectations and their potential pressures, and, consequently, they have not been able to delay the introduction of some modifications. Thus, our tentative conclusion is that some economic and social development is possible without political development, for all of the GCS have achieved a degree of economic and social development under the auspices of their traditional paternalism. As economic and social development continues, however, the pressures for political development tend to grow stronger and to become more effective.

Before the recent Bahraini and Qatari modifications, all of the nine GCS were at almost the same level of political development. Fifty years ago, they all started virtually from the same extremely low point as far as their economic and social development were concerned. In the past half century, they have achieved varying levels of economic and social development, and have reached different points along the development continuum. Why have some been able to achieve more than the others? Bahrain, Qatar, Abu Dhabi and Dubai have progressed farther along the road to development and one would call these states the more successful countries and the others the less successful. A striking difference is that the successful countries have enjoyed the benefits of oil revenues, while the less successful have not, though the latter still have high hopes of striking oil also. Obviously, it is not fair to compare oil-producing countries with nonoil-producing countries; for this would mean comparing the relative success of rich and poor countries, and the conclusions would not be sound. No matter how suitable have been the patterns of government in the less successful countries, their ability to plan, design, organize, and implement economic and social change has been constrained by the scarcity of available resources. While one cannot make a meaningful comparison between the more and the less successful countries, it is possible to make reasonable judgments if one compares the relative situations of the more successful countries with each other.

While all of the more successful countries have been enjoying oil receipts for some time, Bahrain and Qatar have had substantial receipts for a longer period. The length and extent of oil revenues vary from one country to another. Bahrain and Qatar have had oil receipts since the early 1950s, and Abu Dhabi and Dubai have had such revenues only since the early and late 1960s, respectively. Naturally, the amount of receipts and the time during which they have been received must have affected the relative ability of the government of each to achieve development. Thus, even comparing the rate of progress of these four more-successful countries one with another will not provide a reliable indicator of the relative suitability of their governments for achieving development. Bahrain and Qatar seem, however, to offer a reasonable opportunity for appraising the relative contributions of their respective governments to the process of development. It will be helpful to take a period, say 1920 to 1970, and compare their relative success over it.

In 1920, both Bahrain and Qatar suffered from the same level of political, economic and social underdevelopment. Both had a tribal system of government and subsisted on a coastal economy in which fishing and pearl-fishing were their major productive activities. Both were without services in education, electricity, health, housing, water, etc. Thus, 1920 can be considered as a base year—a zero point of development.

By 1970, these two countries had achieved different levels of economic and social development. If the major factors which have influenced and shaped the process of development in each during this time span can be identified, it may be possible to relate some of the variables in a meaningful way.

What are the common and what are the noncommon variables in their cases? In the 1930s, pearl-fishing received a mortal blow at the hands of cultured pearls from Japan; and the impact of the loss of this vital resource on both was roughly equal. Both have enjoyed substantial oil receipts since the early 1950s, but Qatar has been more fortunate since its level of production from 1950 to 1970 has been almost quadruple that of Bahrain. While Qatar had an average of 180,000 US barrels per day, Bahrain had an average output of only 47,000 US barrels per day, as shown by Table 2-16. Since a greater oil output means more resources for development, and since Qatar has been enjoying a higher level of oil production, it should have achieved a higher level of development, other things being equal. In this case, the logic of development does not seem to have coincided with the realities of development, however, for Bahrain has made greater developmental progress. Anyone who visits both Bahrain and Qatar is impressed by the fact that Bahrain appears to be ahead of Qatar in almost all respects. Bahrain gives the impression of being an organized society which is driving in organized fashion toward known objectives. One does not get the same impression in Qatar. Subjective impressions lead one to conclude that Bahrain is more advanced, developmentally, than Qatar. Objectively, Table 4-6 shows that Bahrain is ahead of Qatar in most of the indicators selected. It is true that average per capita income is very high in Qatar; but this does not reflect general

Table 4-6
Selected Indicators of Economic and Social Development, Bahrain and Qatar, 1970

No.	Indicator	Bahrain	Qatar
1.	Population density per square mile	800	20
2.	% of population in cities over 10,000	90	87.5
3.	Per Capita G.N.P. (1968)	$ 390	$3,490
4.	% of male students to population	13	13
5.	% of female students to population	10	9
6.	% of local male teachers to total male teachers	80.9	14.6
7.	% of local female teachers to total female teachers	73.2	6.0
8.	% of local teachers (male & female) to total (male & female)	77.7	11.2
9.	% of students in each level to total students:		
	(a) Primary level	73.1	79.3
	(b) Intermediate level	14.3	12.7
	(c) Secondary level	12.1	8.0
	(d) Higher level	0.5	–
10.	University Graduates per 1000 population	1.3	0.5
11.	(a) Population per hospital bed	220	130
	(b) Population per physician	2,200	1,250
	(c) Population per nurse	500	500
12.	(a) No. of local political weekly magazines	2	–
	(b) Local social weekly magazines	1	–
13.	No. of banks	8	7

Source: Items 1 through 11 are based on previous tables; other items are based on authors' survey.

development, for a large segment of the population is still impoverished. Actually, both Bahrain and Qatar have a redistribution problem since both have extremes of wealth and poverty, but the extent of the problem appears to be less in Bahrain.

Since paternalism has been the basic foundation for government in both countries from 1920 to 1970, the relatively greater success of Bahrain, though it has been working under less favorable financial conditions than Qatar, cannot be ascribed to the pattern of government for both have had the same general political structures. A political system may be viewed as a structure designed to allocate powers, authorities and responsibilities in a given society; but a political structure, like any other structure, is a lifeless thing, it needs the human mind, heart and will to operate it and drive it towards developmental ends. A structure is not better than the human element steering its destiny and directing its available resources. While both political systems were largely identical, the qualities of the mind, the heart and the will which were applied to developmental efforts in the two countries seem to have been different. One could conclude that there may be possible positive relationships between the quality of leadership in Bahrain and the ability of this country to achieve development. But leadership is the product of its environment.

While it is possible to advance a strong case in favor of the apparent role of leadership in development in Bahrain, the role of the people has also been important. Why leadership in Bahrain has shown better vision and greater concern for the development of society may be partly explained by observing that the Bahraini people, themselves, may have been more desirous of achieving change, and consequently the ruler could not but respond to the growing developmental expectations held by Bahraini individuals. Their desire for development has been in part created and stimulated through education. While Bahrain started its education in 1919, and by the early 1950s, free primary and secondary schooling was made available to all potential school children, Qatar embarked on its education program only in 1951. Thus, education could be singled out as a major factor which has contributed to what might be called the political maturity of society. The developmental demands stemming from this maturity could not be ignored by the rulers of Bahrain, and they have had to take a keen interest in the development of their country. Education produces ambitious individuals with new potentialities, wider horizons and expanding needs; and it helps them to develop the capacity within themselves to achieve their desires. In the face of such growing pressures, the institutions of government find it expedient to respond to the new demands and to provide new opportunities. When the expectations of individuals and the opportunities created by the government are not in equilibrium, frustration and tension will develop, and if they continue to build up pressure, drastic change will have to take place either by evolution or revolution.

At this point, it should be repeated that the human element rather than the structure of government has been more responsible for developmental trends in these countries. No matter how advanced and sophisticated a country's political structure, its developmental progress will, to an important extent, be the product of its leadership. Development will proceed at a faster rate where leadership cannot ignore societal needs and aspirations and where it has a high sense of integrity and justice, and a constructive vision of the future. To bring leadership to such a stage, there must be a socially and politically minded society. A politically oriented society can be best cultivated through extensive and appropriate education programs. In the GCS, a significant relationship seems to be discernible between education and political development.

While considering the matter of political development, it seems appropriate to bring up again the often raised question: What is the most appropriate form of government for achieving development? Or, as it is often put, what is the best form of government for development? For such a question, there would seem to be only an indirect answer. There is no single best form of government which is optimal for all developing countries; since the general environment varies among countries and government is a product of the environment. If, instead, the question of what is the best form of government for enhancing development in the GCS were raised, it would be possible to offer some meaningful comments. The GCS, as has been stated, have been operating under paternalistic governments. In all of them, varying degrees of development have been achieved. A possible significant correlation between leadership and development has been indicated by comparing the achievements of Bahrain with those of Qatar. The political systems are not modern in the GCS, but so far they have been more or less adequate for their needs at the stages of enlightenment reached by their citizens. In order to continue to respond to the public's needs, there will have to be modifications, as there have been recently, for example, in both Bahrain and Qatar where traditional paternalism has been infused with some elements of modernization. These countries are promoting economic and social development, and the keen interest they are taking in education, will doubtless lead to the development in their citizens of new capacities and new expectations which will result in demands for new and better opportunities, including the potential to screen what is being decided for them. If they feel that the decisions being taken by government are not in accord with their interests, they will seek additional ways and means of influencing these decisions and directing them in the directions of their interests. This suggests that the political system should be alert to the new demands of the people and should be capable of creating new opportunities to satisfy such demands. Governmental systems which are not responsive become stagnant, and vulnerable to revolutionary change. Given the probable alternative, political evolution seems to be the most appropriate strategy of change for the GCS. Bahrain and Qatar seem already to have recognized the logic of this approach, and the rest of these states would be well advised to follow their pattern.

It is not reasonable or appropriate that these countries should at this point subject their societies to the shock that would be involved in establishing political structures similar to those in modern, highly developed countries simply to realize modern, sophisticated political forms. These countries are underdeveloped and are still far from being politically minded and mature. They cannot leap in one giant jump from almost no political system to an elaborate, modern sophisticated one. Development will suffer if overly drastic changes take place. The process of decision-making under their present system is much easier, simpler and quicker. If the ruler is guided by a sense of justice, honesty, the welfare of his country, and a good vision for the future, development will proceed at a much faster rate than under an elaborate political system where the process of decision-making and allocation of available resources will be lost in a maze of compromises and pressures and counterpressures. Benevolent paternalism or benevolent autocracy would seem to serve best the needs of development in the GCS at the present stage of their development.

At this point, a few remarks on the relationship between some different aspects of development would seem to be appropriate. It has become clear from the previous discussion that economic and social development can proceed without political development; in other words, political development is not a prerequisite for economic and social development. The rate of development, however, might be higher under a somewhat more developed and responsive political system. Economic development makes deep imprints on social development and vice-versa. It is sometimes said that countries need to achieve a balanced development, but this needs to be qualified. Development is not simply the summation of achievement in the political, economic, social, administrative and other areas. It is the resultant of the interaction of all of these together. Whenever there is development, leads and lags in various areas will occur. While social development is crucial to the general developmental process, it is often economic development which leads and sparks development in other areas. Development in these, in turn, has a stimulating feedback effect on economic development. Thus, balanced or imbalanced development relates more to the degree of balance or imbalance and is more of an academic than a practical issue.

What has been said about the political structures in the GCS should not be interpreted to mean that the pattern of government in these countries is ideal, for certainly there are some serious shortcomings as evidenced by (1) the concentration of powers in the hands of the ruler; (2) the position of members of the royal family as a privileged group; (3) the widespread inequality of social and economic conditions, with extreme poverty contrasted with great wealth; and (4) the absence of a significant middle class. These conditions, plus the lack of opportunity for participation by the general public in politics, suggest that economic and social inequality are not likely to be removed or even substantially lessened unless positive political action is taken. Therefore, these countries, and their rulers in particular, would do well to encourage the process of political evolution as an alternative to a political revolution that is otherwise virtually certain to develop in these countries as pressures for modernization mount in the years ahead.

5 Administrative Problems
and Policies

Introductory Comments

Of the nine Gulf city states, only four have been receiving oil receipts. These
"have" states are Bahrain, Qatar, Abu Dhabi and Dubai. The other five, Sharjah,
Ajman, Umm al-Qaiwain, Ras al-Khaimah and Fujairah, which have not struck
oil as yet, are the "have-nots." The countries in both groups have been able to
promote varying degrees of economic and social infrastructural development,
though the level of development in the oil-revenue countries, understandably,
has been higher than that of the others. The oil-producing countries have been
able to finance their own development projects, and they have the financial
capacity to promote further economic and social development. The nonoil-producing countries, as mentioned previously, have not been able to finance the
little development which they have achieved; and their development, so far, has
been largely supported by some of the oil-producing countries of the GCS, and
in some cases, by Britain, Kuwait, Saudi Arabia, and other outside donor
countries.

All the economic and social infrastructural projects which have been carried
out in the oil-producing GCS have been largely state designed, organized and
managed. As the poorer countries among the GCS are able to launch new
development projects, such projects also will almost certainly be state designed,
organized and run. Since the governments of both groups of countries have, in
the past, played a key part in promoting economic and social infrastructural
development, and since they will undoubtedly continue to play a major role in
the future, public administration must be recognized as a vital determinant of
the pace, and direction of development. A sound public administration is a
crucial factor in planning as well as in implementing development. All developing
countries, including the oil-producing ones, have developmental demands which
exceed their limited resources. Advanced countries, also, confront such a
situation; for no matter how advanced they are, they still aspire to achieve
further progress and, consequently, even their abundant resources fail to meet
the ever-increasing demands upon them. Thus, all countries, rich and poor alike,
need to organize and manage their available resources in the most productive
manner. This is of particular importance, however, in the case of countries which
have just begun, or are about to start, their journey along the continuum of
development.

Administration in the Gulf city states has been, and will continue to be in the years ahead, an important aspect of development. While both private and public administration have contributed to development in the GCS, since public administration has played a greater role in the past, and is expected to continue to do so in the near future, the following discussion will focus on this area of public administration. In view of the fact that public administration is so vital in the process of nation-building and development in these tribal societies, it will be helpful to consider its main features, major problems, and the possible approaches which may be followed in order to increase its developmental capacity. For convenience, this discussion will be presented under the headings, environment, organization, management, personnel, and financial administration.

The Environment of Public Administration

The Structure of Society

As a fresh starting point, it will be helpful in introducing the current discussion to review the social structure common to the Gulf city states which was described in an earlier chapter. It has been emphasized that the GCS are basically tribal societies and each is a confederation of many tribes. The size of these tribes varies; some have a small population in the range of tens or hundreds, others have a larger population in the range of thousands. Some tribes hold a superior position in relation to others, just as some families have a higher relative position than others belonging to the same tribe. The ruling family in each state holds a position superior to all other families. In hierarchical terms, there are the family, the tribe, and then the state in an ascending order. The head of the ruling family is the sheik of the tribe to which the superior family belongs; and he is also the ruler of the state. He thus has a triple role.

Members of the ruler's family are expected (and usually they live up to the expectation) to give him strong support, obedience and loyalty. His tribesmen, too, perhaps to a lesser extent, give him support, obedience and loyalty. Other tribesmen are under an obligation as members of a subordinate tribe in society to give loyalty and allegiance to the ruler.

The head of a tribe is usually chosen for his personal qualities; and wisdom, bravery, honesty, generosity and justice are among the basic personal characteristics which qualify an individual to steer the fortunes of his tribe. According to the tribal rationale, age brings wisdom; consequently, the sheik of the tribe is usually an old man, though there are definitely exceptions to this. Once an individual has been chosen for the headship of his tribe, he establishes some sort of divine right for his sons to step up to the headship of the tribe after he steps down for any reason. According to the tribal way of viewing things, the boy is his father's shadow.

Since members of his tribe as well as of other tribes give him allegiance, obedience and loyalty, the ruler is expected, in turn, to carry out some functions and provide certain services. During their early period, the tribal communities which established the tribal centers in what is known today as the GCS led, as has been mentioned, a simple, primitive life. The rulers of those tribal centers had to provide internal security and justice and to protect their communities against the possible external threats of other tribal centers. Their job was relatively simple and easy.

When these tribal centers placed themselves at the hands of Britain in the nineteenth century, that country took over the functions of internal security, justice and defense, and assumed the responsibility for their foreign relations. This situation continued to 1971, when Britain withdrew from its long-standing role in the area.

The Impact of Oil Receipts

When the rulers of some of these countries began to enjoy substantial amounts of oil receipts, their role and the expectations of their tribesmen began to take on new dimensions. Allegiance, obedience and loyalty deserve to be compensated, after all. Before oil receipts began flowing into the treasuries of the rulers, tribesmen were content with the limited functions provided by their tribal governments. The rulers and their tribesmen were in almost the same situation of severe poverty. Rulers had little, if any, funds; hence they were not subject to demands by their tribesmen for rewards in exchange for their support. New sources of wealth opened the doors for new demands, not only from members of the ruling family who are supposed to be partners with the rulers, but also from others.

In all cases, members of the royal family proper were rewarded, or rather they received their share, in the form of direct monthly payments in cash or in kind, or in both. The amounts of such payments varied from one country to another according to the amounts of oil receipts and according to the relative position, age, sex and status of the recipient. The reward to others, that is to the rest of society, took an indirect form. Oil receipts have been essentially divided into two major, but not necessarily equal parts. One portion has been for the ruler and his court, the other for financing development projects. The apportionment of receipts between the two major interest groups has varied from one country to another according to the criteria used by each.

The Need for an Expanding Public Administration

The spending of money by the rulers to perform new functions and services or to improve already existing ones has resulted in the need for establishing and staffing new organizations. Though new governmental employment opportunities began to arise, available manpower in the local labor market lacked the basic minimum skills required for the satisfactory discharge of the duties and responsibilities of the new functions and services in education, health, agriculture, communication, transportation, electricity, water, and other areas. When they embarked on the path of development, none of the GCS local labor markets could provide the government or the private sector with qualified manpower. In fact, local labor markets were not able to provide anything more than the needed unskilled labor.

Since a tribal society is a status-oriented rather than a function-oriented society, loyalty tends to be more important than competence in determining eligibility for work in government. Thus, in many cases, administrative positions in the GCS were filled from the local labor market by persons who lacked any training or experience. Though the rulers in the GCS found it convenient to import a considerable amount of skilled and professional manpower from neighboring Arab countries, in all cases, directors of the newly created departments and offices were recruited from the ranks of the royal family to ensure continuous control over these organizations. The royal family directors, in turn, recruited as officials under them in their departments, persons who showed loyalty to the regime and who knew that they were recruited because of their loyalty. Thus, the loyalty of government administrators is primarily directed not to the functions for which they have been made responsible, but to the official who helped them to get a place in the administration. Under the circumstances, it is not surprising to observe that many of these recruits to the government service consider that they receive their salaries at the end of each month not as a fair compensation for their contributions, but rather as their due share of oil receipts. Since administration in the GCS from its inception has been dominated by personal considerations rather than functional ones, it is not surprising that it has been to a large extent a personal administration catering more to the needs of the privileged few than to the needs of the general public. It has been an obedient and a faithful vehicle used to enhance the image and position of the more fortunate elite. Since the senior officers of the administration, mostly drawn from the ranks of the royal family, participate in the formulation of public policies, *ipso facto*, they have been intimately involved in politics. This means, then, that the political system and public administration have been closely linked in the GCS, and government administrators have been considered not servants of the state, but servants of the ruler. It should be added that Great Britain, as the colonial power, also provided a few advisors and key personnel.

The Organization of Public Administration

An organization may be viewed as a structure involving an arrangement of available resources to achieve desired ends. While an organization as a structure is a lifeless thing, a good structure facilitates the allocation of given resources, human and material, in a productive way. It is an axiom that good organizations breed good people and good people breed good organizations. Also, the quality of an administrative structure is no better than the quality of the people who manage it. So far, the quality of governmental organizations and the people involved in them in the GCS seem to leave substantial room for improvement. It will be helpful to consider the main features of administrative organizations in these states. Since some of them have introduced significant basic changes since 1970, it will be helpful to consider, first, the nature of their organizations before 1970, and then to examine the changes which have occurred since then.

Administrative Organizations Prior to 1970

Before the GCS embarked on economic and social development projects and programs, they had a few simple administrative organizations which were responsible for providing law and order. When, as a result of their improved financial position, they began to assume new functions and services in agriculture, communications, education, electricity, health, housing, transportation, water, etc., they began to establish a new administrative unit for each new function or service. The rapid multiplication of new administrative units paralleled the enlargement and extension of government functions and services and gave rise to a proliferation and fragmentation of government activities.

New administrative units need to be coordinated with each other and with already existing departments as well. Since this has not been done sufficiently in the GCS, proper coordination of governmental activities has been very difficult to achieve, and duplication of activities and responsibilities has frequently occurred. The establishment of structures in this way was, in part, influenced by political considerations. It has been mentioned previously that administration and the political system are closely linked in the GCS. This linkage has left its imprint on the emerging organizational patterns. The multiplication of new administrative units has served best the interest of the political system. Establishing more units has helped the rulers of these states to accommodate the desires of those persons whom they favored. Since each new administrative unit needs a head to manage it, the establishment of new units has made it possible to reward additional faithful supporters. Thus, the creation of new administrative units has too often been a means of finding new jobs for some of the privileged few. Jobs for appointees rather than appointees for jobs has been too much the pattern. As a result of high functional specificity, the overall structure of public administration has assumed a flat pattern. All functional organizations have been placed at the same level with their heads reporting directly to the ruler without any intermediate link in between. It was inconceivable in this culture to place administrative units headed by persons of equal status—all are loyal and close to the ruler—at different levels. All desired to have direct access to the ruler, and, therefore, the structure which has developed reflects their wishes. Instead of organizing around functions, the structure which emerged resulted more from organizing around personalities.

Professor Fred W. Riggs has suggested three models for detecting major difference among traditional, transitional and modern administrative systems.[1] According to his findings, traditional societies have fused structures, while modern societies have diffracted structures and transitional societies have refracted structures. Administrative development will take place, according to his models, when the structures of government become more specialized.[2] Our findings in the GCS point to contradictory results. Administrative structures in these countries initially were highly specialized, and as development has occurred, they have become less specialized. The number of administrative structures in the GCS before 1970 was less than the number after 1970, as will be seen from the following sections which provide a country-by-country review of administrative structures among the Gulf city states.

Bahrain's Administrative Structure to 1970

Government functions in Bahrain have been gradually increasing since it began to receive oil receipts, and consequently the size of the administration has been constantly increasing. As the patriarchal government has exercised increasing sovereignty over the country as a whole, government affairs have become more and more complex. Complexity, however, has not been solely a result of enlargement of the patriarchal government; but it has also resulted from the introduction of new functions and services and the extension of existing ones. Hospitals, clinics, schools, roads, streets, postoffices, telecommunications, water, electricity—all of these and a myriad of other functions and services have been gradually undertaken by government. New administrative units have been added to provide the new functions and services. This process has resulted in the multiplication of highly specialized administrative units.

By the beginning of 1970, Bahrain had 21 major departments undertaking government functions and services. The government of the United States has only 10 major departments. Organization Chart 5-1 depicts the pattern which existed until January 19, 1970. All of the 21 departments were placed at the same level; and the head of each reported directly to the ruler. As such, no hierarchy existed, and, as mentioned before, this kind of administrative structure gives a flat organization. A flat organization may lay a claim to some advantages. Heads of departments have direct access to the ruler without the intervention of hierarchical channels. While this may prove useful to heads of departments, it may not be so to the ruler who has to attend to the overall policies and problems of the country; for he cannot give careful attention to all of these heads who

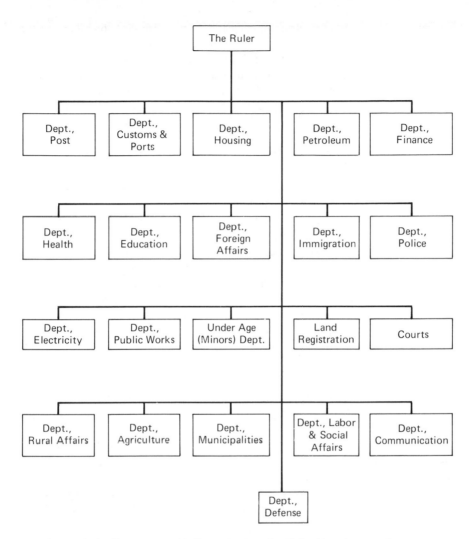

Figure 5-1. Governmental Organization in Bahrain prior to January 19, 1970. Source: Authors' survey.

report to him directly. If one uses the concept of span of control to appraise this model, it becomes apparent that the span of control of the ruler was too wide; and wide spans of control at such a high level are not conducive to effectiveness and efficiency. The explanation for the development of such a pattern in Bahrain and elsewhere among the GCS is found, as discussed previously, in their patriarchal system of government. Administration and government are closely linked in these countries. The ruler does not appoint heads to these departments entirely on the basis of their competence; he simply appoints members of the ruling family and others as a recognition of their due share in government.

The growth of organizations and their proliferation is also explained in political terms. It was not unusual to establish a new department simply to justify the appointment of a favored person. In good administrative practice, the maxim, "appointees for jobs not jobs for appointees," is usually observed.

Qatar's Administrative Structure to 1970

The process of establishing administrative units in Qatar followed a trend similar to that of Bahrain. Continuous enlargement of government and the extension of its functions and services led to the growth of administrative units. The rapid multiplication of new administrative units occurred without adequate efforts to coordinate them with each other or with already existing departments. This proliferation and fragmentation of governmental activities resulted in poor coordination and not infrequent duplication. Until recently, the administrative structure of Qatar was composed of 33 major departments, all placed at the same level and reporting directly to the ruler. Organization Chart 5-2 shows administrative organization in Qatar until March 30, 1970. The pattern shown in the organization chart is revealing. Since similar and related functions and activities were not grouped together under more streamlined and consolidated administrative units, the number of separate units was relatively large and, hence, the span of control of the ruler became unduly wide and difficult.

A ruler may either encourage heads of the departments to have frequent contacts with him for guidance, approval, authority and the like, or he may discourage such contacts. If he follows the first course, he reduces his office to one of daily routine; and if he chooses the second approach, he should delegate adequate authority to the department heads to enable them to run the routine functions of their departments without having to disturb his concentration on the more important issues and overall policy formulation. The first approach, of course, leaves much to be desired, but it is the one traditionally followed in Qatar and the other GCS.

Abu Dhabi's Administrative Structure

Abu Dhabi began to receive oil receipts in the early 1960s, but then ruler, Sheik Shakhbout, was hesitant to use them to transform his country. He did not want to rush it into an affluent life. His brother, Sheik Zayid bin Sultan, who succeeded him in 1966, was determined to enlarge the government and expand its functions and services. With the finances available to him, he began to establish administrative organizations and to entrust each with a specialized

159

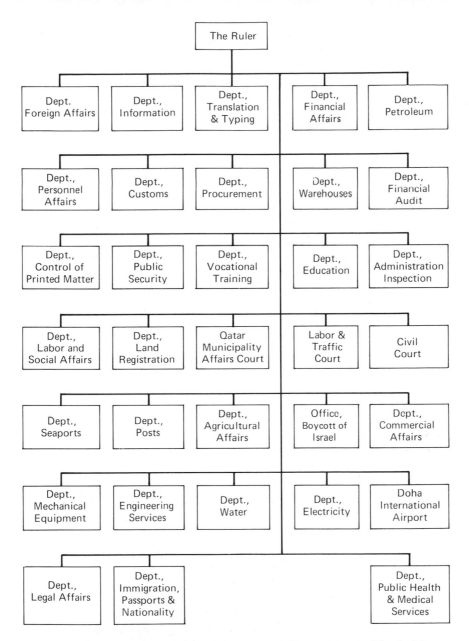

Figure 5-2. Governmental Organization in Qatar prior to March 30, 1970. Source: Authors' survey.

function. He laid the foundations of the present administrative structure soon after his accession to the rulership. On September 18, 1966, he issued Decree Number 3, which created a number of departments and made their heads directly responsible to him. Nine Sheiks from the royal family were appointed to take charge of the created departments as follows:

(1) Sheik Khalifa bin Zayid, Crown Prince, Head of Defense, Viceroy in the Eastern Province and Head of its Courts.
(2) Sheik Hamdan bin Muhammad, Head of the Departments of Education, Health, Public Works and Water.
(3) Sheik Muhammad bin Khalid, Head of the Departments of Finance, Customs and Ports.
(4) Sheik Mubarak bin Muhammad, Head of the Departments of Police and General Security, Nationality, Passports and Residency.
(5) Sheik Tahnoun bin Muhammad, Head of the Departments of Agriculture, Animal Resources and Labor in Al-Ein town.
(6) Sheik Saif bin Muhammad, Head of Abu Dhabi Municipality.
(7) Sheik Khalifa bin Muhammad, Head of the Electricity Department.
(8) Sheik Sroor bin Muhammad, Head of the Justice Department.
(9) Sheik Ahmad bin Hamid, Head of the Departments of Labor and Social Affairs, Information and Personnel.

This pattern of appointments is significant; for the relative positions of the sheiks who were appointed heads of government departments is reflected in it. Sheik Hamdan, for example, has a superior position compared to the other heads. He is next only to Sheik Khalifa bin Zayid, the Crown Prince; and he has charge of the so-called development departments of Education, Health, Public Works and Water.

Between 1966 and 1968, the number of administrative units continued to grow. The ruler passed Emiri Decree Number 14 on March 20, 1968. This created the Supreme Planning Board under his direct control as its president; and the Head of Development, Deputy Head of Finance, Head of Labor and Social Affairs, Head of the Emiri Diwan, Head of the Planning and Coordination Department were appointed as members as well as nine citizens who were selected as members on the basis of their experience. The ruler, apparently, was interested in planning as a means of carrying out his ambitious hopes for economic and social development. Immediately upon the creation of the Board, a five-year plan (1968-1972) was drawn up, approved and promulgated by Emiri Decree Number 5, dated March 20, 1968.

The structure of Abu Dhabi's administrative organization today is as shown on Chart 5-3. There are 33 units directly attached to the ruler. For this country also, the pattern is one of a flat organization, since all units are placed at the same level. The fact that all are headed by sheikhs from the ruling family partly

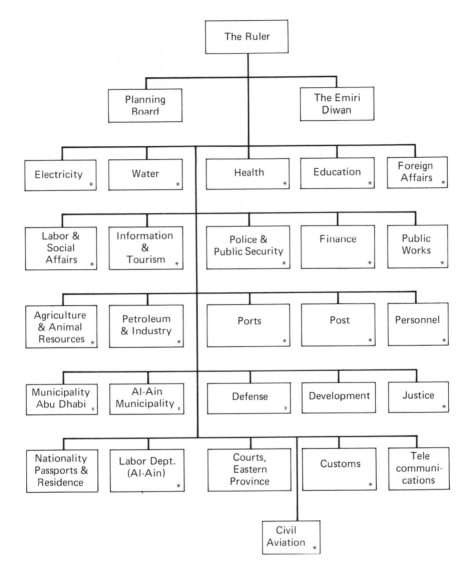

Note: *Starred units are those whose heads are from the royal family.

Figure 5-3. Governmental Organization in Abu Dhabi as of July 1970.
Source: Authors' survey.

explains the fragmented nature of the organizational structure. The ruler, given local customs, had to take into consideration all potential family members aspiring to participate in government. In Abu Dhabi, also, paternalistic politics is closely linked with administration; and the governmental structure here leaves room for improvement. There is strong need for consolidation and coordination. One who is expert in administrative organization should be able to construct a rational organizational structure with an optimum hierarchy which takes into consideration the benefits of separating line and staff functions so they would complement each other in ways which would ensure the smooth running of the organization.

Abu Dhabi, as is the case in the other GCS, suffers from shortages of qualified administrators. In view of this problem, good administrative policy would call for carefully limiting the number of major organizational units in order to keep to a minimum the number of administrators needed. Flat organizations do not suit the local administrative needs in the Gulf city states, though political considerations led to this pattern. More in line with their administrative requirements are hierarchical organizations which have similar and related activities integrated under major units. This type of organizational structure is less demanding on the scarce supply of administrative talent.

Administrative Structure in the Other GCS

In the discussion to this point, consideration has been given to the cases of Bahrain, Qatar and Abu Dhabi. The other GCS so far have not enlarged their governments to the same extent as have these three countries. Only Dubai among them has begun to receive oil revenues, and these date only from September 1969. Whether its organizational pattern will now follow that of Bahrain, Qatar and Abu Dhabi remains to be seen.

The ruler in each of these other Gulf city states runs the affairs of government through the municipality department which is usually attached to him directly. In addition to the municipality department, a few other basic units are also found in each, such as customs, land and property, passports, police, and in some cases, oil affairs. Again in these countries, as in Bahrain, Qatar and Abu Dhabi, the rulers appoint ruling family members to run these units in line with accepted norms of tribal societies and personal bureaucracies.

Organization Chart 5-4 shows the administrative structure in Dubai and Chart 5-5 shows the administrative structure in Sharjah, both as of July 1970. One may well question, in the case of Sharjah, the logic of its 1970 budget which provided BD 920,000 for twelve different departments. Rather than being fused or refracted, the administrative units of this country seem to be too much diffracted, to use Professor Riggs' terminology.

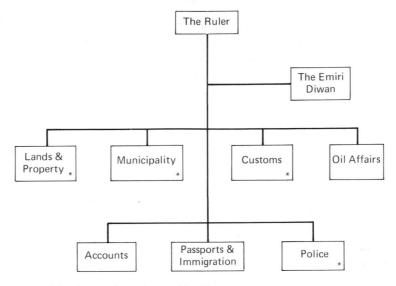

Note: *Head comes from the royal family.

Figure 5–4. Governmental Organization in Dubai as of July 1970.
Source: Authors' survey.

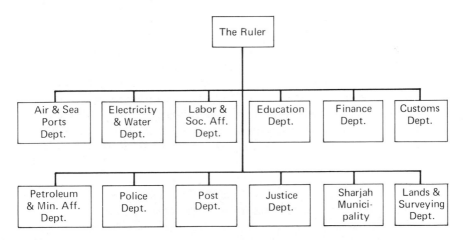

Figure 5–5. Governmental Organization in Sharjah as of July 1970.
Source: Authors' survey.

Administrative Organizational Changes from 1970

The organizational patterns which have been outlined are essentially still in operation in all the countries of the GCS, except in the cases of Bahrain, Qatar and Abu Dhabi where recent changes have taken place. It will be helpful to note the changes in these three countries.

Recent Administrative Changes in Bahrain

Early in 1970, when Bahrain was pondering its future as a result of Britain's decision to withdraw from the Gulf area by the end of 1971, the ruler became convinced that the ability of the country to achieve further economic and social development and to create a modern progressive state would depend on its success in developing a competent governmental administration. Accordingly, he issued Decree Number 2, dated January 19, 1970, which called for the reorganization of Bahrain's bureaucracy as shown in Chart 5-6.

The then existing 21 departments were merged into 11. The Departments of Defense, Foreign Affairs, Information, Education and Health were retained, and each was to be headed by a president reporting to the president of the Council of State. The other sixteen departments were integrated into six departments, each also headed by a president reporting to the president of the Council of State. The integration of these departments has been as follows: Finance, Petroleum, Housing, Customs and Ports, and Post were merged into a Department of Finance and National Economy. Police and Immigration were merged into one department; and Public Security, Courts, Land Registration and Minors' Property were combined into a Department of Justice. Public Works, Electricity, Water and Communications were consolidated in a Department of Development and Engineering Services; and Municipalities, Agriculture and Rural Affairs were brought together under a Department of Municipalities and Agriculture.

It should not be concluded that the recent reorganization has resulted in an optimum organization. In fact, the new organizational structure still leaves much to be desired; and a closer look into the internal organization of these departments reveals that the mergers have not been in line with some of the generally accepted criteria of organization. For example, similar or related functions have not been grouped under the same department in all cases. Also, the distinction between line functions and staff functions has not been accorded due consideration. While it falls outside the scope of this study to dwell on such problems, it should be noted that there is a need for extensive research on the administrative structures of these countries in order to determine a sound and efficient organizational pattern for them.

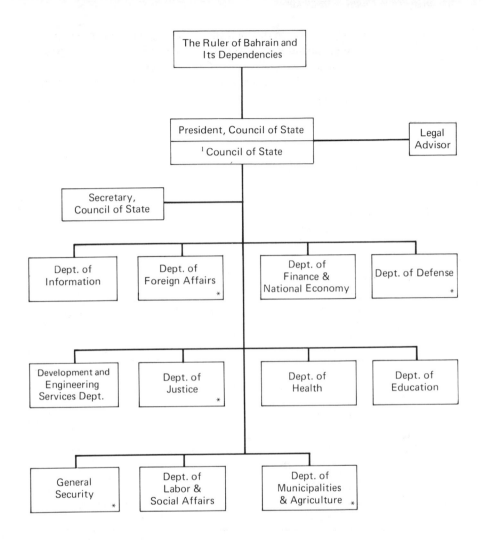

Notes: *Head comes from the royal family.
[1] It is composed of all heads of departments (11), the legal advisor and the president. All members are appointed or released by a decree issued by the ruler.

Figure 5-6. Governmental Organization of Bahrain as of June 1970. Source: Authors' survey.

Administrative Changes in Qatar

In April 1970, when Qatar was contemplating embarking on a new development era, administrative reorganization received the close attention of the government. Thirty specialized departments out of the then existing 33 were reorganized into ten ministries and three departments. The new structure is shown in Chart 5-7.

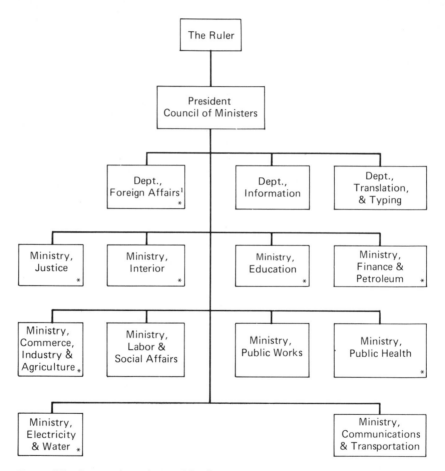

Notes: *Head comes from the royal family.

[1] Raised to ministerial level on September 3, 1971, when Qatar became independent.

Figure 5-7. Governmental Organization of Qatar, as of July 1970. Source: Authors' survey.

The three Departments of Foreign Affairs, Information, and Translation and Typing were retained. The eight departments of Financial Affairs, Petroleum Affairs, Personnel Affairs, Customs, Procurement, Warehouses, Financial Audits, and Administrative Inspection were combined in a Ministry of Finance and Petroleum. The Departments of Public Security, Immigration, Passports and Nationality were merged into a Ministry of Interior. The Civil Court, the Labor and Traffic Court, the Legal Affairs Department, and the Department of Land Registration were merged into a Ministry of Justice. The two Departments of Engineering Services and Mechanical Equipment were combined into a Ministry of Public Works.

The Departments of Commercial Affairs, Boycott of Israel, and Agricultural Affairs were consolidated into a Ministry of Commerce, Industry and Agriculture; and Post, Ports and the Doha International Airport were merged into a Ministry of Communications and Transportation. The two Departments of Electricity and Water were integrated into a Ministry of Electricity and Water.

Similar organizational defects to those which remained after the administrative reorganization in Bahrain are also found in Qatar. The grouping of functions and services under ministries overlooked the importance of integrating departments performing similar or related work. Also staff and line distinctions have not been carefully observed. The reorganization attempt, in itself, is a step in the right direction. It is to be hoped that the Qatari government is contemplating a further review of the administrative structure which may lead to additional changes which will result in the kind of administrative organization which will best serve the needs of its transitional society.

Administrative Changes in Abu Dhabi

The major administrative and political changes in Abu Dhabi have been the establishment of the Consultative Council and the Cabinet as of July 1, 1971.[3] As a result of the creation of the Cabinet, the various government departments have been integrated into thirteen ministries as shown in Chart 5-8.

The Present Situation

Table 5-1 is revealing. First, it shows that the privileged few still dominate the administrative scene. In all of the countries listed in the table, the percentage of heads of departments drawn from the royal family is high. Second, there does not seem to be a significant relationship between the number of administrative units and the level of government expenditure among these countries, which is not surprising in view of the marked differences in their oil revenues. These

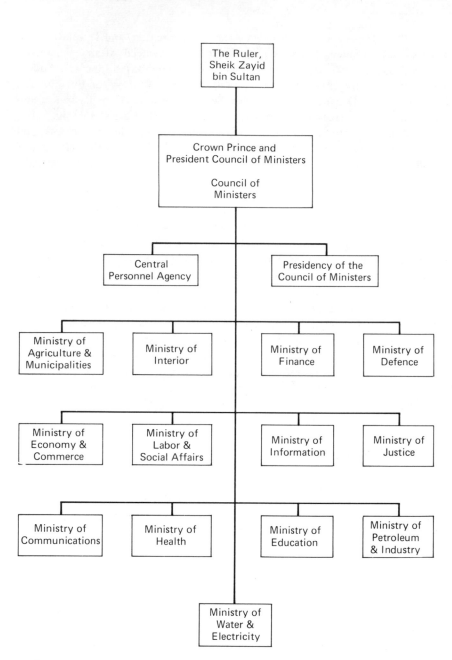

Figure 5–8. Governmental Organization of Qatar as of July 1, 1971.
Source: Authors' survey.

Table 5-1
Governmental Administrative Units by Number and State Expenditures for Selected Gulf City States

Country	No. of Administrative Units	State Expenditures (Thousand B.D.)
Bahrain	11	14,750 (1969)
Qatar	10	n.a.
Abu Dhabi	25	73,513 (1968)
Dubia	7	12,450 (1970)
Sharjah	12	920 (1970)

Source: Previous charts and tables.

societies seem to be, as are other transitional societies, structurally rather than content oriented.

Before closing this discussion on administrative organization, it is interesting to note that the recent attempts to integrate and consolidate administrative structures in Bahrain, Qatar and Abu Dhabi do not support Professor Riggs' findings of the prismatic model, especially in connection with the number of administrative units.

Administrative Management in the GCS

Introductory Comments

The tribal nature of society, the linkage of government and administration, and the local labor market have each influenced, shaped and left deep imprints on the quality of management in the GCS. When the GCS began to undertake social and economic projects and programs, their indigenous populations lacked the minimum qualifications required for the satisfactory discharge of the duties and responsibilities of the newly created positions. This unfortunate situation applied to all categories of personnel, clerical, semiskilled, skilled, technical, professional and administrative. As has been mentioned in a previous chapter, of the nine GCS, Bahrain began its education program considerably earlier than any of the others—the first primary boys school was opened in 1919, the first secondary school was inaugurated twenty years later, and technical education was initiated in 1936.

Qatar started its first public school in 1950, and its regular system of education for boys went into operation in 1956. The first primary boys' school was opened in Abu Dhabi in 1958, and the other Trucial States—Dubai, Sharjah, Ajman, Umm al-Qaiwain, Ras al-Khaimah and Fujairah—began receiving Kuwaiti support for education in 1953. From these relatively recent dates, it can be readily assumed that the local labor markets in these states have not been able to supply either the government or the private sector with the trained manpower they needed.

Because of the tribal nature of society in the GCS and the linkage of government and administration, the problem of administration has not been adequately approached. A tribal society is a status rather than an achievement-oriented society; who you are is more important than what you can do. Since these governments staffed higher levels without due consideration to merit, spoils appointments infiltrated down the line. Administrators were drawn from the ranks of the privileged few, mainly from the royal families, to manage the activities of newly established administrative units; they were selected and appointed not on the basis of qualifications, but because of political consider-ations. Thus, key personnel who were supposed to give life and meaning to their respective units were lacking in training and experience. These heads, em-powered in most cases to hire and fire their subordinates, also hired from the local market without much attention to the requirements of merit. Therefore, an administrative gap was created from the very beginning; and as government functions and services increased in variety and complexity, the administrative gap also became more and more acute.

While officials were able to draft many from the local market to staff government positions, they could not ignore totally the requirements of the highly technical and professional jobs. To staff these, they imported foreign talent from the neighboring Arab countries. The colonial power, Britain, also naturally helped them in recruiting some British advisors and other key personnel. Subordinates, no matter how well qualified, need the guidance and direction of a good leadership to be of optimum effectiveness. Since heads of departments were not chosen on the basis of their merit and qualification, they were often far from being effective leaders. Given the political rather than functional considerations which had brought them to positions of administrative authority, direction and control, it is readily understandable that management problems were compounded.

When schools and vocational training centers in these states began to graduate better qualified personnel, the local labor markets showed improvement; but they have not improved sufficiently to meet the actual needs of government and the private sector. As recently as 1965, 71% of Bahrain's population in the age group 15-years-and-over was illiterate and only 29% was literate (Table 3-8); and in the Trucial states, 79% of the age group 15-years-and-over was illiterate and 21% literate in 1968 (Table 3-7). The quality of a country's administration is closely related to the general level of literacy; and most government employees in the GCS have had only a meager amount of formal education.

In 1965, the level of education of government employees in Bahrain was as follows: 59.8% had no education, 15.8% had a primary education, 19.0% had a secondary or a technical education (Table 2-6), and only 5.3% had received a university education. The educational level of government employees in the Trucial states in 1968 was even lower, for 65.6% had had no education, 14.6% had received primary schooling, 13.5% had a secondary education, 0.4% had a technical training, and 6% were university trained (Table 2-7). The relatively high ratio of university education in the case of the Trucial states in comparison with Bahrain requires clarification.

Most of the university graduates who work for the Bahraini government are natives, while almost all university trained personnel working for the governments of the Trucial states are expatriates. Bahrain actually enjoys the highest standard of education of the native population among the GCS, including higher education. As shown in Table 5-2, by the end of 1969, Bahrain had 263 university graduates and a number of its students were receiving university training abroad; Qatar had 42 graduates and 175 students abroad; and Abu Dhabi had only 4 graduates and 64 students being trained abroad.

Managerial Shortcomings in the GCS

The foregoing comments help to identify some basic problems of management of public organizations in the GCS. There are also a number of other managerial

Table 5-2
Number of Students Receiving University Education abroad and Number of University Graduates in the GCS

Country	Number of students receiving university education abroad	Number of university graduates in the country
1. Bahrain (1969)	n.a.	263
2. Qatar (1969)	175	42
3. Abu Dhabi (1969)	64	4
4. Dubai	n.a.	–
5. Sharjah (1969)	110	17
6. Ajman (1970)	–	3
7. Umm al-Qaiwain	–	–
8. Ras al-Khaimah (1970)	38	2
9. Fujairah	–	–

Sources: Govt. of Bahrain, Dept. of Finance and National Economy, *Statistical Abstract 1969*, Aug. 1970, p. 14;
Ministry of Education, Qatar;
Govt. of Bahrain, Dept. of Education, unpublished education statistics, p. 11;
Al-Shirook, Municipality of Sharjah, Vol. No. 2, July 1970, p. 46;
Government of Ras al-Khaimah (unpublished material).

problems which confront the GCS. These are summarized briefly under the the following seven headings.

Too Much Political Support

To perform their duties and assume their responsibilities effectively and efficiently, administrators in general should enjoy adequate political support. But too much support is as bad as too little support. Administrators, as heads of the major national departments, reflect the sentiments of the ruler in each of the GCS. They are partners in governance. Though they serve at his pleasure, when they are in office they enjoy wide discretion over their respective departments. In many cases, such latitude of freedom of action is used to further personal interests rather than the public interest. In the absence of standards of performance and uniform personnel and budgetary practices, these actions tend to overshadow the very objectives for which their administrative units have been established.

Master not Service Orientation

Administrators who are serving in the GCS at the pleasure of the ruler have succeeded not because of their loyalty to the objectives and goals of their organizations, but because they have showed unfailing personal loyalty to their superiors. Administrators, in turn, have appointed subordinates because of their loyalty to them. The subordinate appointees serve at the pleasure of the administrators; and their stay, promotion, etc., will depend largely upon satisfying their bosses. As a result, they are more loyal to their superiors than to the requirements for the efficient and effective discharge of their duties and responsibilities. This suggests that the officials and their subordinates are not adequately responsive to the citizens' needs—they tend to be not servants but masters of their societies.

Excessive Concentration of Authority and Control

Administrators who are mostly political appointees and who have appointed their subordinates not on the basis of merit, are very often hesitant to delegate authority to their subordinates. They do not trust the judgment of these appointees and are hesitant to rely on them. Such a climate leads to undue delay in the processing of transactions, no matter how routine they may happen to be. Cumbersome procedures are the price for concentrating routine decision-making at the highest administrative level.

Shortage of Qualified Manpower

It is not necessary to dwell much more on this aspect of administration in the GCS. It has already been shown how low the level of education of government employees is throughout the administrative structure. But generally speaking, administration at the middle level will continue to suffer most. The school systems in the GCS may be adequate to provide the needed quality of personnel to work at the lower operational level in government, but they have not matured to the point where they can provide competent supportive personnel to meet the needs at the middle administrative level. Since university training abroad will undoubtedly help them to staff some of the higher positions, it seems likely that unless appropriate measures are taken quickly, the trend will be toward administrations more adequately staffed at the lowest and highest levels than at the middle level which constitutes the backbone of any administration.

Unclear Definition of Goals and Objectives

Administrative units are not ends in themselves; they are the means of achieving desired ends. Thus, organizations will operate much more effectively if their goals and objectives are made clear to the administrators and their staffs. In the GCS, in most cases, organizations are first established and then administrators start speculating on what the goals and objectives are. Even when goals are assigned to existing organizations or to newly created ones, they are usually expressed in very general and often quite vague terms. It is not unusual to appoint personnel to certain organizations without knowing what they are expected to do. In the absence of a clear interorganizational and intraorganizational allocation of duties and responsibilities, excessive duplication is virtually certain to occur, and coordination will be difficult, if not impossible.

Inadequate Organization

Where there is an inadequate structural arrangement, individual administrative units will not be related to each other and to the whole administrative structure in an optimum way. Inadequate attention to staff and line functions and organizations adds to the complexity of the management function.

In the GCS, an adequate appreciation of the need for bringing together staff and line officers, functions and organizations in a harmonious way has not been developed. Very frequently, line and staff organizations are placed at the same level without establishing adequate and effective vertical and horizontal channels of communications. In other words, these states do not seem to appreciate fully, as yet, the inescapable administrative reality that staff and line functions and organizations are equally important for the realization of the objectives of administration. Structural flaws and managerial shortcomings compound administrative problems and result in a management process which leaves much to be desired. Duplication of activities, blurred lines of communications, delays in decision-making, weak coordination, low morale and frustration are not uncommon features of such unsatisfactory organization.

Empire-Building

In many cases, heads of governmental units in such administrative environments as those found among the GCS will tend toward empire building, and the evils described by Parkinson's Law will be experienced. This has been particularly the case in Abu Dhabi, when between 1966 and 1969, the rate of increase in the number of state employees exceeded all reasonable bounds. In fact, late in 1969, the government of Abu Dhabi realized that its administration was overstaffed and started to terminate many of its employees, only to begin shortly thereafter the recruiting of many newcomers. On analysis, it seems that only those employees who were not supported by their heads, that is those who for one reason or another could not maintain their links with their heads or other influential officials, were terminated and then soon replaced.

Further Comments on Managerial Problems in the GCS

It should be mentioned here that management flaws are inseparable from organizational ills. After all, administrative organization whether in Abu Dhabi or in any of the other Gulf city states has responded to the personal rule and tribal nature of these societies. Organizations were created all too often to reward an influential person, and it is not surprising, therefore, to find that the notion of personal rewards infiltrated from the highest level to the rank and file at the bottom of the hierarchy. Corruption breeds corruption and bad organization generates bad management philosophy and techniques.

While focusing on the inadequacy of organization and management practices in the Gulf city states, it is appropriate to dwell on the inevitability of what has evolved. Good people create good organizations; they also help to develop and enhance the capabilities of people, and ultimately this leads to better processes of management. The Gulf city states have not been able, so far, to rid themselves of an unfortunate organization-management-people interdependent triangle; they have tended to float in a vicious circle. They do not have good organizations because they do not have trained people who know how to establish and run good organizations. The problem, therefore, is how to break through. Some of the GCS have been totally dependent for a long time on expatriates to staff their different organizations. By no means are all of the imported expatriates top-quality civil servants; many of them could not meet the requirements for the public service in their own countries. In addition, those few who are qualified are likely to be placed under the direct control of incompetent local officials and their potential for fruitful contribution is thus often greatly diminished. Not given the opportunity to make their full contribution, they become easily frustrated and consequently their productive ability begins to decline.

What is needed is a genuine determination on the part of the governments of these states to create a favorable management climate. First and foremost, each government should determine the range of functions and services to be undertaken. Based on this, an administrative reorganization should then be carried out which would take into consideration the need for division of work and coordination. The grouping of functions must be decided on the basis of similar or related work, and certainly, the human factor must be given due recognition in the process of reorganizing. While organizing around functions, the human element which actually gives life to the organization cannot be ignored. Appointments to the various positions at the different levels throughout the administration must be guided by the principle of merit, "The right man for the right job." If these states can create the proper kind of organizational structure needed to push forward their development efforts, and if they can staff adequately such organizations, authority and responsibility should be consistent with the responsibilities assigned at each level. When this is achieved, the decision-making process will become faster and more rational; and the targets of development will begin to fall within the reach of the administration.

Budgeting in the GCS

Before oil receipts, duties imposed on imports and transshipments in the case of some countries of the GCS constituted the major source of the ruler's income. This was, as it still is today in the poor states, a very thin source which hardly provided the funds needed by the leader to maintain a simple law-and-order machinery. With oil receipts flowing since the 1950s in Bahrain and Qatar, since the early 1960s in Abu Dhabi, and since the late 1960s in Dubai, the rulers in these countries have been enjoying substantial amounts of income. As mentioned previously, these receipts have been considered by the rulers to be their own personal money and no distinction was established, as such, between their private treasury and that of the states. No clear lines existed to indicate how much of the income should be used for public purposes. Some rulers, guided with a sense of justice and a vision for the future, decided to promote development projects capable of transforming their tribal societies into modern progressive states. To do this, they had to use oil receipts for financing public projects. In creating the necessary organizations and in the recruitment of staff to help in the promotion of development, the rulers have found that they have had to allocate funds to support these organizations. What the ruler would take and what he would give for the support of governmental organizations, was a personal decision. To keep records of public expenditures, accounting units were created to trace receipts and expenditures, that is, the inflow and outflow of cash.

The expansion of functions and services in some of these countries placed a strain on the treasury of the ruler and this forced some of them to make more careful decisions concerning the manner of allocating revenue receipts among the various competing interests. In some countries, receipts were allocated according to certain standards found most convenient by the ruler.

Budgeting in the modern sense was an innovation unheard of in the GCS, until recently. Of the nine Gulf city states, only Bahrain and Abu Dhabi have some kind of budgeting. Table 5-3 shows the budget of Bahrain for 1968 and 1969, and Table 5-4 shows the budget of Abu Dhabi for 1967 and 1968. Although these two countries have budgets, they are still far from following modern budgetary practices and techniques. Actually, their budgets are simply an extension of their accounting practices. The budget is not considered more than an accounting device for keeping an essential balance between the inflow and outflow of cash. They tend to attach much more importance to the figures in the document than to what the figures stand for. Since these two countries, as well as the other seven Gulf city states, need to promote very extensive programs of development, they all need modern budgeting to help ensure the use of their resources in an optimum way. Unless they follow good budgetary principles, practices and techniques, they will not be able to maximize the returns from their limited and badly needed resources.

A budget is but a plan of action for a forthcoming fiscal year; the figures represent desired functions and services to be achieved during the period in question. As such, budgeting involves political, technical and administrative insights. The determination of projects to be undertaken is certainly a political decision in the final analysis; the evaluation of the relative importance and contribution of potential development projects by economists and other experts as an aid to the establishment of priorities is a technical matter. Sooner or later, and better sooner, these countries must recognize that they need to review their budgeting conceptions and practices. Among other things, they need to create special budget units separate from their already existing accounting units.

It is easy to enact a decree calling for the creation of a budget office or department and to place it at the highest level of authority to give it the influence and respect it deserves; but creation of a budget organization will not automatically lead to improved budget practices. The staff of such an organization will be a key element in determining its failure or success. Since they lack any previous experience, these countries do not seem to have the kind of budget

Table 5-3
Budget of the Government of Bahrain, 1968 and 1969 (BD '000)

	1968	1969	% of Total 1969 Expenditure
Current Expenditures			
Central services, finance, customs, judiciary, etc.	1,076	1,155	7.8%
Municipality grants	128	150	1.0%
Agriculture & Rural affairs	215	230	1.6%
Education	2,900	3,200	21.7%
Health	2,460	2,700	18.3%
Housing	200	200	1.4%
Public Security	1,600	1,950	13.2%
Public Works & Water Supply	800	960	6.5%
Defense Force	–	1,250	8.5%
Miscellaneous	650	785	5.3%
	10,029	12,580	85.3%
Capital Expenditures			
New government offices & work in progress	942	980	6.6%
Development:			
Power Generation	1,250	840	5.7%
Water Supply	180	200	1.4%
Port Storage	80	150	1.0%
Total Expenditures	12,431	14,750	100.0%

Revenue	1968	1969	(BD '000) % of 1969 Revenue
Oil Receipts	8,000	8,870	69.6%
Custom Dues	2,250	2,250	17.6%
Rents, leases, etc.	750	750	5.9%
Other revenue	481	880	6.9
Total Revenue	11,481	12,750	100.0%

Source: Middle East Economic Digest and Arab Report and Record Survey, *Bahrain 1969*, December 1969, p. 9.

talent and experience needed. They should guard against being too naive in creating budget units and entrusting them to unqualified persons; for this may easily do more harm than good. To be realistic, they should plan to develop as rapidly as possible, budget units adequately staffed both in numbers and in quality of personnel. Since the budget, especially where it is based on sound budgetary principles and techniques, is a short-term plan, budgetary develop-

Table 5-4

Expenditures and Revenues of the Government of Abu Dhabi, 1967 and 1968 (Bahraini Dinars)

Department	1967	1968
Agriculture	33,320	122,505
Civil Aviation	20,116	125,752
Civil Service Commission	7,453	33,756
Customs	94,023	125,567
Defense Force	1,218,762	5,606,892
Development Headquarters	20,432	98,674
Education	129,442	657,905
Electricity	146,220	462,693
Finance	36,510	156,344
Guest House	99,322	112,171
Health	319,996	1,289,197
Justice	35,171	71,085
Labour	22,959	103,706
Municipalities	168,808	1,155,871
Petroleum Affairs	36,962	131,664
Planning and Co-ordination	7,672	29,267
Police and Public Security	642,285	1,503,015
Post Office	66,213	86,584
Public Works	215,675	842,187
Water Supply	155,988	346,834
Privy Purse	12,691,827	18,324,511
Miscellaneous	9,546,081	10,522,072
Development (see Table 81)	16,037,659	30,512,225
Intelligence	–	39,031
Labour and Social Affairs	–	27,807
London Office	–	11,364
Palace Office	–	811,156
Ports and Harbours	–	225,782
Telecommunications	–	6,056
Total Expenditure	41,752,896	73,512,864

Source of Revenue	1967	1968
Customs	275,639	534,299
Civil Aviation	21,360	46,435
Interest on Public Account and investment income	804,205	830,276
Electricity Supply	25,249	38,399
Health	–	5,229
Justice	4,998	28,826

Table 5-4 (Cont.)

Source of Revenue		1967	1968
Labour		1,177	1,374
Municipality		100,686	155,807
Post Office		80,077	115,412
Police and Traffic Fees		16,256	34,302
Water Supply		44,297	31,915
Petroleum Royalties and Taxes		49,592,865	71,607,972
Miscellaneous		19,924	337,118
Donation by H.H. the Ruler		2,007,000	–
Total Revenue	B.D.	52,993,733	73,767,362

Note: All items are given to the nearest BD.
Source: Government of Abu Dhabi, *Statistical Abstract*, Vol. 1, July 1969, pp. 47-48.

ment would be enhanced if it is closely linked to development planning. A word of caution must be inserted here. These countries should not be too ambitious in trying to establish planning organizations without first improving their budgeting capabilities. Good budgeting will facilitate and enhance planning; the reverse is not true, however.

Personnel Policies in the GCS

Good organization and good people are the two most important aspects of management. No organization can be completely successful without both. An organization without people is a structure without life; in reality, it does not exist. An organization chart usually depicts the nature and method of inter-action of people working within the formal structure which it illustrates. Its people give an organization its life and blood; for any organization without the necessary staff cannot achieve its mission. Its ability to achieve and realize its designated goals and objectives depends, finally, on the quality of its staff. The quality of the people working in any organization, in turn, is dependent upon the quality of the policies, laws, methods and procedures used in recruiting, selecting, appointing and retaining personnel. This is true of any organization, be it private or public.

On the whole, the Gulf city states have not developed adequate personnel policies, laws, organizations and the required staff for the proper management of the important personnel function. Though Bahrain, Qatar and Abu Dhabi seem to have discovered the urgent need for improving the quality of designing and managing personnel policies, the other six states have not as yet felt the need, probably because their scale of operations has not increased to the level at which hundreds or thousands of employees need to be recruited. These others are still able to cope with personnel requirements along traditional lines; but Dubai is now enjoying oil receipts, and it will soon discover the need for personnel standards for recruiting and retaining different categories of personnel required by the new functions and services which are being introduced by the government as a result of the improved financial situation.

Because of the close similarities among the nine Gulf city states, it is safe to assume that personnel policies and laws which are capable of meeting effectively the needs of any one of them would be useful to any of the other countries in the group, probably with some minor modifications.

At this point, it will be useful to develop an overview of the nature of the public personnel problem in Bahrain, Qatar and Abu Dhabi. For the past twenty years or so, government services in Bahrain have been increasing; and the number of organizations and the number of government employees have also been increasing. During the initial stages, public employees were few in number, but today there are several thousand persons working for the government. Because it is a tribal society and operating under a patriarchal system of government, no attempt was made during the earlier period to establish personnel policies and laws; in a status-oriented society, it is very difficult to establish standards which cut across tribal boundaries. A sound personnel law would have weakened the prerogative of the ruler and his direct aids in staffing; and it would have interfered with their recruiting and appointing close loyal supporters, regardless of their potential ability to assume the duties and responsibilities of the jobs to which they were to be assigned. Personal loyalty, not functional loyalty, determined one's opportunities for entry into government service.

The attempt in Bahrain to establish known guides in personnel administration took place in July 1964, when the so-called "Personnel Law" was passed. According to this law, there are a number of levels of government employees: the first level includes the junior employees such as messengers, janitors and the like; the second level includes artisans and mechanics; the third includes clerks; the fourth includes pharmacists, X-ray technicians and health inspectors; the fifth level comprises supervisors; the sixth covers the police service; the seventh concerns the nursing profession; the eighth and ninth deal with European and non-European electrical engineers; the tenth and eleventh sections cover schools; and section twelve is a special section on administrative personnel. While the law has divided government employees into these numerous categories, it has not established minimum qualification requirements, or grade or compensation levels. The law emphasized seniority in line with the tribal nature of society where age brings wisdom. Personal attributes, not merit considerations are highly prized in recruitment and promotion. In 1970, however, almost all senior officials in government still did not know whether the law is in force or not; they commented at length on its shortcomings and inadequacy and claimed that recent developments have rendered its provisions obsolete. Whether uniform personnel policies and standards are observed or not is a matter of speculation.

Some government employees at various levels seem to be discontent with existing personnel practices and they are seriously concerned about the need for reconsidering personnel policies, laws and regulations in the light of present and potential levels of economic and social development.

In Qatar, the status-oriented society managed to operate without personnel policies and codes until June 19, 1967, when its first personnel law was enacted by Emiri Decree Number 9. The law consists of 110 articles on various aspects of personnel policies and practices. The most important aspect of the law, aside from its establishing for the first time uniform personnel standards, is the limiting of entry to government service to those who meet the minimum requirements for the different positions.[4] As shown in Table 5-5, the law classifies government positions into four major groups. The first group consists of one grade for senior experts, technicians and specialists; the second group comprises four grades for higher positions; the third group covers five grades for intermediate-level positions; and the fourth group includes two grades for laborers. A university degree is a minimum requirement for groups one and two; an intermediate certificate is required for group three; and group four has no minimum education requirement.

On November 25, 1967, Emiri Decree Number 21 revised the classification

Table 5-5

Grades and Monthly Salaries of Government Personnel in Qatar (in QDR)

Category	Grade	Salary	Salary and Steps within Grade					
			1	2	3	4	5	6
I		4,000						
(Sr. Experts	—	to						
and Specialists)		5,000						
	1	3,200	3,300	3,400	3,500	3,600	3,700	—
II	2	2,600	2,700	2,800	2,900	3,000	3,100	—
(High-Level	3	2,000	2,100	2,200	2,300	2,400	2,500	—
Positions)	4	1,500	1,600	1,700	1,800	1,900	—	—
								—
	1	1,250	1,300	1,350	1,400	1,450	—	—
III	2	950	1,000	1,050	1,100	1,150	1,200	—
(Intermediate-	3	700	740	780	820	860	900	—
Level Positions)	4	520	550	580	610	640	670	—
	5	400	425	450	475	500	—	—
								—
IV	1	270	295	320	345	370	395	—
(Laborers)	2	165	180	195	210	225	240	255

Source: Emiri Decree No. 9, 1967.

pattern as shown in Table 5-6. Group four has been divided into two major parts. Part A covers supervisors and laborers, and lists five grades; and part B consists of drivers, and includes three grades. Emiri Decree Number 20 of November 27, 1967, promulgated required regulations for implementing provisions of the law.

Generally speaking, the law and its accompanying regulations provide, at the formal level, for the adoption and implementation of merit principles in personnel administration. Organizing entry to government service on the basis of qualifications is called for, and the law is designed to regulate the life of the employees once they are inside the government machinery. Thus, its intentions are meritorious. What is true in theory, however, is not necessarily so in practice. Not too much can be expected of a tribal society which is just struggling to break away from tribal ties; it cannot, overnight, rid itself of traditions which have been in the culture of the society for centuries. At best, it can gradually leave some traditional elements behind and replace them by

Table 5-6
Grades and Monthly Salaries of Government Personnel in Qatar (in QDR)

Category	Grade	Salary and Steps within Grade							
		1	2	3	4	5	6	7	8
I		4,000							
(Higher-Level									
positions)	–	5,000							
	1	3,200	3,300	3,400	3,500	3,600	3,700	–	–
II	2	2,600	2,700	2,800	2,900	3,000	3,100	3,200	–
(High-Level	3	2,000	2,100	2,200	2,300	2,400	2,500	2,600	–
positions)	4	1,500	1,600	1,700	1,800	1,900	2,000	–	–
	1	1,250	1,300	1,350	1,400	1,450	–	–	–
	2	950	1,000	1,050	1,100	1,150	1,200	–	–
III	3	700	740	780	820	860	900	–	–
(Intermediate-	4	520	550	580	610	640	670	–	–
level positions)	5	400	425	450	475	500	–	–	–
	6	240	260	280	300	320	340	360	380
	1	700	740	780	820	860	900	–	–
IV-A	2	510	535	560	585	610	635	660	–
(Supervisors and	3	385	410	435	460	485	–	–	–
(Laborers)	4	270	285	310	335	360	–	–	–
	5	165	180	195	210	225	240	255	–
	1	335	350	365	–	–	–	–	–
IV-B	2	290	305	320	–	–	–	–	–
(Drivers)	3	245	260	275	290	–	–	–	–

Source: Emiri Decree, No. 21, 1967.

modern elements, as and when it becomes feasible to do so. These countries cannot, and probably they should not, effect drastic changes overnight; for this would be highly likely to lead to undesirable, disruptive social explosions.

Abu Dhabi embarked on its development programs after 1966, and suddenly various categories of personnel—clerical, administrative, technical and professional—were much in demand. None of these skills was available in the local labor market. Importing the needed personnel from the outside, mostly from the Arab countries, was the only alternative for Abu Dhabi if it were to be able to push ahead with its development plans. Since no personnel law or standards had existed before, haphazard methods were used in recruiting, selecting, grading and compensating personnel. The personnel practices of those who have been commissioned by the government and his aids to staff government departments leave much room for justifiable concern. It was not uncommon to give different grades and salaries and other fringe benefits to persons who are performing similar functions in the same government department. Many expatriates discovered after they had been recruited that they were underpaid compared to others in the same department or in another department. Rather than applying uniform standards to matters related to recruiting, selecting, appointing and compensating personnel, personal whims and wishes and bargaining were the rule, not the exception. Few administrators knew or tried to know their actual staff requirements. In 1969, financial pressures caused Abu Dhabi to fire hundreds of employees who had been labeled redundant.

Bahrain, Qatar and Abu Dhabi have personnel units that claim to have governmentwide jurisdiction. In Bahrain, a personnel department is located in the Ministry of Finance and Petroleum, and Abu Dhabi has a personnel department directly attached to the Emiri Diwan. Their location is not important; but the fact that they exist is encouraging.

Because the GCS are developing countries and are continuously introducing development projects, the need will continue to arise for recruiting more and more personnel. The local market, except in the case of Bahrain, cannot meet the growing demand for almost all types of personnel. Where there is no central personnel unit, if each government department is empowered to hire and fire, conflicting standards will prevail. This will create confusions and frustrations and will certainly lower the morale of the employees. Ultimately, it will lead to lower productivity. To function properly and to render more than lip service to personnel administration, personnel units need to have adequate political support and suitable policies and laws. If properly manned, they can render the greatest service in recruiting and retaining competent manpower for the various government departments.

Where to Go from Here

It should be emphasized again that the pace of a country's economic and social development depends heavily upon its success in developing a suitable administration. To be sure, the GCS have been able to achieve some development and will undoubtedly realize further progress, but creating a sound public administration will enhance their development efforts and maximize the returns from their resources. As has been shown, public administration in these countries leaves much to be desired. Their organization and management, as well as their budgeting and personnel approaches and practices, need further modernization to bring them up to a desirable level. They face problems in doing this, as has been mentioned, but these problems are not so deep rooted that positive actions to overcome them cannot bring real improvement. Such actions should be taken, and the sooner the better. In short, the GCS would be well advised to consider the following matters.

Reorganization

Existing governmental structures should be the subject of comprehensive surveys by qualified analysts to determine the most appropriate possible allocation of functions, authorities and responsibilities. At present, none of the GCS has the required organization (O) and manpower (M) experts who are qualified to undertake such surveys. Their O and M problems, however, are much too acute for them to wait until they have developed their own local O and M talent. They need to act soon, and to do so, they would have to import the required specialists. Soon these countries will receive back some of their students who have been taking university training abroad. Some of these may have received training which would enable them to benefit from working with the O and M experts as aids or trainees. In a sense, they could be used as counterparts who, while learning, could provide imported experts with insights, ideas and thoughts about the local scene. Adequate knowledge about the local conditions increases the ability of outside experts to handle problems of the administration. In order to institutionalize the O and M function and ensure its continuity after the foreign experts have served their term and left, the creation by the GCS of O and M offices at the highest possible level is highly recommended. Each O and M office can acquire experience during the time of the survey and will be in a better position to develop policies and methods for the proper handling of O and M functions in the years ahead.

Training

Since almost all present government employees lack both education and experience, the need for designing and implementing optimum training policies and practices is overwhelming. A governmentwide survey should be undertaken to determine the nature and level of training needs. This must be followed by the planning of training to ensure the creation of an adequate program for the training of present and future staff.

Central Personnel Agency

The desirability of establishing competent central personnel agencies in the GCS cannot be ignored. Such units should have a key role in determining training needs and possible approaches to satisfy them.

Budget Department

No matter how well organized and staffed the various administrative units of government are, they cannot function effectively unless adequate funds to finance their activities are allocated to them. Thus, the inflow and distribution of funds need to be carefully planned and regulated. There is no substitute for preparing good yearly consolidated estimates for revenue receipts and expenditures. Some of the GCS have already embarked on the preparation of crude budgetary figures which leave much to be desired. Such estimates, where they exist, are being prepared by existing accounting offices and not by specialized budget departments. The budget function is different from the accounting function and, therefore, if accounting offices continue to handle budgetary questions, the budget will become an extension of the accounting system and will undoubtedly fail to achieve its objectives. The time is ripe for the GCS to consider the establishment of competent, specialized budget departments.

Coordinating the Brains

Three urgently needed governmental departments have been recommended for the GCS—an O and M department, a central personnel department and a central budget department. It is true, of course, that there is interdependence as far as the activities of these three key departments are concerned, and adequate attention should be given to the matter of relating them to each other. While all should be located at the highest possible level where they can be assured continuous, effective political support, their location should also facilitate their coordination.

Need for an Honest Middle-Man

Finally, the GCS will be well advised to seek the services of a nonprofit body of the highest professional standing to help them identify, select and appoint qualified, honest and sincere consultants who can plan, organize and implement administrative reform with paramount consideration for the needs which these states have to build effective and efficient development administration systems.

Problems of Federation

Cooperation–An Alternative to Colonization

Britain's announcement in 1968 of its intention to withdraw from the Gulf area by the end of 1971, prompted rulers of the nine GCS to consider how political stability could be maintained and sustained thereafter. Anticipating a potential vacuum after the termination of Britain's military presence in the Gulf, the rulers quickly responded and started to get together to consider possible approaches to overcome potential threats. Under its treaty obligations, Britain had assumed foreign affairs and defense responsibilities on behalf of the Gulf states for many years. In Britain's absence, individually or collectively, they would have to assume these responsibilities themselves. But the vacuum is not confined to these two functions alone; for though Britain was for a long period an effective stabilizing factor in the Gulf, traditional rivalries and tribal feuds have not been entirely overcome. Only a major power, like Britain could have suppressed such deep-rooted development-retarding elements. Some of these countries, the smaller ones in particular, know that their chances of becoming viable political units are very slim, while each of the larger states aspired to play a key role in the area in the absence of a big power like Britain. The impact of Britain's withdrawal will not be confined to the nine Gulf city states however; for other Arab and non-Arab countries also consider that they have stakes involved. Given the crisis which they could sense approaching, the rulers have had to put their heads together and to seek to achieve a solid front.

The Trucial States Council

The seven Trucial states—Abu Dhabi, Dubai, Sharjah, Ajman, Umm al-Qaiwain, Ras al-Khaimah and Fujairah—had been discussing their outstanding common problems in the Trucial States Council (TSC), established in 1952. The TSC provided a center for the development of cooperation among the individual states; but cooperation took on a new dimension from 1965, when the Trucial States Development Fund (TSDF) was formed.[1]

The Trucial States Council consisted of rulers of the seven Trucial states who had equal weight in it. The British political agent presided over the Council until March 1966, when Sheikh Saqr bin Muhammad al Qasimi, ruler of Ras al-Khaimah, took over following his election as chairman. Sheikh Khalid bin

Muhammad al-Qasimi, ruler of Sharjah was its chairman from October 1968, when he was elected to succeed Sheik Saqr.[2]

The Trucial States Development Fund

When the Development Fund was established under the Development Office, the Trucial States Council began to consider interstate and intrastate development projects such as linking the coastal capitals of the Trucial states, providing basic necessities like water and electricity for the poorer states, constructing low cost housing, as well as a number of other development projects which have been financed by the Development Fund.[3] When it was formed in the summer of 1965, the Development Fund received capital contributions from Britain (£1,000,000), the ruler of Qatar (£250,000), the ruler of Abu Dhabi (£100,000), and the ruler of Bahrain (£40,000). Further contributions have also been received.[4]

From its inception until 1970, the Development Office received a total of BD10.3 million, of which Abu Dhabi contributed more than 70%.[5] Without the

Table 6-1

Trucial States Council Development Expenditures for Various Periods by Major Development Programs

Major Program	Total to end 1968 BD	Expenditures in BD 1969	1970	Total to end 1970 BD	% of Grand Total[1]
1. Technical Education	232,836	35,089	144,000	411,925	5.37
2. Health	192,829	348,919	588,500	1,130,248	17.74
3. Agriculture	541,829	240,803	247,000	1,029,632	13.43
4. Fisheries	—	142,515	119,000	261,515	3.41
5. Harbors	229,055	3,270	96,200	328,525	4.28
6. Trunk Roads	732,905	228,157	745,000	1,706,062	22.25
7. Town Roads	145,308	2,876	30,000	178,184	2.32
8. Town & Village Water Supplies	636,660	137,751	422,000	1,196,411	15.60
9. Electricity	680,130	280,480	168,000	1,196,411	15.60
10. Housing	62,600	13,436	23,000	99,036	1.29
11. Urban Development	93,333	35,424	12,000	140,757	1.84
12. Telecommunications	49,465	2,429	—	51,894	0.68
13. Miscelianeous	2,683	—	3,000	5,683	0.07
Grand Total	3,599,633	1,471,149	2,597,700	7,668,482	100

[1] Percentage figures may not add to 100 because of rounding.

Source: Development Office, Trucial States Council, Round-Up News for the Month Ending 28th February 1970, n.d. (unpublished material).

Table 6-2
Trucial States Development Office Income, 1965-1970

Contributions	1965 BD	1966 BD	1967 BD	1968 BD	1969 BD	1970 BD	Total BD
The Ruler of Abu Dhabi	266,625	666,600	1,819,762	337,662	1,700,000	2,500,000	7,290,649
The Ruler of Qatar	333,250	–	–	–	–	–	333,250
The Ruler of Bahrain	53,298	–	–	–	–	–	53,298
Britain-Annual Grant	322,720	266,600	196,768	278,597	114,000	–	1,178,685
Initial Capital	399,900	533,199	85,725	257,175	171,000	–	1,446,999
Grand Total	1,375,793	1,466,399	2,102,255	873,434	1,985,000	2,500,000	10,302,881

Source: Unpublished Report, Development Office, Trucial States Council, n.d., p. 43;
Unpublished Material, Development Office, Round-Up of News for 1969 and 1970.

cooperative spirit of the "haves," the poorer states would still not have the few services they enjoy today. Rulers of the poorer states undoubtedly recognize that achieving further development or even maintaining the present status quo is largely dependent upon their ability to cultivate and nurture the good will of the more affluent countries.

Movements toward Federation

Abu Dhabi and Dubai were the first to spark the movement for cooperation. On February 18, 1968, the rulers of the two countries decided to federate and agreed to share a common policy in the areas of foreign affairs, defense and citizenship, though the two states would continue to look after their own internal and judicial affairs. The agreement also covered border demarcation adjustments which have since been carried out. This agreement was the immediate precursor of the Nine-State Federation announcement and of the more recent federation developments.[6]

Article 4 of the Abu Dhabi-Dubai bilateral Agreement invited the other Gulf states to discuss it and to participate in it. The rulers of Bahrain and Qatar in particular, were invited to deliberate on the future of the area and to join in a unified front.[7] Rulers of the nine GCS, in quick response to the invitation of Abu Dhabi and Dubai, met in Dubai on February 25, 1968, to consider the future of their countries after Britain's withdrawal from the Gulf.[8] A three-day series of deliberations culminated in a Federation Agreement which was signed by the nine GCS rulers on February 27, 1968. The Federation Agreement was to go into effect at the end of March 1968.[9] It is important to note the major features of the federation which was proposed.

Identity and Role

The rulers of the nine GCS agreed to give the name, "Federation of the Arab Emirates," to the proposed union. They conceived of the proposed federation as a suitable vehicle for enhancing cooperation and establishing closer ties among them which would ultimately increase their economic and social development potential. They also considered their action a positive step toward achieving wider cooperation and realizing the greater Arab unity. They agreed to the sharing of foreign policy and defense activities.[10]

Top Federal Political Authority

The Federation Agreement invested ultimate political authority in a supreme council composed of the rulers of the nine GCS; and this body was made responsible for formulating overall policies on political, economic and social affairs. Chairmanship of the Council rotated annually among its members; and the chairman represented the Federation both internally and externally.[11] Whether by coincidence or design, the Supreme Council, as the highest body in the Federation, carried with it its own seeds of destruction, for its decisions were to be taken by a unanimous vote. Thus, the Supreme Council could not act should any one of its members decide to vote against or withhold support from any matter under consideration.

The Federation Agreement seems to have failed in finding a practical solution to the problem posed by conflicting concerns among various countries. A country the size of Ajman (pop. 5,500) and a country the size of Bahrain (pop. 205,000) cannot logically be given the same weight. Viewed from another angle, any of the smaller and poorer countries such as Ajman, Umm al-Qaiwain and Fujairah had a veto over the decisions of the Supreme Council. Granted that this probably was inevitable, initially, in order to enlist their cooperation and support, the fact remains that decisions of the Supreme Council should not have required a unanimous vote—a majority vote should have been adequate. The experience of the Supreme Council clearly showed how difficult it was to reach common agreement on issues discussed by the Council. As a result, the Council was not able to reach a decision to bring into reality the proposed Federation of the Nine.

Federal Executive Authority

Executive authority of the Federation of the Arab Emirates was assigned to a federal council which would serve as an executive arm of the Supreme Council. The federal council was not empowered to make final decisions. It could make recommendations to the Supreme Council; and its actions had to conform to policies and laws laid down by the Supreme Council. The Federation Agreement was silent on questions related to organization and composition of the federal council.[12] This, again, handicapped the process of implementation as the Supreme Council was not able to reach an agreement on these matters. It is easier, it seems, to frame a law than to implement it.

Finances of the Federation

The Federation Agreement dealt with the budget of the proposed federation in a very general and vague way. The Supreme Council as the highest federal authority was empowered to issue the budget, but the more difficult questions concerning the sources of revenue receipts and the contributions of each of the member states were not dealt with in a satisfactory way. The Federation Agreement provided that "the sources of revenue and the share to be contributed by each of the Emirates shall be fixed by law."[13] Again in this case, the Agreement seems to have carried enough seeds of contention to prevent its implementation. The experience of the Supreme Council during its period of activity, as will be seen in the following pages, is revealing. It was not able to resolve the varied, and in most cases conflicting, views on these as well as many other equally important issues.

Defense

The Federation Agreement provided that the parties to it should cooperate to strengthen their individual and collective defense capabilities. While it made it a common responsibility of all of them to repel any armed aggression to which any one of them might be subjected, the Agreement gave no clear indication as to whether they had agreed to develop a common defense force.[14] Since defense was one of the two main functions which they had agreed to unify, it should have received more attention in the Federation Agreement to prevent future questions of interpretations which could have hindered implementation.

Federal Justice

The Federation Agreement called for the establishment of a "Supreme Federal Court." Its functions, organization and jurisdiction were left to be defined by law.[15]

Capital of the Federation

The location of the permanent Federation headquarters was left to be determined by the Supreme Council.[16] Since the location was not determined at the time of the drawing of the Federation Agreement, it became a source of friction and speculation. When members began to come down to earth and to attempt to carry out provisions of the agreement, their competing ambitions led to the proposing of many conflicting solutions.

Some Observations on the Federation Agreement

When the nine rulers met in Dubai on February 25, 1968, to consider how they could pool their resources to form a solid front that would neutralize possible threats which might develop after Britain's withdrawal from the Gulf, they seem to have responded each according to his own evaluation of the nature and seriousness of the issue at hand. They apparently were talking the same words but with different meanings. Their words and concepts seem to have lacked the requirement of operational definitions. In a three-day meeting, they were able to draw up the Federation Agreement and they rejoiced in its signing. But for more than four years, they were not able to implement what they reached a general agreement on in three days. Undoubtedly, drafting the Federation Agreement in such general and vague terms and leaving final decisions on the more important issues for future decision to be taken by the Supreme Council, where actions required unanimous votes, helped the rulers to overcome their differences, at least temporarily. Each must have interpreted the Agreement in his own way and counted on his veto power in the Supreme Council. The veto provision paralyzed the Council and prevented it from taking the steps needed to put the objectives of the Agreement into operation. It will be helpful to consider the major potential obstacles to the Federation of the Nine.

Major Obstacles to the Federation of the Nine

Before examining the kinds of problems which have prevented and may continue to prevent the rulers from taking positive action toward finalizing a union of the nine, it is appropriate to assess potential problems which would influence, at least indirectly, the flexibility or rigidity of individual governments concerning union issues. These problems relate to area, population, wealth and foreign claims. Not a single country can claim superiority in all of the factors of size of territory, size of population, wealth, and foreign claims of influence. Of the four most developed countries, on which the future of a union of nine would depend, Bahrain is the smallest (256 sq. miles), Abu Dhabi is the largest (26,000 sq. miles), Dubai is the second smallest (1,500 sq. miles), and Qatar is the second largest (4,000 sq. miles). There is no doubt that the size of individual countries is important, but how much weight should it be given?

Among these four, Bahrain is the most populous country (205,000), Abu Dhabi is the smallest (60,000), Qatar is the second largest (80,000), and Dubai is next to the smallest (75,000). In terms of their wealth as measured by present levels of production and the potential for further increase, Bahrain is the poorest, and Abu Dhabi is the wealthiest, followed by Qatar and then Dubai, in that order.

Of the big-four countries, Qatar and Dubai have not faced any serious political problem; but Bahrain has had the Irani claim outstanding for a long time, and Abu Dhabi has a dispute with Saudi Arabia over al-Buraimi.

First Meeting of the Supreme Council

Because more than one country claimed to be the first among equals, the proposed Federation of Nine, as such, was not brought to fruition. All kinds of problems were raised during the various meetings of the Supreme Council held to put into effect the Federation Agreement. The first meeting of the Council, held in Abu Dhabi on July 6-7, 1968, uncovered rivalry between the competing would-be leaders, as Bahrain and Qatar reciprocated their opposition to each other from the very beginning of the meeting.[17] During the meeting, Bahrain nominated Dr. A. Bazzaz, an Iraqi ex-Prime Minister to be appointed as the Federation's legal advisor responsible for drafting the Federation constitution. Qatar immediately rejected the nomination and made a counterproposal to appoint Dr. Hassan Kamel, an Egyptian, instead. Influenced by Kuwaiti wishes, Abu Dhabi nominated Dr. A. Sanhouri as a compromise. At the same meeting, Qatar nominated its then deputy Ruler and heir apparent, Sheikh Khalifa bin Hamad Al-Thani, for the presidency of the Federal Council. Bahrain rejected the nomination on the grounds that the President of the Federal Council should be one who could devote full time to the position. Again, Abu Dhabi mediated and Bahrain tabled its objection.

While the first meeting provided an opportunity for the rulers to exchange ideas about the prospects and future of the area and the potential role of the Federation in maintaining and sustaining political stability, it revealed that Qatar and Bahrain were the two opposite poles. It also saw Abu Dhabi emerge as an accepted mediator between the two. Bahrain and Qatar were in the race of the first among equals. Bahrain was more developed than Qatar in many respects; but Qatar had seen much progress over the past twenty years and its oil income was more than triple that of Bahrain. The mediator, Abu Dhabi, also aspired to have a key role in the Federation. It was encouraged in this by its large size and new-found wealth—its oil production was more than double that of Bahrain, Qatar and Dubai combined.

Second Meeting of the Supreme Council

During the second meeting of the Supreme Council, held in Doha, Qatar, during October 20-22, 1968, friction between Bahrain and Qatar proved unavoidable, and Abu Dhabi continued its role as moderator and mediator. During this meeting, Bahrain raised a really tough issue in suggesting that the next meeting be held in Manama, its capital city. Bahrain in making this request must have wanted to test the seriousness and sincerity of the Federation in supporting it against the Irani claim. Had they agreed to hold the meeting in Bahrain, they would have shown their serious intentions to support Bahrain all the way through. But Iran had, as it has today, friendly relations and close ties with a number of the GCS, and, therefore, Bahrain's bid to hold the third meeting of the Supreme Council failed to receive a unanimous vote.

Two main issues were also discussed, but no agreement was reached on either one. Qatar laid claim to the capital and the chairmanship of the Supreme Council, and predictably, Bahrain rejected this and specified its justification for the refusal. Vested interests of external powers began to surface during the second meeting of the Supreme Council. Saudi Arabia indirectly worked to support the Qatari claims to the chairmanship and the capital; and Dubai and Ras al-Khaimah, both friendly with Saudi Arabia, followed the same line. Kuwait was opposed to any intervention, regardless of its source, in the affairs of the proposed federation and therefore opposed the Saudi influence. As a result of such conflicts, mainly between the two major contesting parties, Bahrain and Qatar, the second meeting of the Supreme Council did not push forward the proposed Federation significantly. It culminated in the formation of a committee composed of Bahrain, Qatar and Abu Dhabi which was charged with the responsibility of discussing the unresolved items.[18]

Third Meeting of the Supreme Council

The third meeting of the Supreme Council held in Doha May 10-14, 1969, was no more successful than the previous meetings. During its first session, Qatar submitted an agenda of 20 items for the meeting, but Bahrain not only quickly rejected the proposed agenda but submitted a counteragenda for the meeting.[19] The seeds of conflicts and disputes were present from the very beginning of the meeting and thus it was doomed to failure.

Fourth Meeting of the Supreme Council

The fourth meeting of the Supreme Council which opened in Abu Dhabi on October 21, 1969, agreed on the following points.[20]

1. Sheikh Zayid, ruler of Abu Dhabi, was selected to become the first chairman for two years, and Sheikh Rashid bin Said al-Maktoum, ruler of Dubai, was selected deputy chairman. It is interesting to note that neither Qatar nor Bahrain succeeded in gaining the chairmanship. Instead, the mediator and moderator of the previous meetings, Abu Dhabi, won the contest.
2. Sheik Khalifa bin Hamad al-Thani, Deputy Ruler of Qatar, was appointed Prime Minister of the proposed Federation. It is interesting to note here that Bahrain had originally rejected the appointment of Sheikh Khalifa on the grounds that he could not become a Prime Minister of the Federation since he was also Deputy Ruler in Qatar and, as such, could not devote full time to the Federation.
3. It was agreed that Abu Dhabi town should serve as the Federation Capital until a new capital could be built on the border between Abu Dhabi and Dubai.
4. It was further agreed that each of the nine member states would have an equal number of representatives in the proposed Federal Council. Realizing that it would be most difficult to decide on the more crucial issues and still satisfy both Bahrain and Qatar, since each was still claiming to be the first among equals, the members at their October 1969 meeting agreed to rely on their deputies who would meet to prepare the groundwork for the following meeting of the Supreme Council.

Political Developments in 1970 and Their Impact on the Proposed Federation

Internal Political Developments

Between the October 1969 meeting of the Supreme Council and the end of 1970, both Bahrain and Qatar witnessed certain political developments which might have influenced the future of the proposed Federation. Early in 1970, Bahrain, as mentioned previously, modified its paternalistic system of government. A Council of State vested with executive powers and composed of heads of the operating departments was established. In addition, it also took further steps to streamline and modernize its administration. In the process, the Departments of Foreign Affairs and Defense were established. It is very difficult to find out the exact reasons for creating either of these two departments since the proposed Federation was supposed to assume the functions of foreign affairs and defense. It does suggest, however, continuing differences between Bahrain and Qatar.

Qatar followed the Bahraini example and in April 1970, its fundamental law defining powers and authorities of the various organs of the state was enacted. The Qatari fundamental law created the first cabinet in the GCS. In contrast to Bahrain, however, Qatar at that time had not created ministries for defense and foreign affairs, though it has recently done so. Two reasons could be advanced for this. The first is that Qatar had not lost hope for the proposed federation which was supposed to handle foreign affairs and defense. The second is a technical one and involves the fact that since Britain under its treaty obligations was responsible for foreign affairs and defense, Qatar presumably would take over these responsibilities only gradually as Britain withdrew in accordance with its end-of-1971 deadline.

The two developments in Bahrain and Qatar, important as they are, may not have influenced the course of the proposed federation as much as the United Nations decision in favor of independence for Bahrain which seemingly ended the long outstanding Irani claim.

Abu Dhabi, Dubai and Qatar had friendly relations with Iran and, therefore, they were not pushing hard for a federation which included Bahrain. They were not willing to antagonize Iran; and also, they were conscious of the possibility that Iran might create problems for a federation which included Bahrain. In fact, a federation without Bahrain might have been more attractive to the other GCS.

Bahrain probably saw the problem in a different perspective. From its standpoint, if the federationists were serious about forming the kind of union which would be capable of taking care of the interests of the area and which could act on a threat such as that of Iran to Bahrain, then they should be prepared to face the matter of the Irani claim. This problem, which could have weakened Bahrain's position and strengthened that of Qatar, was resolved in May 1970, when the United Nations Security Council acted on the report of the

Personal Representative of the Secretary General and voted for independence for Bahrain.[21]

External Political Developments

The rulers of the nine Gulf states originally agreed to hold their fifth meeting in Dubai during the first part of June 1970, to continue their deliberations on the federation. Their deputies met in Abu Dhabi shortly prior to the scheduled meeting to prepare the ground. In this meeting, the deputies agreed to recommend to the Supreme Council that the selection of ministers for the Council of Ministers be carried out on the basis of nominations to be made by member states. Under this procedure, each state would be permitted to submit a list of three potential ministers.[22]

Knowing that the British elections were approaching, the rulers preferred to delay their fifth meeting until after they had been held. The British general elections took place on June 18, 1970, and brought about a different political situation since the Conservative Party gained power. Some of the GCS, it is reported, were pleased that the Conservatives had won. At heart, such countries hoped that success for the new Conservative government would bring a serious attempt to reverse the 1968 policy announcement calling for British withdrawal from the Gulf by the end of 1971. Though the rulers of the GCS were anxious to have Britain stay in the Gulf beyond 1971, other Arab as well as non-Arab countries were against Britain's presence in any form beyond the already announced deadline. Iran, Iraq, Kuwait, Saudi Arabia and the U.A.R., among others, openly rejected the idea of extending Britain's stay beyond 1971, whether on its own initiative or at the request of the GCS themselves.[23]

After the Conservatives came to power, the Gulf area has witnessed continuous diplomatic missions and visits. The diplomats gave assurances that they were doing their best to help the GCS finalize the proposed Federation of Nine.

Iran, Kuwait and Saudi Arabia, in addition to Britain, showed great concern about the future of the GCS federation. Following talks between the Kuwait and Irani foreign ministers during a three-day visit by Mr. Zahidi, Iran's Foreign Minister, to Kuwait, a communique was released which supported a federation as the best possible means for maintaining and sustaining the political stability which was fundamental to further progress and prosperity in the area.[24] Early in July 1970, Sir Alec Douglas Home, Britain's new Conservative foreign secretary, met the Shah of Iran in Europe and exchanged with him views on the future of the Gulf area. Sir Alec told a press conference afterwards that Iran, Saudi Arabia and the rulers of the Arabian Gulf States were equally concerned about this.[25] He also told the press that he would have talks with Saudi Arabia and the rulers of the GCS simultaneously. Although Sir Alec did not explain the nature of his talks, political analysts concluded that he was trying to collect reactions from Iran about the possibility of Britain's maintaining a military presence beyond

1971.[26] This was essential to the new Conservative government before a move to reverse the decision of the former Labor government could be taken.

Kuwait was opposed to Britain's staying in the Gulf and requested that Britain's new Conservative government honor the Labor government's commitment on withdrawal.[27] Kuwait did not believe that there would be a so-called vacuum in the area after a British withdrawal; for it felt that the peoples of the area could defend their independence and safeguard their sovereignty.[28]

Iran and Saudi Arabia also were not quiet on the issue. They had a number of diplomatic contacts, and both agreed to build pressure for a British withdrawal.[29] Iraq too, did not spare efforts to show its concern about the Gulf area situation. In a public speech on July 17, 1970, Mr. Ahmad Hassan Baker, the Iraqi president, called for the creation of a defense alliance combining Kuwait, Saudi Arabia, Iraq and the nine Gulf city states. Kuwait rejected the Iraqi proposal when it was discussed in its Council of Ministers in its session on July 19, 1970.[30] Iraq was not pleased with the Kuwaiti response to its proposal and invited all progressive powers and organizations in the Arab countries to be prepared to meet their Gulf responsibilities.[31]

Diplomatic contacts within and outside the Gulf area during the month of July 1970, convinced Britain that Iran, Saudi Arabia and Kuwait were against any British presence after 1971. Britain also established diplomatic contacts with the U.A.R. on the issue, again with a negative reaction. Late in August 1970, Mr. William Loss, the Personal Representative of the British Foreign Secretary, started a three-week visit to Saudi Arabia, Kuwait, the Gulf city states, Iran, the U.A.R. and Iraq. At least Iran, Kuwait, Saudi Arabia, and probably Iraq, were in earnest in deciding to refer the case to the International Court if Britain insisted on staying in the area beyond 1971. They threatened to take measures against Britain, including the cutting off of oil and diplomatic relations, unless the U.N. Security Council took a strict decision on the issue.[32]

The new Conservative government knew well that Iran, Kuwait and Saudi Arabia would only accept talks with Mr. Loss on the issue of withdrawal, and on nothing else. But the new government hoped to find a way to reverse the decision of the Labour government, since some of the rulers of the Gulf city states showed a serious readiness to finance the stay of British forces and urged the new government to keep British forces in the area. A three-week visit by Mr. Loss did not result in any progress; for Iran, Kuwait and Saudi Arabia were not very receptive and did not change their minds.[33]

The status of the proposed federation was not discussed by the GCS rulers or their deputies during the period of July to September 1970. Discussions were resumed in October when Sheikh Zayid, ruler of Abu Dhabi, paid a visit to Bahrain. The latter state indicated its interest in a meeting of the rulers to discuss the prospects of the proposed federation and suggested delaying the time of the meeting until more consultations on the questions of the Federation capital and representation in the proposed Federal Council had been concluded.[34] Instead of a rulers' meeting, their deputies met in Abu Dhabi late in October 1970. The deputies failed to agree on the capital of the Federation and on representation in the Federal Council.[35] Although Bahrain had agreed during the October 1969 meeting that a new capital should be built between Abu Dhabi and Dubai, in this later meeting, it withdrew its previous agreement. Bahrain was ready to accept a recommendation submitted by Mr. Loss and agreed to by Qatar, Abu Dhabi and Dubai, regarding a three-level representation in the Federal Council. According to this suggestion, the big four, Bahrain, Qatar, Abu Dhabi and Dubai, would each have six representatives; Ras al-Khaimah and Sharjah would each have four; and the rest would each have three representatives.[36] No action was taken and the dispute continued to hamper the Federation. The conflict which emerged at this meeting is indicative of the underlying problems which prevented finalizing the proposed Federation of Nine.

During his three-week visit to Kuwait, Saudi Arabia and the other Gulf States, Mr. Loss, as the personal representative of the British Foreign Secretary, exchanged ideas with the parties concerned and the rulers agreed on a number of issues. Mr. Loss, as a result of his visit, concluded that Britain:

1. Supported the establishment of an effective Federation as soon as possible;
2. Considered that the location of the capital of the Federation should not be a real problem;
3. Supported a three-level representation in the Federal Council under which Bahrain, Qatar, Abu Dhabi and Dubai would have six seats each; Sharjah and Ras al-Khaimah would have four seats each; and each of the remaining GCS would have three seats;
4. Supported economic unity among the Emirates to enable the Federation to play its expected development role.[37]

Though it proved impossible to bring the originally proposed Federation of the nine GCS to a successful conclusion, the efforts were by no means entirely wasted for the rulers of six of the Trucial states were finally able, after some eighteen months of preparatory work and discussions, to agree to join together in a federation known as the United Arab Emirates. The U.A.E. came into existence on December 2, 1971, and the seventh Trucial state, Ras al-Khaimah, was admitted on February 13, 1972. Ras al-Khaimah had originally refrained from joining, among other reasons, in protest against the allocation of seats in the al Majlis al Watani al Ittihadi (The National Assembly of the U.A.E.) which is the legislative branch of the U.A.E. and consists of forty representatives. The allocation of seats is eight each for Abu Dhabi and Dubai, six each for Ras al-Khaimah and Sharjah, and four for each of the other states. Each member country may either elect or appoint its representatives, the only requirement being that of citizenship in the country concerned.

When the U.A.E. was established in late 1971, Ras al-Khaimah pressed for the same representation as that of Abu Dhabi and Dubai, but it ultimately agreed to its present level of representation.[38] It has been said that Ras al-Khaimah had requested before joining the U.A.E. that the member countries support its claim for recovery of the two small islands, Greater and Lesser Tunb, which it claimed and which had been occupied by Iran on November 30, 1971, one day before Britain's withdrawal of its military presence in the Gulf.[39]

Iran's unilateral occupation of these two islands claimed by Ras al-Khaimah plus its occupation at the same time of a third island, Abu Musa, claimed by Sharjah—apparently with at least the partial consent of the Ruler of the latter country—created serious tension in the Gulf area.[40] Iraq reacted strongly and broke off diplomatic relations with both Iran and Great Britain as a result of the occupation; and other Arab countries expressed their grave concern. The occupation seems to have become a *fait accompli*, at least for the time being.

Both Bahrain and Qatar refrained from joining the U.A.E., apparently at least in part because they could not get the extent of representation and control which they desired. As a result, these two states are going their own way, and both have become members of the United Nations.[41] The U.A.E. has also joined the U.N. For reasons discussed later, it is to be hoped that in time Bahrain and Qatar will join the U.A.E.

The National Assembly of the U.A.E. serves as the legislative branch of the government. It has the responsibility of helping the Majlis al Wuzara (the Council of Ministers) draw up legislation for submission to the Supreme Council of rulers for their consideration for ratification. Under the temporary Constitution of the U.A.E., the Assembly is accorded the right to discuss draft legislation submitted by the Council of Ministers and to propose amendments before such legislation goes forward to the President and the Supreme Council of rulers for ratification.

The temporary constitution also states that the Assembly can discuss government matters in the presence of the Council of Ministers; and that the Assembly must be informed of any international agreements or treaties entered into by the Supreme Council of rulers. This latter body is to be represented at meetings of the Assembly by the Prime Minister or by a member of the Council of Ministers.

Officers of the Assembly include its president, currently from Dubai, and two vice-presidents, currently both from Abu Dhabi. The Assembly will hold annual sessions of six months' duration, normally starting in November.[42]

The Assembly held its first meeting in Abu Dhabi on February 13, 1972. The session was opened by the president of the U.A.E. who presented a statement of the federal government's policies with regard to both internal and external affairs. Internal matters touched upon in his statement included the point that primary education in the U.A.E. would be compulsory and education at this and higher levels would be free. Medical services and various social services were also to be provided by the federal government. As a further matter of internal policy, the new government is committed to encouraging economic growth and development in order to achieve prosperity in the member states.

In regard to external policy, the president's statement emphasized that the U.A.E. supported Arab and Islamic causes and that it sought friendly relations with peoples and countries throughout the world in keeping with the charter of the United Nations. As part of its foreign policy, the new federal government has become a member of both the Arab League and the United Nations.

By the time of the first meeting of the Assembly, the government of the U.A.E. had taken steps to establish an official gazette, had adopted a national flag, had developed arrangements for a common defense force, and had instituted the Ministry of Foreign Affairs, which among other things, would provide diplomatic representation for the U.A.E. in the U.N. and in various countries throughout the world.[43]

The formation of the U.A.E. initially by six of the Trucial states, but soon by the addition of the seventh as well, was a progressive and very wise step which showed great statesmanship on the part of the rulers of the member states. It is to be hoped that Bahrain and Qatar, as well, perhaps, as Muscat-Oman, may also become members in the course of time. In federation or union, there are the political advantages of strength and protection for these small states; and there are also major economic and social benefits to be realized as well. Potential gains from federation are considered in some detail in the following chapter.

7 Potential Gains from Regional Economic and Political Integration

Historical Background

For more than a century, Britain played a guiding role in the nine Gulf city states. In conducting its obligations with them, it recognized each as a separate political entity. In theory, Britain did not consider any of them as the first among equals. Vertical relationships between each of the GCS and the greater political entity, Britain, were essentially of a subordinate-superior nature; while horizontal relationships between any two of these small states have been contacts between equal partners. It can be assumed that this pattern served the interests of both Britain and the Gulf city states. As a colonial power, it was easier for Britain to deal with each unit alone rather than to deal with them combined in a larger unit.

It is not clear whether Britain originally carved out the artificial boundaries among these states to facilitate the not uncommon colonial strategy of divide and rule. In this case, however, it would seem that colonial motives coincided with the interests of the colonized. When Britain first established its position in the Gulf states, tribal rivalries were strong, especially among the ruling families, and even today, rivalries have not been entirely overcome. Such rivalries created both the need and the opportunity for close cooperation between the different rulers and the British political resident in the Gulf. Britain could play a game in which each of the nine Gulf states was an equal partner; but since Britain has terminated its role, the parties to the game have inevitably discovered that they are not *de facto* equal partners.

Isolation versus Cooperation

Britain in leaving the Gulf at the end of 1971 made it clear that its military presence in the area would not be extended beyond the deadline. In fact, Iran, Kuwait and Saudi Arabia agreed on insisting that Britain honor its commitment to withdraw. They also seemed to be agreed that cooperation among the nine Gulf city states in the proposed federation would be the most appropriate course of action to help maintain and sustain political stability in the area after the British withdrawal.

In the absence of Britain, each of the nine Gulf city states was faced with the alternative of isolation or cooperation. Rather than assessing the potential input which each country can contribute to some form of regional integration, it will be more revealing, first, to assess the isolation potential of each. In this analysis, these states will be considered one-by-one.

Fujairah

Fujairah does not seem to stand any reasonable chance of becoming a viable political unit by itself. Its total population is approximately 10,000, and it is very difficult to see how it could realize genuine autonomy and isolation. In fact, the little urban infrastructural development which was promoted in this small city state in the 1960s was organized and financed by the Development Office of the Trucial States Council. During the period 1965-1968, Fujairah received BD 94,749 to finance low-cost housing, a water system and a supply of electricity.[1]

Fujairah's public revenues from 1966 to 1968 are shown in Table 7-1. This level of income hardly enabled the ruler to maintain himself and his tribal machinery.

Estimates of revenues for the period 1971-74 are shown in Table 7-2. Even with the slight increasing trend projected, it is very difficult to see how the ruler could finance any development projects unless he receives external support.

Table 7-1
Fujairah's Public Revenues, 1966-68

Source	(In BD Million)		
	1966	1967	1968
Oil Concession	0.48	0.14	0.14
Stamps and other income	0.07	0.08	0.10
Total	0.55	0.22	0.24

Source: Middle East Economic Division, British Embassy, Beirut, "An Economic Survey of the Northern Trucial States," 1969 (unpublished), Vol. 1, p. 12.

Table 7-2
Estimates of Fujairah's Public Revenues, 1971-74

Source	(In BD Million)			
	1971	1972	1973	1974
Oil	0.14	0.14	0.14	0.14
Other	0.13	0.14	0.15	0.16
Total	0.27	0.28	0.29	0.30

Source: Middle East Economic Division, British Embassy, Beirut, "An Economic Survey of the Northern Trucial States," 1969 (unpublished), Vol. 1, p. 33.

Expected growth in the ruler's income does not cover the anticipated growth in operating expenditures needed to keep his governmental machinery running. Also, since health and education have been organized and financed by Kuwait from the beginning of their development in Fujairah, the scope of the problems the ruler would have faced would have been much greater had he decided to take the route of isolation rather than cooperation and have lost this outside support as a result. Even considering the oil receipts which could flow in if oil finds are confirmed in its territory, it is not unrealistic to say that Fujairah would not be likely to be able to become a viable state, given its small size and population. On the whole, the ruler of Fujairah would seem to have made a wise decision in choosing the path of integration.

Ras al-Khaimah

Ras al-Khaimah, also, does not seem to have the potential for political and economic viability. The size of its population, its area and its known economic resources are far from being adequate to achieve this. Some urban infrastructural development has taken place in this little city state; for between 1965 and 1968, the ruler received a total of BD 875,953 from the Development Fund of the Trucial States Council to finance electricity, the water supply, town roads, telephones, a trade school and some clinics.[2] If it had not been for the financial assistance provided by the Development Fund, it would not have been possible for the ruler to introduce any of these badly needed development projects. The level of state revenue receipts does not allow the ruler to think beyond maintaining his simple law-and-order machinery. Without external assistance, it would be very difficult, if not impossible, for the country to embark on developmental projects.

Ras al-Khaimah's public revenues from 1966 to 1968 are shown in Table 7-3. Estimates of revenues for the period 1971-74 are shown in Table 7-4.

Table 7-3
Ras al-Khaimah's Public Revenues, 1966 to 1968

Source	(In BD Million)		
	1966	1967	1968
Oil Concession	0.10	0.10	0.10
Stamps and other income	0.12	0.16	0.18
Municipal Revenue	0.02	0.02	0.02
Total	0.24	0.28	0.30

Source: Middle East Economic Division, British Embassy, Beirut, "An Economic Survey of the Northern Trucial States," 1969 (unpublished), Vol. 1, p. 12.

Table 7-4
Estimates of Ras al-Khaimah's Public Revenues, 1971-74

Source	(In BD Million)			
	1971	1972	1973	1974
Oil Concessions	0.13	0.13	0.13	0.13
Stamps and other revenue	0.21	0.22	0.23	0.24
Municipal revenue	0.02	0.03	0.03	0.04
Total	0.36	0.38	0.39	0.41

Source: Middle East Economic Division, British Embassy, Beirut, "An Economic Survey of the Northern Trucial States," 1969 (unpublished), Vol. 1, p. 33.

The small anticipated improvement in the financial position of Ras al-Khaimah is not sufficient to enable it to undertake any major development project. If it had tried to be isolationist, its present level of income or that expected over the coming five years, would hardly have supported the administrative machinery needed to keep the state moving. Had it insisted on being really independent and establishing relationships with other countries, it would have had neither the money nor the trained personnel needed to carry out such ambitious objectives. It is true that it, as well as others of the tiny Trucial states, hopes to strike oil in the near future; and if its hopes are realized, it could perhaps solve its financial problem; but it is unlikely that it would be able to cope alone with potential political and administrative problems, even so. If oil is not found soon, the people will be looking to the other richer GCS—some of them have already done so—where they can find better work opportunities and enjoy living in more developed towns and cities.

It seems clearly in the interest of the people of the smaller states to work with the other Gulf city states within the framework of the U.A.E. In doing so, they can identify themselves with this larger political entity which will be better qualified to provide them with more favorable opportunities for achieving their hopes and aspirations. The rulers of the tiny states, on the other hand, know that cooperation will place them in tough competition with the other rulers who have better chances of supporting their claims to first-among-equals status. Their alternatives, however, would seem to be far less desirable.

Umm al-Qaiwain

One could understand that Ras al-Khaimah might consider the possibility of independence and the maintenance of an autonomous political unit; but it is almost beyond imagination that Umm al-Qaiwain could aspire to and work toward becoming an independent national entity. Umm al-Qaiwain is just 300 square miles in size with a total population of 4,500. It is an extremely poor country where almost the entire population subsists on fishing. The Development Fund of the Trucial States Council has financed the little urban infrastructural development which has taken place. Between 1965 and 1968, Umm al-Qaiwain received BD 367,831 to finance projects such as electricity, the water supply, town roads, telephones, wharf facilities and a clinic.[3] Left alone, the ruler could do little for his community, and at best he would be able to maintain his law-and-order municipal administration. His domestic financial sources are barely adequate to meet his operating expenses, and they cannot be stretched to cover development projects. Total state revenue receipts accruing to the ruler in the years 1966 to 1968, are shown in Table 7-5; and estimates of his revenues for the period 1971-74 are presented in Table 7-6.

If oil is struck and the country starts to enjoy substantial oil receipts, this may make it financially viable, but the ruler even then probably would not be able to transform his tiny community into a viable political unit. Also, psychologically, the people are likely to want to belong to a larger entity. The ruler has demonstrated his vision of the future in realizing that joining the U.A.E. rather than isolation is an important step toward meeting the growing needs of his community.

Table 7-5
Umm al-Qaiwain's Public Revenues, 1966 to 1968

	(In BD Million)		
Source	1966	1967	1968
Oil Concessions	0.03	–	–
Stamps and other income	0.06	0.07	0.08
Total	0.09	0.07	0.08

Source: Middle East Economic Division, British Embassy, Beirut, "An Economic Survey of the Northern Trucial States," 1969 (unpublished), Vol. 1, p. 12.

Table 7-6
Estimates of Umm al-Qaiwain's Public Revenues, 1971-74

	(In BD Million)			
Source	1971	1972	1973	1974
Oil Concessions	0.04	0.04	0.04	0.04
Other revenue	0.11	0.12	0.13	0.14
Total	0.15	0.16	0.17	0.18

Source: Middle East Economic Division, British Embassy, Beirut, "An Economic Survey of the Northern Trucial States," 1969 (unpublished), Vol. 1, p. 32.

Ajman

Ajman is quite similar to Umm al-Qaiwain. It is a country of 100 square miles with a total population of 5,500, and being so small, it, too, could not think seriously of isolation. Neither its size nor its level of wealth would qualify it to follow the course of an independent national entity. Through cooperation and not isolation, Ajman has been able to promote some urban infrastructural development. From 1965 to 1968, BD 217, 871 was given to Ajman from the development fund of the Trucial States Council to finance development projects such as electricity, the water supply, town roads, telephones and its wharf.[4] The income of the ruler hardly finances his tribal small-scale law-and-order administration; and it would have been difficult for him to raise the resources that would have enabled him to finance any projects which might have had developmental significance had he followed an isolationist course.

Ajman's public revenues from 1966 to 1968 are shown in Table 7-7; and its income estimates for 1971-74 are presented in Table 7-8. Taking into consideration the physical and financial circumstances of Ajman, it is indeed appropriate that it has chosen to join the U.A.E.

Table 7-7
Ajman's Public Revenues, 1966-68

	(In BD Million)		
Source	1966	1967	1968
Oil concessions	0.02	—	—
Other income	0.06	0.07	0.08
Total	0.08	0.07	0.08

Source: Middle East Economic Division, British Embassy, Beirut, "An Economic Survey of the Northern Trucial States," 1969 (unpublished), Vol. 1, p. 12.

Table 7-8
Estimates of Ajman's Public Revenues, 1971-74

	(In BD Million)			
Source	1971	1972	1973	1974
Oil concessions	0.02	0.02	0.02	0.02
Other income	0.11	0.12	0.13	0.14
Total	0.13	0.14	0.15	0.16

Source: Middle East Economic Division, British Embassy, Beirut, "An Economic Survey of the Northern Trucial States," 1969 (unpublished), Vol. 1, p. 33.

Sharjah

Compared to Fujairah, Ras al-Khaimah, Umm al-Qaiwain and Ajman, Sharjah is more affluent. It is not difficult for the traveler who passes through these particular countries to observe that Sharjah is more developed than the others. It has town roads, modern buildings, busy bazaars, banks, automatic traffic lights, etc. In area, it is larger than any one of these four other small countries, and it is about the size of Ras al-Khaimah, Umm al-Qaiwain and Ajman combined. Its population is also larger than that of any of the other four states, for it is about the size of that of Fujairah and Ras al-Khaimah together, or of Ras al-Khaimah, Umm al-Qaiwain and Ajman combined.

Though these factors give Sharjah a more favorable position, it still has a basic deficiency shared by all of the other four countries as well. This is the absence of the required foundation to support an independent national entity. In Sharjah's case, also, it is thanks to the Development Office of the Trucial States Council that financing for its development projects has been made available. From 1965 to 1968, a total of BD 831,236 was given to Sharjah to finance the water supply, electricity, town roads, town development, its jetty, a trade school, the Mileiha agricultural scheme, etc.[5]

As with the other four poor states, Sharjah has not been able to raise the domestic resources needed to finance development projects and it is unlikely that it will be able to do this in the near future, unless oil is found in commercial quantities. From 1966 to 1968, its revenue receipts were steadily increasing, but not enough to leave a surplus over current expenditures for investment in development projects. Its estimated domestic revenues for the years 1966 to 1974 are presented in Table 7-9.

The British base in Sharjah has been a major source of income, but since Britain's withdrawal, the loss to some extent has been compensated for by an increase in other income, mainly receipts from electricity and water payments;

Table 7-9
Estimates of Sharjah's Public Revenues, 1966-74

Source	(In BD Million)								
	1966	1967	1968	1969	1970	1971	1972	1973	1974
Rents	0.14	0.14	0.14	n.a.	–	–	–	–	–
Oil Concessions	0.05	–	–	0.09	0.09	0.09	0.09	0.09	0.09
Municipal revenue	0.08	0.09	0.12	n.a.	0.14	0.15	0.16	0.17	0.18
Other income	0.35	0.40	0.46	n.a.	0.69	0.74	0.65	0.70	0.75
Total	0.62	0.63	0.72	n.a.	0.92	0.98	0.90	0.96	1.02

Source: Middle East Economic Division, British Embassy, Beirut, "An Economic Survey of the Northern Trucial States," 1969 (unpublished), Vol. 1, pp. 10 and 32.

but it is not likely that there will be any surplus over recurrent expenditures for investment in development projects. In 1968 for example, its income amounted to BD 720,000, while its recurrent expenditures reached 860,000, for a deficit of BD 140,000.[6]

Although Sharjah is just 12 km. from Dubai, a more affluent state, it, too, has an airport. Sharjah is also dredging its seaport to be able to receive large ships, in spite of the fact that Dubai is completing the largest and best equipped port in the Gulf area. Sharjah's imports have been steadily increasing, and they now exceed BD 305,950 per year.[7]

Given its financial inability to support its own development, and its relatively small population, Sharjah has done well to throw in its lot with the other Trucial states in forming a federation. The people of Sharjah have nothing to lose; and they certainly have more to gain from having joined the U.A.E. in which they can identify with a larger entity, benefit from a relatively larger market, and share the blessings of oil receipts that are pouring into the oil-producing countries.

Dubai

Of the nine Gulf city states, only Dubai has been able in the past to promote a significant level of urban infrastructure without oil receipts. Its entrepot trade, thanks to its geographical location, has provided an important source of income which only recently has been augmented by oil royalties. Duties imposed on imports were formerly the major source of state income. Government revenues for the period 1966 to 1968 are shown in Table 7-10. This level of income was not sufficient, however, to enable the ruler to sponsor many of the development projects which were badly needed to transform his tribal society into a modern national entity. He found it necessary, in addition, to call on the Trucial states Development Fund, and between 1965 and 1968, Dubai received a total of BD 194,614 to finance development projects.[8] If it had not been for Kuwait's

Table 7-10
Dubai's Public Revenues, 1966-68

Source	(In BD Million)		
	1966	1967	1968
Duties	1.10	1.60	2.80
Oil Concessions	0.19	0.31	0.31
Stamps and Misc.	0.10	0.13	0.17
Municipal Revenue	0.21	0.28	0.45
Total	1.60	2.32	3.73

Source: Middle East Economic Division, British Embassy, Beirut, "An Economic Survey of the Northern Trucial States," 1969 (unpublished), Vol. 1, p. 9.

assistance, it is difficult to see how Dubai would have been able to provide much in the way of health or education services.

Dubai's recent entry into the group of oil-producing and oil-exporting countries, has certainly opened new hopes and horizons. Its revenue estimates over the period, 1971-74, are presented in Table 7-11. If other factors remain constant, its oil receipts, if devoted to financing development projects, should give good prospects for further economic and social progress.

Since Britain's departure, Dubai, if it had decided to try to follow the path of independence, would have had to conduct its own foreign affairs and law-and-order functions which were in the past assumed by Britain. In addition, it would have had to find some new means to provide for its own defense. Although oil receipts are expected to double by 1974, with a predicted increase from BD 10.05 million in 1970 to BD 19.79 million in 1974, this seemingly large increase might still be insufficient to finance a national bureaucracy which also had to staff a foreign affairs operation. In addition, in following an isolationist policy, Dubai would have had to build its own armed forces for defense purposes. Even with its anticipated oil revenues, this would almost certainly have been beyond its capability.

From a purely financial viewpoint, then, Dubai would have been in a dubious position to achieve independence. In view of this, cooperation rather than isolation certainly seems to be in its best interest. Even if it is assumed that Dubai will become financially qualified to meet the needs of independence, it would still be most difficult, if not impossible, for it to meet any time soon the manpower requirements which this would entail. It would not be able to staff quickly the required government machinery even if the bureaucracy should be kept to a minimum. In addition, its population could not provide the manpower for more than a very modest military defense force.

The people, themselves, seem likely to gain as a result of joining the U.A.E. They will have more mobility, a larger market and, above all, they will be able to identify with a larger entity. The ruler and the ruling family have demonstrated statesmanship in rising above parochial interests.

Table 7-11
Estimates of Dubai's Public Revenues, 1971-74

Source	(In BD Million)			
	1971	1972	1973	1974
Oil concessions	13.88	19.79	19.79	19.79
Duties	1.50	1.50	1.50	–
Municipal revenues	0.70	0.80	0.90	1.00
Other income	0.35	0.40	0.45	0.50
Total	16.43	22.49	22.64	21.29

Source: Middle East Economic Division, British Embassy, Beirut, "An Economic Survey of the Northern Trucial States," 1969 (unpublished), Vol. 1, p. 32.

Abu Dhabi

Of the seven Trucial states, only Abu Dhabi has not received external financial assistance; in fact, it has contributed more than 80% of the Development Fund of the Trucial States Council which has financed many intrastate and interstate development projects. Its territory comprises 26,000 square miles which makes it not only the largest country in the group, but, in addition, its area is more than double the total area of all the other eight Gulf city states combined. Its oil receipts are also more than double the total oil receipts of Bahrain, Qatar and Dubai. For 1970, the oil receipts of these three countries were estimated at about $110 million, as compared with the estimate of $240 million for Abu Dhabi.

Not only is Abu Dhabi the richest country in the Gulf on a per capita basis, but it is also the richest in the world, for its average per capita income of well over $4,000 is higher than that of Kuwait or the United States. Abu Dhabi is a newcomer to the field of development, however, for it was only in 1966 that it began to promote urban infrastructural development to transform its tribal society into a modern national state.

But financial qualifications are not enough for statehood in isolation. Had Abu Dhabi elected this route, it would have been impossible for it to meet all of its needs on its own. It lacks the manpower needed to operate and defend a state dependent only on itself. It could have tried going this route by importing the needed trained manpower from other countries; but there would be serious dangers in its taking such a step at such an embryonic stage of its development. Wisely, Abu Dhabi has shown a continuing interest in the approach of cooperation among the Gulf city states. Its generous contributions to the Development Office of the Trucial States Council since its inception in 1965 strongly confirms this interest, as does the leading role which it played in the formation of the U.A.E. Abu Dhabi is to be congratulated for having supplied the first president of the union.

Qatar

Of the nine Gulf city states, Qatar is second in the size of its territory and its population. It is second to Abu Dhabi in area and to Bahrain in population. Qatar is also the second richest country, being not far behind Abu Dhabi in this regard. In fact, on a per capita basis, it is the third richest country in the world with an estimated per capita income of $3,490 in 1968. Thus, financially, Qatar is qualified to meet independence obligations. It has been promoting urban infrastructural development for the past two decades, but it still needs to undertake further economic and social development projects to achieve complete transformation from a tribal order of life to a modern one.

Of all the Gulf states, Qatar alone has a cabinet and a fundamental law defining the powers and authorities of government. It also has the nucleus of a national bureaucracy; but it still lacks the qualified manpower to run the machinery of government under conditions of independence. No matter how rich Qatar is, in view of its limited manpower resources compared to those needed for its national development as a fully independent state, a policy of cooperation would clearly seem in its best interests. It is to be hoped that Qatar will soon be able to overcome whatever barriers may have prevented it from joining the U.A.E. so far.

Bahrain

Bahrain is the most populous country in the group, and 40% of the total population of the Gulf city states lives in its small area of 256 square miles. Its oil receipts are not large, being about $20 million per year, but it has been able to attain a reasonable level of economic and social infrastructure. As mentioned in an earlier chapter, Bahrain has a well-developed education system that compares well with those of other countries in the Middle East.

In comparison with Qatar, Abu Dhabi and Dubai, Bahrain is a poor country, for its per capita income in 1968 was estimated at $390, or just about one-tenth that of Qatar. It has a reasonable nucleus for a national bureaucracy, and unlike the other Gulf city states, it does not suffer from acute manpower problems; though it could not man a very sizeable defense force. It is difficult to see how Bahrain can afford to continue indefinitely its course of isolation given its strained financial position. It is hardly able to finance the present level of operations; and it will be most difficult for it to meet the costs of conducting foreign affairs and defense. Given the relative advantages and disadvantages, it would seem clearly in Bahrain's best interest to join the U.A.E. as soon as possible.

Recapitulation

The preceding survey to determine whether or not, individually, the nine Gulf city states could readily exist as full-fledged states has led to the conclusion that while some of them may have most of the necessary qualifications, none of them appears fully able to do so. The inescapable conclusion is that it would be to the advantage of every one of them to be part of a larger political entity. The seven Trucial states have already wisely recognized this fact by joining together in the promising U.A.E. It would seem in the interest of Bahrain and Qatar to join also.

Potential Gains from Integration

The nine Gulf city states can be grouped in different categories. First, they can be divided into the "haves" and "have-nots." Bahrain, Qatar, Abu Dhabi and Dubai fall in the have group; and all of the rest would be included among the have-nots.

Second, they can be divided into larger states and smaller states from the standpoint of the size of their territories and population. According to size, Abu Dhabi, Qatar, Dubai and Sharjah, *relatively* speaking, are large states, while all the rest are small. In regard to their population, again in relative terms, Bahrain, Qatar, Abu Dhabi and Dubai fall under the large group, while all the other states would be classified as small.

Essentially, these nine states fall into two different groups regardless of the criteria used; four states would come under one group and five under the other, though the composition of the groups changes somewhat with the different criteria considered. This suggests that in a federation of all nine, they would complement each other in many respects. The nine would—as will the seven in the U.A.E.—benefit from economies of scale in organizing and operating a number of fundamental state functions and services that would otherwise have to be performed and rendered by each of them, individually, under independence conditions. Similarly, the members of the U.A.E. will be able to avoid some of the diseconomies of small scale. It will be useful to consider some of the mutual gains which will accrue from cooperation.

Foreign Affairs

A highly significant qualification of any viable political entity is its capacity to enter into relations with other political entities. To be able to engage in foreign relations, each state needs to organize and operate a foreign service at home and abroad. Granted that all of the GCS are theoretically qualified to do this, they do not all have the financial and manpower resources to do so. Joined in a federation, they can benefit from one foreign service which can service the entire group. Instead of having nine separate services, there would be just one. The overhead cost would be greatly reduced and competent manpower, which is very scarce in all of them, would be used in the most efficient and effective manner. The image and prestige of the service would be considerably enhanced; for a foreign service assuming foreign relations for a state of about half a million people would certainly have more weight and status than a service conducting foreign relations for a country of 5,000, 10,000 or even 50,000. The seven states in the U.A.E. are already benefiting from a unified foreign service.

Defense

An independent state tends to have to organize an army no matter how small the country might be. The cost of defense, even with limited armed forces, can absorb a large portion of a smaller state's ordinary budget. Most of the nine Gulf city states are not qualified, financially or in terms of manpower, to organize and maintain armed forces. It will be relatively cheaper to organize one central force to assume defense responsibilities for the entire group. The cost to each state per unit of equipment and per soldier will be smaller as it is shared by a larger group. Also, each state will feel, at least psychologically, more secure to know that it is defended by a relatively larger army than it, alone, could muster; and unfriendly states will be more impressed by the size of the defending forces with the group-defense approach.

Education

All of the GCS need to improve the quality and quantity of their educational services. The sheer numbers of the potential consumers of these services would allow economies of scale to be realized under cooperation, for this would allow the spreading of overhead costs over the units served. The overhead-cost-to-operating-cost ratio would be much smaller with cooperation. Aside from the benefits derived from reductions in per-student overhead costs, there are certain specialized education functions, such as vocational training, that have to be provided for the citizens of any state. Though it would be unrealistic to establish a vocational training center, for example, in Ajman to serve a population of only some 5,000 persons, regional vocational centers could be highly effective in meeting such training needs. It would also be infeasible for any one state to establish a male or female teacher training college, a university or other higher education facility which may be needed to upgrade the quality and quantity of education available to its citizens. Again, a unified approach would be appropriate.

Of great importance in the area of education, integration will provide the GCS with a unique opportunity to review their curricular designs and to develop an appropriate common one to be used by all. The present differences in the structure and content of education do not reflect different local needs. Their needs are similar, if not the same, and, therefore, they could tailor a set of curricula which would be quite appropriate for all of them. More uniform educational curricula will help to enhance regional integration.

Health

As in education, so also in health, the GCS can derive great benefits from pooling their resources. It is unlikely that Umm al-Qaiwain, a country of about 5,000 people, could justify the establishment of a nursing school or highly specialized hospital. Such a small country does not provide an optimum size for many health services. While all of them need to maintain clinics to cope with the more routine health cases, one central hospital could be established at an optimum location to handle the more difficult cases which require sophisticated equipment and highly specialized medical staff. A fleet of ambulance aircraft could provide patients of each country with quick access to it. Since all of these countries need to train badly needed nurses, they could also benefit from a central nursing school.

The GCS can advantageously reconsider their overall health policies on a regional basis. A good philosophy of health must consider both preventive and curative areas of medicine. In the case of both areas, major economies of scale are possible through an integrated approach.

Public Administration

In any independent state, there will be functions and services that have to be organized and performed which will give rise to the need for organizing and operating a number of government line and staff agencies. The GCS need some outside help in organizing and establishing operating policies and systems for such a machinery. To the extent that broad administrative cooperation can be achieved among these states, the operating costs of government will be kept to a minimum. If each state attempted to bring in the needed outside experts to advise on organization, management, budgeting and a myriad of other administrative problems; the cost would be much greater than would be the case if they acted cooperatively. The same personnel law, the same organization guides, etc. could readily be applied in all of these countries. The creation of central staff units such as a budget office, a planning unit, a personnel agency, an inspection office and the like would be more economical since the scope of their coverage would be wider.

Those countries which have already established some sort of national bureaucracy, or those which will be establishing one in the near future, need training facilities to upgrade the level of their civil servants. An institute of public administration which would serve the needs of the entire area would be desirable, for none of these states is in a position to organize and run such an institute on its own. It would be wise to try to establish one central institute to meet the needs of all.

Industry

In most industries, the productive capacity or scale of individual plants has a direct bearing on the unit cost of production. At the same time, the market determines the range of productive capacity appropriate for a plant. In the GCS, if several countries should establish the same industry, the productive capacity and the market for each plant would be very limited and such industries would not be able to benefit from economies of scale. Thus, the efficiency of such facilities would not be as great as that of a similar factory which is geared to a larger market. Establishing industries in the GCS at optimum locations and with regard to optimum scale of plants would result in the realization of substantial economies of production.

As an example of a current trend toward inefficiency through duplication, Ras al-Khaimah is planning a cement factory whose production will be more than enough to meet the requirements of all the Trucial states in spite of the fact that Dubai has already initiated efforts to establish a cement factory with a planned productive capacity which would leave a large surplus over its needs; Qatar already has a cement factory which overproduces; Abu Dhabi seems also to be planning one; and so on. Another important industry which is already in operation and which may benefit from centralization is the fishing industry. For example, both Bahrain and Qatar have factories for processing fish and shrimp for export to foreign markets. Coordination, if not complete merger, would result in a reduction in overhead costs and in better marketing policies and facilities.

Trade

Bahrain has a modern seaport; Qatar has completed a modern deep water port; Dubai is building a 15-berth quay; and Abu Dhabi is also building a seaport. The combined capacity of these port facilities is far greater than the present or expected future actual needs of the Gulf countries. Each country decided to build its own facility without adequate consideration of its own needs and the plans of the other states. The result, in the end, is likely to be idle facilities which have absorbed large amounts of money that otherwise could have been invested in more urgently needed development projects.

As another example of duplication of facilities, there is no point in maintaining a major airport at Sharjah which is just 12 kilometers from Dubai where there is a first-class international airport. In fact, the runways of the Dubai international airport hit the boundaries of Sharjah. Instead of each country's seeking to establish a first-class jumbo jet airport, it would be more appropriate to establish different levels and sizes of airports in the area with an optimum location selected for each type.

Radio and TV

The Kuwaiti Radio and TV presently cover all of the six most northern Trucial states. Also, Abu Dhabi and Qatar have radio and TV stations, and Bahrain has a radio station. Some consolidation and the development of one major set of radio and TV facilities to serve the entire area would be more economical; for the total cost would be much less than the cost of the present multiplicity of local stations.

Concluding Comment

Larger political and economic units tend to be able to accomplish more than small ones. In view of this, the average Gulf citizen should derive more pride and satisfaction from a political and economic structure which encompasses a larger area of territory and a larger population. Such a structure will provide better defense opportunities, enhance stability in the area, and contribute to a faster rate of social, economic and administrative development.

Each Gulf state claims to be imbued with the spirit of Arab nationalism which has overall Arab unity as its ultimate goal. Regional cooperation among the seven Gulf city states comprising the U.A.E. already represents a step toward the goals of Arab nationalism and Arab unity.

Further, a larger entity embracing all nine Gulf city states would provide an even greater possibility for reducing localism and narrow interests. The development of such a larger entity may take some time, but until then, every possible effort should be made to support and sustain the development of the U.A.E. Without ignoring the right of self-determination, leaders should continue efforts to bring Bahrain and Qatar under the umbrella of the U.A.E. In addition, the U.A.E. would be further strengthened and regional integration extended if Muscat and Oman should also become a partner in the union.

The Price of Non-Integration

Problems of Integration

Following the British Labour government's announcement in January 1968 that Britain would leave the Gulf area by the end of 1971, the rulers of all nine Gulf states—Bahrain, Qatar, Abu Dhabi, Dubai, Sharjah, Umm al-Qaiwain, Ras al-Khaimah and Fujairah—reached an agreement in February 1968, to form a federation. The political shock generated by Britain's decision to withdraw from the Gulf, pushed the rulers to work together to face possible potential threats. The political uncertainty and social unrest which followed Britain's announcement brought to the fore the need for cooperation. Then known as well as unknown internal and external potential threats forced their quick and positive response.

While the nine rulers, initially, had all perceived the dangers of potential threats when the announcement was first made, the rulers of Bahrain and Qatar later reappraised their positions and ultimately refrained from joining the U.A.E. when it was first established. Whatever their individual perceptions, the fact remains that a potential threat was brought about by Britain's announcement; and the threat is still there, with such force that cooperation represents the best route to ensure the political stability and to further the economic and social progress of all nine of the GCS.

Unfortunately, what is true in logic and theory is not always easily realized in practice. When the GCS actually began to try to establish the proposed federation, their individual motivations and interests began to interfere, and progress toward implementing the federation was slow. When the rulers met in Dubai in February 1968, and quickly agreed to form a federation, they carried with them to the meeting their own perceptions and evaluations of the prevailing situation; but later, internal and external forces developed which caused some of the rulers to adjust their attitudes accordingly. During the meeting of the Supreme Council in Abu Dhabi in October 1969, five major items were discussed:

1. a proposed interim constitution;
2. the election of a president and a vice-president for two years;
3. the federation capital;
4. the formation of a council of ministers; and
5. the possibility of creating a national consultative council.

The Council agreed in principle on the following:

1. the election of the ruler of Abu Dhabi to serve as president for two years;
2. the selection of Abu Dhabi City as a temporary capital; and
3. equal representation in the proposed national consultative council.

No agreement was reached in connection with the other items.

At the time of the fourth meeting of the Supreme Council, Bahrain for example, was willing to accept almost anything in order to stay in the federation. The Irani claim to Bahrain was still unsettled and while the other Gulf states wanted to have Bahrain in the federation, they did not want to sever their good relations with Iran, which is a major Gulf power. It is probable that they were not enthusiastic about Bahrain's joining the federation; and that they did not feel it was possible for them explicitly to admit this. Instead, they tried to deprive that country of possible leading roles. The very few items agreed upon in this meeting were not signed by the rulers. While they were meeting, the British political agent in Abu Dhabi delivered a message from Britain to the rulers requesting them to conclude a quick and definite agreement on establishing the federation. The ruler of Ras al-Khaimah considered the message direct interference in the affairs of the federation and left the meeting to be followed by the ruler of Qatar. The meeting was postponed for a time, to be scheduled later.

It will be helpful at this point to examine the major forces that have had a direct bearing on the more recent attitudes of the rulers and which have slowed progress towards achieving the membership of all nine states in the federation.

Bahrain's International Status

When Bahrain signed the Federation Agreement and showed rather a lenient attitude toward the various items discussed during the subsequent meetings of the Supreme Council and of the rulers' deputies, it was in a relatively weak position as a result of the Irani claim. Its position and attitude have changed markedly since the U.N. Security Council voted for Bahrain's independence in its fifteen-hundred-and-thirty-sixth meeting on May 11, 1970. Since then, the mood of the country has changed; and as a result of the apparent removal of this potential threat, Bahrain has become more sensitive to having a key role in the Federation which its population and level of development would seem to justify. In short, the country's cost-benefit equation calculations have changed. Previously, it was willing to pay a higher price for joining the Federation; but now, the calculations seem to have led to a different conclusion so far as its interpretation of sacrifices and anticipated benefits is concerned.

The Conservative Government in Britain

The Conservative government which succeeded the Labour government in England in June 1970, brought with it new political dimensions. Some of the GCS had exerted all kinds of pressures on the Labour government to extend its stay in the area, but the government was not willing to give concessions. Thus, some of the GCS, the authors have been told, went to the extent of helping to finance the Conservative campaign in the hopes that a Conservative government would reverse the former Labour government's decision to withdraw forces. The Conservatives came to power in June 1970, and soon gave the Gulf problem special attention. Sir Alec Douglas Home, the new Secretary of Foreign Affairs, appointed Mr. William Loss as his personal representative in charge of Gulf affairs. Mr. Loss, as mentioned previously, was commissioned to undertake a diplomatic tour to Teheran, Cairo, Baghdad, Kuwait, Riyadh and the Gulf city states to collect first-hand information on the political situation and to discover potential problems and possible solutions for them.[1] While it is very difficult to establish the real motives and objectives of this tour, the then-prevailing political situation seems to have convinced the Conservative government that it could not reverse the Labour government's decision and that it should support the union of the nine Gulf city states. Therefore, although initially the change of power in Britain seemed to open new political possibilities for the area and in a way scaled down the enthusiasm of the rulers for implementing the Federation Agreement in the hopes of an extended British presence in the area beyond 1971, these possibilities soon appeared to become increasingly remote. Therefore, strategies which were originally based on possible Conservative government policy changes in the area needed to be reconsidered by the GCS rulers, since there appeared to be nothing in the air to support their desire for a British presence beyond the scheduled deadline for its removal.

Muscat and Oman Coup

In July 1970, a palace coup overthrew the highly traditional 60-year old ruler of Muscat and Oman and brought his son, Qabus, 28, to power. The coup opened new political horizons in the area and brought with it a number of factors which may, over time, either enhance or retard the possibilities for integration of the nine GCS. The seven Trucial states and Muscat and Oman form one geographical unit, and they could form a viable political unit. An important difference between them is that a significant amount of urban infrastructural development has taken place in the Trucial states, while Muscat and Oman has been essentially insulated against any external influence and, until the change in rulers, this country had not manifested any significant prospects for economic and social development. Its backwardness could tend to handicap or block its participation in the U.A.E.

Qabus, who succeeded his father, is an Oxford graduate and is determined to transform his country from an extremely backward, traditional tribal society, to a modern progressive one. The new regime in Muscat and Oman, with its potentialities, not only has created new political dimensions in the Gulf, but it has also aroused political interest externally. Britain quickly recognized the new regime; and Sheikh Zayed, the Ruler of Abu Dhabi, was the first Gulf ruler to visit Oman and exchange ideas with its ruler.[2]

Following his accession to the rulership, Qabus appointed his uncle, Tarik bin Taymour, Prime Minister.[3] On August 16, 1970, Tarik appointed the first four ministers in his government to head the Ministries of Justice, Health, Education and Interior.

Britain seems to have been pleased by the new changes in Oman, since these changes, it was felt, would help in determining a definite policy in the Gulf. Britain also seems to have thought that the new changes would enhance the efforts toward implementing the Federation Agreement.[4] The speculations on the possible participation of Oman in the proposed federation as the tenth member state came to an end when Tarik, the prime minister of Oman, announced that his country was not yet ready to join the proposed federation, though it might consider joining a union of some Gulf states.[5] The Oman palace coup seems to have delayed the prospects of implementing the Federation of all nine GCS as a result of the political forces which it has brought with it.

The three major political factors which have tended to retard progress toward the full federation have been, then, the removal of the Iranian threat to Bahrain's independence, and the changes of government in Britain and in Muscat and Oman. In addition, there are a number of regional political forces which still directly and indirectly impede progress toward a broadening of the U.A.E. Some of these are described briefly below.

Iran and Saudi Arabia

Saudi Arabia and Iran are the two largest neighbors of the GCS, and they both expect to retain their influence in the region. Apparently, they cooperated in building pressure for British withdrawal and also for the implementation of the proposed federation of the nine Gulf city states. Whether the latter is a genuine interest or not is very difficult to determine.[6]

Although Iran's claim to Bahrain has been settled, it is claiming and has occupied the islands of Abu Musa and the Grand and Minor Tunb located near the strait of Hormuz. The first island belongs to Sharjah, the latter two, to Ras al-Khaimah. Also, Saudi Arabia claims the Al-Buraimi Oasis, and thus has a special dispute with Abu Dhabi.

Interests of the two major Gulf powers will tend to keep either one from cultivating its own influence and interests without the explicit or implicit approval and support of the other. It may also result in the two agreeing on some dimensions of their interests. The only loser in this event will be the Gulf city states themselves.

Iraq

Iraq is also a Gulf power that has not been isolated from the political tensions surrounding the future of the Gulf city states; and it has its own ideas and strategies. To fill the military vacuum after the British withdrawal from the Gulf, Iraq proposed a defense alliance of the Arabian gulf states. Had it been accepted, this suggestion would have left Iran out of such an alliance and would ultimately have led to a new chain of unfavorable political elements in the area, some observers believe.[7]

Kuwait

If Iran and Saudi Arabia have their own good reasons to be interested in the future of the GCS, Kuwait can claim an even stronger interest since it has been financing, organizing and managing education and health services throughout the Trucial states, except in Abu Dhabi. It is likely, therefore, that Kuwait would object to political developments that are not in harmony with its own aspirations and expectations. Kuwait will support the proposed federation, but it will wish to insure that it has an influence at least equal to that of Saudi Arabia and Iran. To keep down the influence of outsiders on the Gulf city states will be a minimum political target for Kuwait.

Evaluation of Alternatives to the Proposed Federation of Nine

If the nine Gulf city states cannot resolve their latent and overt disputes, most of which are related to the respective role Bahrain and Qatar aspire to play in the U.A.E., there are alternative routes which may be followed. Some alternatives and the potential problems and opportunities for success associated with each are discussed below.

The United Arab Emirates

A more limited integration has brought together the seven Trucial states. It is to be hoped that they will profit by the lesson to be learned by the failure of the federation of all nine states caused by the desire of both Qatar and Bahrain to play the leading role in it. A federation without these two major contesting parties certainly has possibilities of success, but how practical an alternative is it? The answer would seem to be that it will be a practical alternative if the seven states of the U.A.E. can rise above any petty differences and can avoid serious disputes of leadership status such as that which developed between Bahrain and Qatar.

The size of its territory and its rich oil fields inevitably give Abu Dhabi an important position in the United Arab Emirates. It has been the major contributor to the Development Fund of the Trucial States Council since the Fund's inception in 1965; and the Development Office has financed all of the development projects which have been promoted in five of the Trucial states—Sharjah, Ajman, Umm al-Qaiwain, Ras al-Khaimah, and Fujairah. Some help also went to Dubai.

Since Abu Dhabi has contributed more than 80% of the total receipts of the Development Fund from its inception to date, this means that if it had not been for its substantial and generous contributions, five of the Trucial states would not have experienced any significant urban development. Undoubtedly, the rulers and the people of these states give credit to the ruler of Abu Dhabi for his continuous financial help. If these states do not strike oil, it would be most difficult for them to make any headway on their own; and, in such a situation, they would have to look to a potential source of development help such as Abu Dhabi.

But Dubai, also, is a country of growing significance among the seven. It has a larger population and has achieved a higher level of urban infrastructural development than other Trucial states. It is the most developed country among the newly integrated seven, and since 1950, it has been the most active trading center in the area. It has built its wealth on its entrepot trade. In addition to being one of the most active gold-trading centers in the world, Dubai also has begun to enjoy oil revenues, and it expects substantial increases in these in the near future. Both Dubai and Abu Dhabi have a paternalistic system of government, and traditional rivalries have not entirely been overcome.

The unresolved dispute between Saudi Arabia and Abu Dhabi over al-Buraimi could prove a source of difficulty for Abu Dhabi. Before the formation of the U.A.E. during meetings of the Supreme Federation Council, Saudi Arabia directly and indirectly sponsored and supported Qatar's efforts to be the undisputed leader in the proposed federation. Qatar and Dubai have a very close and friendly relationship, so, indirectly, the U.A.E. with Abu Dhabi and Dubai as the two leading countries might create the opportunity for Saudi Arabia to press further its claims to al-Buraimi which has been a source of dispute with Abu Dhabi.

These and other difficulties may arise and interfere with the continuation and development of the union of the seven Trucial states. But even in the absence of such difficulties, the members, individually and collectively, would be better off as members of a federation of all nine Gulf city states. The reasoning behind this conclusion is presented below.

Extent of Political Viability

A union of the Trucial states comprises less territory and less population; for the population of all seven of the Trucial states exceeds the population of Bahrain by only about 20,000. Thus, a political unit composed of the Trucial states is much smaller than a political unit which included all seven of them plus Bahrain and Qatar, as well, would be. We are living in the days of political power blocs. Psychologically speaking, belonging to a larger political unit is more satisfying than belonging to a smaller one. The size of the political unit helps to determine the size of the armed forces which it is potentially possible to support; and a federation of all nine Gulf city states would be able to build a larger army. Even if it is assumed that the level of professional competence of the army in both cases would be the same, the image and weight of the larger force representing a federation of the nine states would be greater than that of the military force raised by the U.A.E.

The ability of the United Arab Emirates to command respect and to prevent the infiltration of external influence is likely to leave much to be desired. For example, the U.A.E. could not stop Iran's occupation of the islands of Abu Musa and the Grand and Minor Tunb; nor has it been able to shut off the Saudi claim to al-Buraimi. Furthermore, even if it is assumed that the union of the seven can exercise effective sovereignty over its defined territory, it will still find it difficult to assume and maintain foreign relations with other political entities. This stems from the fact that all seven of these Trucial states suffer from an acute scarcity of qualified manpower and will continue to do so for some time to come.[8] Since it will be a number of years before they will be able to depend on local trained manpower, a federation even of the nine Gulf states would not be able to solve this key problem immediately. A federation with Bahrain in it, however, would help to alleviate the relative intensity of the problem. Either federation would have to depend largely on imported trained manpower, but the already-available trained native Bahraini manpower would help to inject a significant local element among the imported personnel.

To sum up, a union limited to the seven Trucial states will almost certainly encounter varied and complex internal and external problems which will pose major threats to its viability. It will be difficult for such a limited federation to achieve and maintain a satisfactory rate of economic and social progress. A federation of all nine Gulf city states would benefit more from economies of scale. In government, in trade and in industry, the relative productivity of their inputs would be much higher. Although there is a strong case for a federation of the nine, still there may be other unseen considerations to which these countries may attach heavy weights. These could possibly swing the balance in favor of a more limited federation.

A Federation of the Six Most Northern Trucial States

It is greatly to be hoped that no problems will develop between any members of the U.A.E. which would lead over time to a breakdown of the present structure; but should this happen, another alternative might, at first glance, seem to be the establishment of some sort of federation or union of the tiny states of Sharjah, Ajman, Umm al-Qaiwain, Ras al-Khaimah and Fujairah, perhaps under the leadership of Dubai. In such a case, the influence of Abu Dhabi in these states, except for Dubai, could not be ignored, however; for it has been supporting the Development Fund which is to be credited with helping the poor countries of Sharjah, Ajman, Umm al-Qaiwain and Fujairah in promoting the little urban infrastructural development which they have been able to achieve. It is true that Dubai has also become an oil-producing country, but its level of production over the coming five years, according to present estimates, would hardly enable it to meet obligations it has already contracted for planning and implementing its own development projects; and it would be most difficult, if not impossible, for it to contribute to the poorer states. Thus, financially, a limited union which excluded Abu Dhabi would not be able to stand on its own feet and meet even its current obligations. To build defense forces and assume foreign relations would definitely be beyond the reach and competence of such an artificial political unit. If created, such a unit would also be subject to potential outside influence. It would tend to be merely a tiny political entity which would have to look to a larger political state or bloc to give it moral, and most probably financial and security support, as well.

Qatar and the Seven Trucial States

A federation of all nine Gulf city states seems, as mentioned several times, to face problems stemming from the rivalry between Bahrain and Qatar, since each has insisted on being the first among equals. It has been said that the rulers during their fourth meeting in Abu Dhabi in October 1969, were maneuvering to ease Bahrain out and to form a federation of the remaining eight states. This federation composition is also among the possible alternatives should the present union of seven not prove viable. In such a federation, would Qatar have a potential claim to a leadership position? It has, after all, realized much economic and social progress during the past two decades. In terms of size, it has the largest population, and the size of its territory is second only to that of Abu

Dhabi. Its oil receipts are substantial, though they fall much below those of Abu Dhabi. Also, Qatar was the first Gulf state to take a major step in organizing its society along modern lines. In April 1970, the ruler passed what is called the "Interim Fundamental Law for Rule in Qatar," in which he defined the powers, authorities and jurisdiction of the state and its agencies. The executive branch has been reorganized into ten ministries, each entrusted with a special function. Qatar has been the first Gulf state to have a council of ministers similar in theory to those of modern countries. Given these factors, Qatar could make a strong argument in favor of its assuming a leading role in a federation of eight.

But Saudi Arabia, as has been indicated, has strong ties with Qatar, Dubai and with some of the smaller Trucial States. It also has an unresolved territorial dispute with Abu Dhabi, as mentioned previously. Saudi Arabia and Iran, the two largest neighbors, are interested in the future of the area. Iran claims and has recently occupied the islands of Abu Musa and the Grand and Minor Tunb; the former has belonged to Sharjah, and the latter two to Ras al-Khaimah. Would the two major Gulf powers, Iran and Saudi Arabia, suppress their claims and allow a federation of eight to proceed in view of their friendly ties with some of the member-states? If not, would the proposed federation be able to face their claims and prevent potential threats? It is very difficult to answer such questions, but whatever the case might be, if Iran and Saudi Arabia should have a disagreement, their subsequent mood and attitude would influence the course of events before and after any possible establishment of a federation of eight of the Gulf states. It can be assumed that such a union could be achieved; but, again, a union which also included Bahrain would seem to be a more favorable one than any of the possible more limited federations.

With Bahrain, the federation could benefit more from economies of scale, for it would be larger in territory and in population; and it would have a broader image which would enable it to command greater respect. A federation of the nine would be better able to resist potential outside influences, regardless of their source. And of course, a federation of ten which included Muscat and Oman would offer even better prospects.

Bahrain and Qatar

If Qatar should not join some federation of the Trucial states, it would be most difficult, if not impossible, to effect a union between Bahrain and Qatar. Instead, each would tend to try to continue its own independence as a state, but this will mean that each will have to allocate substantial resources to finance new functions such as defense and foreign affairs. This will put great strains on their financial resources, particularly in the case of Bahrain. Both need to introduce many development projects; and the allocation of substantial resources for other purposes will delay the undertaking of projects with the result that national development will be retarded. Even if they could assume the new functions with no financial strains, it would be most difficult to assume them without manpower problems. Even Bahrain, which has celebrated the fiftieth anniversary of the founding of its first school, will find it too demanding to staff a ministry of foreign affairs at home and embassies, consulates, etc. abroad. Both states are inexperienced in these matters and will need a long time before they will be able to perform effectively in them. Assuming that they could overcome such problems in time, they still could become, at best, only weak political units which would be wide open for outside influence. It is doubtful, indeed, whether they could continue on the path of nation building without encountering serious difficulties.

A Major Gulf Power Alternative

If parochialism and traditionalism should continue to impede the progress of implementing a union of all nine Gulf city states, if the union of the seven Trucial states should prove to be not viable, or if a union of Qatar and the seven Trucial states could not be effected, would it be possible to establish a union of all nine Gulf city states under the leadership of an outside power? Specifically, these nine states are Arab states which, generally speaking, still lack some of the basic ingredients needed to form a solid political unity and which need competent help and guidance. Saudi Arabia is a major Arab Gulf state which has some forty years of experience behind it. It shares with the nine Gulf city states the same religion, the same language, similar climate, similar traditions, etc. It is also an oil-producing country, and essentially has an oil economy similar to those of some of the nine Gulf city states. The size of its territory is almost twenty-five times larger and its population is eight times larger than the nine Gulf city states combined. In addition, its oil revenues are much greater than those of the nine GCS together.

If the nine GCS fail to achieve a union among themselves, would it not be worth their while to consider the potentialities of an approach to regional economic and political integration involving Saudi Arabia?

The Price of Parochialism

If a federation of all nine Gulf states is not implemented and if the U.A.E. should not prove viable, a number of smaller political entities are likely to emerge. Such new-carved entities would be more artificial than real; and some external powers which have already indicated concern about the future of the area, would be given the opportunity to cultivate their own influence, probably for a cheap price, and each according to its own way and interests. Non-Gulf major powers would also have an opportunity to show their concern and to join the race for influence and control. The U.S.A., the U.S.S.R., and now Communist China, would each have its own reasons for keeping a close check on developments. The Arab world in general, and the U.A.R. in particular, also would not simply stand by and watch. If the nine Gulf city states or the U.A.E. should fail in their efforts to integrate, they will expose the Gulf area to a potential political instability which would undoubtedly disrupt developmental efforts and lead to other highly undesirable consequences.

In establishing two or more smaller political units, traditional rivalries and destructive competition are likely to flourish among the GCS. As one manifestation of this, they may try to compete with each other in the introduction of development projects. This has been the case already to a certain extent. But this type of attitude will distract their attention from the most fruitful development projects and will lead to unproductive expenditures, which will result in their having even less funds for investment in development projects after their defense and foreign affairs expenditures which will, after all, swallow a major portion of the receipts available or made available to them.

Also of great importance is the effect which the failure to develop a broad and sound federation would have upon the private sector of the economy, for entrepreneurs are highly sensitive to political instability. The level of private participation would be seriously curtailed in the presence of political uncertainty, and employment would also be adversely affected. Foreign capital which might otherwise flow into the region would be hesitant to accept the risk of political uncertainties. In brief, political uncertainties and instability would create internal and external economic shocks which would hold down the level of economic activity and have a negative impact on the process of development. Thus, economic stagnation is the second major price which would have to be paid for noneffective federation.

Isolation, it should be noted, also conflicts with the declared motives of the rulers, all of whom seem to be imbued with a touch of Arab nationalism. Their cooperation in implementing a federation of all nine Gulf city states would tie in nicely with the aims of Arab nationalism; for it would facilitate subsequent larger unions which would be necessary steps toward the still greater goal of an overall unity of Arab countries.

A third price to be paid for parochialism could well be revolution instead of evolution. Implementing the full federation of nine should contribute importantly to evolution. Should they fail to achieve this, they will be running the risk of inviting external influence and the consequences which this might bring.

Now that Britain has withdrawn from the area, the Gulf city states are very much on their own. One can only hope that they will make the most of their opportunities so they can achieve their aspirations for favorable development within the framework of relative political independence. The formation of the U.A.E. is an encouraging step forward. If this can be quickly expanded into a stable and effective federation of the nine, or even ten, or more, the prospects for the future of the Gulf city states will be even brighter.

Notes

Notes

Chapter 1
An Overview

1. It should be noted that the term "Gulf states," as it is traditionally used, is a broader term which is meant to include all of the states bordering the Arabian Gulf. The seven Trucial states—Abu Dhabi, Dubai, Sharjah, Ajman, Umm al-Qaiwain, Ras al-Khaimah and Fujairah—joined together during the period 1971-72 in a union known as the United Arab Emirates, often referred to in the western press as the Union of Arab Emirates.

2. Only a few days before his death in September 1971, Dean Acheson, former Secretary of State of the United States, wrote an article for the *New York Times* in which he commented upon Russia's penetration in the Middle East and upon the fact that reopening the Suez Canal "... would give her [Russia] naval dominance in the Persian Gulf and Indian Ocean and power to control the movement of Persian Gulf oil to Europe, East Asia, and North America." See *New York Times*, 14 October 1971.

Chapter 2
Economic Foundations

1. Figures are not available for Qatar, as mentioned in Table 2-1.

2. One hectare equals 2.47 acres.

3. Survey conducted by the British Ministry of Overseas Development covering the Northern Trucial States (unpublished).

4. One Bahraini Dinar is equal to approximately U.S. $2.00.

Chapter 3
Social Development

1. Ratios for each level, primary, intermediate and secondary, are shown in Tables 3-29, 3-30, and 3-31, respectively.

2. Barasti is a straw and mud type of construction.

3. QDR stands for Qatar-Dubai Riyal. QDR 1.00 equals approximately U.S. $0.20.

4. Qatar Department of Labor and Social Affairs, *Annual Report*, 1969, p. 96.

5. Ibid.

Chapter 4
Political Foundations

1. Milton J. Esman, "The Politics of Development Administration," in *Approaches to Development: Politics, Administration and Change*, John D. Montgomery and William J. Siffin eds. (New York: McGraw-Hill, 1966), p. 87.

2. George Grassmuck, "Polity, Bureaucracy and Interest Groups in the Near East and North Africa," Comparative Administration Group (CAG) Occasional Paper, Indiana University, Bloomington, Indiana, revised draft, June 1965, pp. 11-24.

3. Ibid.

4. See also, R.G. Fenelon, *The Trucial States: A Brief Economic Survey*, Beirut: Khayats, Second Edition, Revised, 1969, pp. 13-16.

5. Ibid.

6. Middle East Economic Digest and Arab Report and Record Survey, *Bahrain 1969*, December 1969, pp. 6-7.

7. The text of the exclusive agreement is given in Husain M. Albaharna, *The Legal Status of the Arabian Gulf States*, Manchester University Press, 1968, pp. 313-314.

8. Middle East Economic Digest and Arab Record Survey, *Qatar 1969*, October 1969, p. iv.

9. Ibid., p. iv.

10. Albaharna, p. 314.

11. Ibid., pp. 316-317.

12. Middle East Economic Digest and Arab Report and Record Survey, *Bahrain 1969*, Dec. 1969, p. 9.

13. Middle East Economic Digest and Arab Report and Record Survey, *Abu Dhabi*, June 1969, p. 222.

14. Hereditary rights belong to the brother or son of the ruler.

15. In April 1970, the ruler of Qatar enacted what is called the "Temporary Fundamental Regulations for Rule in Qatar," which will be examined later.

16. Middle East Economic Digest and Arab Report and Record Survey, *Bahrain 1969*, December 1969, p. 5.

17. Ibid., p. 5.

18. An-Nahar, *Special Issue on Bahrain*, June 1970, pp. 19-20.

19. Ibid., p. 20.

20. Articles 1, 4, 5, Decree No. 1, 1970.

21. Article No. 6, Decree No. 1, 1970.

22. Article No. 2, Decree No. 1, 1970.

23. Article No. 7, Decree No. 1, 1970.

24. Article No. 9, Decree No. 1, 1970.

25. Report of Mr. Guicciardi to the United Nations Security Council on May 11, 1970.

26. This law was enacted by an Emiri Decree on April 2, 1970, and it was promulgated in the Qatari Official Gazette No. 4, April 2, 1970.

27. He became ruler in February, 1972.

28. Arab Report and Record, *Abu Dhabi*, London, June 1969, p. 222.

Chapter 5
Administrative Problems and Policies

1. Fred W. Riggs, *Administration in Developing Countries* (Boston: Houghton Mifflin Co., 1964), p. 25.

2. Ibid., p. 422.

3. *An-Nahar*, July 2, 1971.

4. Article No. 6, Personnel Law, 1967.

Chapter 6
Problems of Federation

1. Unpublished report by development office, Trucial States Council, no date, p. 2.

2. Ibid.

3. See Table 6-1.

4. Unpublished report by Development Office, Trucial States Council, n.d., pp. 2-3.

5. See Table 6-2.

6. Arab Report Record, *Abu Dhabi*, Special Issue—June 1969, p. 225. (See also footnote 2.)

7. Chamber of Commerce, *Iktisadiat Imarat Al-Khaleej (Economics of the Arabian Gulf Imirates)*, a special issue, Cairo, 1969, p. 14.

8. Ibid.

9. Article 12 of the Federation Agreement. See MEED ARR Survey, *Dubai 1969*, July 1969, p. iv and Chamber of Commerce, op. cit., pp. 14-18, for the text of the Agreement.

10. Article 1.

11. Articles 2 and 3.

12. Articles 5 and 6.

13. Article 4.

14. Article 7.

15. Article 8.

16. Article 9.

17. Riyadh Najib Al-Rayyes, *The Federation of the Arab Emirates*, Beirut, no publisher listed, n.d., pp. 7-13.

18. Ibid., pp. 14-20.

19. Ibid., pp. 24-32.

20. Middle East Economic Digest and Arab Report and Record Survey, *Bahrain 1969*, December 1969, p. 7.

21. Department of Information, *Bahrain News*, May 1970 and June 1970.

22. *The Daily Star*, May 29, 1970; see also *An-Nahar*, June 16, 1970.

23. *The Daily Star*, June 29, 1970, July 9, 1970, July 10, 1970; see also *An-Nahar*, July 22, 1970 and *Al-Anwar*, August 25, 1970.

24. *The Daily Star*, July 13, 1970.

25. *The Daily Star*, July 10 and 11, 1970.

26. *Al-Nahar*, October 12 and November 2, 1970.

27. *The Daily Star*, July 10 and 13, 1970 and *Al-Anwar*, August 25, 1970.

28. Ibid.

29. *The Daily Star*, July 13, 1970.

30. *The Daily Star*, July 15 and 22, 1970.

31. *An-Nahar*, July 21, 1970.

32. *The Daily Star*, July 10, 1970.

33. *Al-Nahar*, October 12, 1970.

34. *Al-Nahar*, October 24, 1970.

35. *Al-Nahar*, October 27 and 28, 1970.

36. *Al-Issbou' Al Arabi (The Arab Weekly)* No. 595, November 1970, pp. 15-17.

37. Ibid.

38. *The Daily Star*, Beirut, February 11, 1972.

39. *The Daily Star*, Beirut, February 5, 1972.

40. Sheik Khaled bin Mohammed who was ruler of Sharjah at the time of the annexation of Abu Musa Island by Iran, was assassinated in late January 1972, in a coup attempt which failed.

41. *The Daily Star*, Beirut, February 5, 1972.

42. *The Daily Star*, Beirut, February 14, 1972.

43. For an interesting account of the first meeting of the Federal National Consultative Assembly, see ibid.

Chapter 7
Potential Gains from Regional Economic and
Political Integration

1. Unpublished Report, prepared by Development Office, Trucial States Council, n.d., p. 41.

2. Unpublished Report, p. 37.

3. Unpublished Report, p. 34.

4. Middle East Economic Division, p. 32.

5. Middle East Economic Division, p. 27.
6. Middle East Economic Division, p. 10.
7. *Al-Shirook*, Vol. 1, 1970, p. 85.
8. Middle East Economic Division, op. cit., p. 26.

Chapter 8
The Price of Nonintegration

1. *Al-Arab Weekly*, No. 595, November 1970, pp. 15-17.
2. *An-Nahar*, August 11, 1970.
3. Ibid., August 7, 1970.
4. Ibid., July 29, 1970.
5. Ibid., Oct. 21, 1970.
6. *Daily Star*, July 13, 1970.
7. *Daily Star*, July 22, 1970.
8. In this connection, it is interesting to note that the United Arab Emirates has employed an outsider, Mr. Adnan Pachachi of Iraq, to serve as its representative in the United Nations. He is also serving as the Minister of State of Abu Dhabi. See, *New York Times*, December 26, 1971, p. 2.

Bibliography

Bibliography

Dean Acheson. *New York Times*. 14 October 1971.

Fereydoun Adamiyat. *Bahrain Islands*. New York: Praeger, 1955.

Al-Anwar. 25 August 1970.

Husain M. Albaharna. *The Legal Status of the Arabian Gulf States*. Manchester University Press, 1968.

Al-Issbou' Al Arabi (The Arab Weekly). No. 595, November 1970.

Al-Nahar. 12, 24, 27, 28 October and 2 November 1970.

Riyadh Najib Al-Rayyes. *The Federation of the Arab Emirates*. Beirut: no publisher listed, n.d.

Al-Shirook. Vol. 1, 1970, and Vol. 2, 1970.

An-Nahar, 16 June, 2, 21, 22 July, and 11 August 1970.

An-Nahar. Economic and Financial Supplement. 29 November 1970.

An-Nahar. *Special Issue on Bahrain*, June 1970.

An-Nahar Survey. Qatar, September 1970.

Arab Report and Record. *Abu Dhabi*. 1 June 1969.

Arabian American Oil Company. *Aramco Handbook: Oil and the Middle East*. Dhahran, 1969.

Aramco Handbook. 1966.

ARAMCO, Research Division. *Oman and the Southern Shores of the Persian Gulf*. Cairo: Imp. Mist SAE, 1952.

Arbitration Concerning Buraimi and the Common Frontier between Abu Dhabi and Saudi Arabia. Memorial submitted by the Government of the United Kingdom of Great Britain and Northern Ireland. London, 1955.

Bahrain, Qatar and the Trucial States. London: British Information Services, 1965.

The Bahrain Islander. Bahrain Petroleum Company. 17 October 1946-19 June 1952 (biweekly), 19 June 1952–after April 1954, a monthly pictorial and a news sheet.

Bahrain Trade Report. India, Political Agent, Bahrain. Simla, Printed by the Manager, Government of India Press, annual.

Charles Belgrave. *The Pirate Coast*. London: Bell, 1966.

Jean Jacques Berreby. *Le Golfe Persique*. Paris: Payot, 1959.

Richard Bowen. "The Pearl Fisheries of the Persian Gulf." *Middle East Journal* V (Spring 1951).

British Petroleum Company. *World Petroleum Statistical Review*. 1970.

Sir Reader Bullard, ed. *The Middle East: A Political and Economic Survey*. 3d. ed. London: Oxford University Press, 1961.

Chamber of Commerce. *Iktisadiat Imarat Al-Khaleej (Economics of the Arabian Gulf Imirates)*. A special issue, Cairo, 1969.

George B. Cressy. *Crossroads*. New York: Lippincott, 1960.

The Daily Star, Beirut, 29 May, 29 June, 9 July, 10 July, 11 July, 13 July, 15 July, 22 July 1970 and 5 February, 14 February 1972.

Department of Information. Government of Abu Dhabi. *Abu Dhabi: Yesterday and Today*. n.d. (in Arabic).

Department of Information. *Bahrain News*. May 1970 and June 1970.

Development Office, Trucial States Council. "Round-Up News for the Month Ending 28th February 1970." n.d. (unpublished material).

Economist Intelligence Unit Ltd. *Oxford Regional Economic Atlas: The Middle East and North Africa*. London: Oxford, 1960.

Milton J. Esman, "The Politics of Development Administration." In *Approaches to Development: Politics, Administration and Change*, edited by John D. Montgomery and William J. Siffin. New York: McGraw-Hill, 1966.

Abbas Faroughy. *The Bahrain Islands*. New York: Verry and Fisher, 1951.

K.G. Fenelon. *The Trucial States: A Brief Economic Survey*. 2d. ed. rev. Beirut, Khayats, 1969.

Financial Times Survey. Abu Dhabi. 25 February 1970.

David H. Finnie. *Desert Enterprise*. Cambridge, Mass.: Harvard University Press, 1958.

W.B. Fisher. *The Middle East*. 3d ed. London: Methuen, 1957.

Karl Gabrisch, ed. *Trucial States, Muscat and Oman*. Vienna: Redaktion, 1960.

Government of Abu Dhabi. Department of Health. 1970 (unpublished material).

Government of Abu Dhabi. Education Department. (unpublished material).

Government of Abu Dhabi. *Statistical Abstract*. Vol. 1, 1969.

Government of Bahrain. *Administrative Report for the Years 1926-1937*.

Government of Bahrain, *Census, 1950*. Bahrain 1950.

Government of Bahrain. *Census, 1965*.

Government of Bahrain. Education Department, Curriculum of the Secondary School (1968-1969) (unpublished).

Government of Bahrain. *Fourth Census of Population, 1965*. Manama: Government of Bahrain, Finance Department [between 1965 and 1969].

Government of Bahrain. *Report*. Bombay: Times of India Press, Annual.

Government of Bahrain. Statistical Bureau. *Statistical Abstract*. 1967 [Manama] Annual.

Government of Bahrain. Statistical Bureau. *The Fourth Population Census of Bahrain, A Brief Analytical and Comparative Study*. Manama, 1969.

Government of Bahrain. *Statistical Abstract*. 1970.

Government of Dubai. Port and Customs Department. *Statistics Report 1968*.

Government of Qatar. Customs Department. *Summary Bulletin of Statistics*, 1969.

Government of Qatar. Ministry of Education (unpublished material).

Government of Qatar. Ministry of Health. 1970 (unpublished material).

Government of Ras al-Khaimah (unpublished material).

George Grassmuck. "Polity, Bureaucracy, and Interest Groups in the Near East and North Africa," rev. draft. Comparative Administrative Group, American Society for Public Administration (CAG), Occasional Papers. Bloomington, Indiana: Indiana University, June 1965.

Great Britain, Foreign Office. *Handbook on the Persian Gulf.* London: Foreign Office, 1953.

Great Britain. *Memorial of the Government of the United Kingdom of Great Britain and Northern Ireland on Arbitration Concerning Buraimi and the Common Frontier Between Abu Dhabi and Saudi Arabia.* 2 vols, 1955.

Great Britain, Reference Division, Central Office of Information. *The Arab States of the Persian Gulf and South-East Arabia.* London: Swindon Press, 1959.

Great Britain, Treaties, etc., 1952 Arbitration Agreement between the Government of the U.K. (acting on behalf of the Ruler of Abu Dhabi and His Highness the Sultan Said bin Taimur) and the Government of Saudi Arabia, with exchange of notes, Jedda, July 30, 1954. London, H.M. Stationery Office, 1954.

Sir Rupert Hay. "The Impact of the Oil Industry on the Persian Gulf Sheikhdoms," *Middle East Journal* IX (Autumn, 1955).

Sir Rupert Hay. *The Persian Gulf States.* Washington, D.C.: Middle East Institute, 1959.

Sir Rupert Hay. "The Persian Gulf States and Their Boundary Problems." *Geographical Journal* CXX (December 1954).

J.B. Kelly. "Buraimi Oasis Dispute." *International Affairs* XXXII (July 1956).

J.B. Kelly. *Eastern Arabian Frontiers.* London: Faber, 1964.

J.B. Kelly. *The Legal and Historical Basis of the British Position in the Persian Gulf.* Vol. IV of St. Antony's Papers, London: Chatto and Windus, 1958.

Kuwait Office in Dubai. July 1970 (unpublished material).

S.H. Longrigg. *The Middle East, A Social Geography.* Chicago: Aldine Press, 1964.

Clarence Mann. *Abu Dhabi: Birth of an Oil Sheikdom*, 1st ed. Beirut: Khayats, 1964.

John Marlowe. *The Persian Gulf in the Twentieth Century.* London: Cresset Press, 1962.

Alexander Melamid. "Oil and the Evolution of Boundaries in Eastern Arabia." *Geographical Review* XLIV (June 1954).

The Middle East and North Africa: 1969-70, 16th ed. London: Europa Publications Limited, 1969.

Middle East Economic Digest and Arab Report and Record Survey. *Abu Dhabi.* June 1969.

Middle East Economic Digest and Arab Report and Record Survey. *Bahrain 1969.* December 1969.

Middle East Economic Digest and Arab Report and Record Survey. *Dubai 1969.* July 1969.

Middle East Economic Digest and Arab Report and Record Survey. *Qatar 1969*. October 1969.

Middle East Economic Division. "An Economic Survey of the Northern Trucial States." Beirut: British Embassy, 1970.

S.B. Miles. *The Countries and Tribes of the Persian Gulf*, 2d. ed. London: Frank Cass, 1966.

Adnan Pachachi. *New York Times.* 26 December 1971.

Report of Bahrain to the Food and Agriculture Organization. 4th Session of the Near East Commission on Agriculture Planning. Baghdad, 23 March to 2 April, 1968.

Report of Mr. Guicciardi to the United Nations Security Council on 11 May 1970.

Fred W. Riggs. *Administration in Developing Countries.* Boston: Houghton Mifflin Co., 1964.

Dr. R. Roolvink, et al. *Historical Atlas of the Muslim Peoples.* Amsterdam: Djambatan, 1957.

'Aziz S. Sahwell. "The Buraimi Dispute." *Islamic Review* XLIV (April 1956).

Richard H. Sanger. *The Arabian Peninsula.* Ithaca, New York: Cornell University Press, 1954.

Saudi Arabia. Memorial of the Government of Saudi Arabia. Arbitration for the settlement of the territorial dispute between Muscat and Abu Dhabi on one side and Saudi Arabia on the other. Cairo, 1955.

Benjamin Shwadran. *The Middle East, Oil and the Great Powers*, 2d ed. New York: Council for Middle Eastern Affairs Press, 1959.

Statistical Abstract of Abu Dhabi, Vol. I, 1969 (Directorate General of Planning and Coordination, Abu Dhabi).

Survey conducted by the British Ministry of Overseas Development covering the Northern Trucial States, 1968, Vol. II (unpublished).

Trucial States Council. *Census Figures, 1968.*

John Tunstall. *Vanishing Kingdoms.* London: Macdonald, 1966.

Maureen Tweedy. *Bahrain and the Persian Gulf.* Ipswich, England: East Anglian, 1952.

United Nations. *Studies on Selected Development Problems in Various Countries in the Middle East.* 1969 and 1970.

H. Woyse-Bartlett. *The Pirates of Trucial Oman.* London: McDonald & Company, 1966.

Arnold T. Wilson, *The Persian Gulf*, 2d. ed. London: George Allen and Unwin, 1954.

Index

Abdul-Azziz ibn Saud, 10

Abu Dhabi, 4, 6, 7, 8, 22, 41, 223; and
continental shelf claims, 8; and United
Arab Emirates (U.A.E.), 13, 199–200,
212, 224; and Demography and population, 15–17, 212; discovery of oil, 18,
27, 145, 151, 175, 212; GNP, 19, 20;
development in, 22, 24, 139–140, 232;
and developmental assistance to poorer
countries, 24 (see also Trucial States
Development Fund below); political
system, 24; economic status of population, 28, 29, 30, 32; employment in
agriculture and fishing, 33, 34, 36;
employment in manufacturing, 37;
employment in construction, 37–38;
employment in oil industry, 38; employment in trade, 38; banking in, 39, 40;
transportation and communication
sector, 39; government sector, 41; education of workers, 42; oil production, 43,
45; agriculture in, 46, 47; and foreign
trade, 49–51, 53, 55–57, 217; import
duties, 56, 57; industrialization, 58, 61,
217; education, 70–71, 87, 89, 90, 92,
99, 169; school curricula, 79–81, 82, 83;
availability of education, 87–89; student-
teacher data, 91, 92, 93–97; cost of
education in, 97–99; health services, 99–
104; housing, 106–108, 110–111; social
security programs, 111; British colonial
heritage, 118; ruling family, 122; tribal
population, 125; political development,
138–140, 142, 144, 226; paternalism,
143, 224; administrative structure, 158–
162, 167, 174; university graduates, 171;
budgeting in, 176, 178–179; public personnel policies, 179, 180, 183; and
Trucial States Council, 187; and Trucial
States Development Fund, 188, 189;
and federation, 190, 193, 194, 195, 196,
199–219, 226; and isolation vs. integration, 212, 214; and radio and TV, 217;
and al-Buraimi, 223, 224, 227

Abu Dhabi city, 17, 22, 195

Abu Dhabi Petroleum Company, 107

Abu Musa, 5–6, 200, 222, 225, 227

Administration, public, 151–186; and social
structure of GCS, 152–154; need for
expansion of, 153–154; and British
advisors, 154, 170; organization of, 154–
169; in Bahrain, 156–158, 196; in

Qatar, 158; in Abu Dhabi, 158–162; in
other GCS, 162; recent changes in, 164–
168; management, 169–183; and literacy
level, 170; problems of 172–175; budgeting, 175–179; personnel policies, 179–
183; authors' recommendations, 183–
186; and integration, 216. See also
Management

Affluence, 24; and imports, 51

Administrative Council, Bahrain, 128–129

Agriculture, 6, 14, 23, 24, 41, 45–48, 59,
113, 121, 154; employment in, 32–37;
Bahrain, 127; and administration, 155

Agricultural schools, 74

Ahbab tribe, 125

Airports, 21, 22, 210; duplication in construction of, 56, 58, 61, 217

Ajman, 4, 43, 45, 151; and U.A.E., 13;
population, 15, 16, 17, 208; GNP, 20;
development, 22–23, 224; economic
status of population, 28, 29, 30; employment in agriculture and fishing, 33, 34;
employment in manufacturing, 37;
employment in construction, 37; employment in oil industry, 38; employment in
trade, 38; and banking, 39, 40; transportation and communications sector, 39;
government sector, 41; educational level
of workers, 42; and agriculture, 46; and
fishing, 48; industrialization, 58; education, 70, 89, 90, 169; school curricula,
81; student and teacher data, 91, 92, 93–
97; health services, 99–104; housing,
107, 109, 110; British colonial heritage,
118; ruling family, 122; tribal population, 125; political development, 141,
208, 226; and paternalism, 143; university graduates, 171; and Trucial States
Council, 187; and federation, 191, 226;
isolation vs. integration, 208; public
revenues, 208

Ajman City, 17, 18

Al-Ain, Abu Dhabi, 111

Al-ali tribe, 125

Al Awamir tribe, 125

Albaharna, Dr. Hussein M., 130

Al-Bida, Qatar, 132

Al-Buraimi, 139, 193, 222, 224, 225

Al bu Shamis tribe, 125

Al-Ein, Abu Dhabi, 160

Algeria, 113, 114; GNP, 115; illiteracy, 1116

Al-Hasa, 10, 132–133

About the Authors

Muhammed T. Sadik has taught in the Graduate Program in Development Administration at the American University of Beirut since 1967. From 1962 to 1968 he served as senior expert in public administration in the Kingdom of Saudi Arabia. He is the author of a book and numerous articles on public administration in developing Arab countries.

Professor Sadik received the B.A. and M.A. degrees from the American University of Beirut and is currently working for his Ph.D at Harvard. He has participated in and contributed to a number of local, regional, and international conferences and congresses dealing with various problems of development.

William P. Snavely has taught at the University of Connecticut since 1947, and served as Department Head from 1966 to 1972. He received the B.A., M.A., and Ph.D degrees from the University of Virginia and did postdoctoral work at Harvard.

Professor Snavely has served as a Ford Foundation consultant to the Jordan Development Board, to the Lebanese Ministry of Planning and to the Graduate Program in Development Administration at the American University of Beirut, and recently has served as a United Nations consultant to Jordan's National Planning Council. He is the author of numerous books and articles on economic systems, economic development planning, and related topics.